DEAD IN THE WATER

DEAD
IN THE
WATER

A TRUE STORY OF HIJACKING, MURDER, AND A GLOBAL MARITIME CONSPIRACY

MATTHEW CAMPBELL
AND KIT CHELLEL

PORTFOLIO · PENGUIN

PORTFOLIO / PENGUIN
An imprint of Penguin Random House LLC
penguinrandomhouse.com

Copyright © 2022 by Matthew Campbell and Kit Chellel
Penguin supports copyright. Copyright fuels creativity, encourages diverse
voices, promotes free speech, and creates a vibrant culture. Thank you for buying
an authorized edition of this book and for complying with copyright laws by
not reproducing, scanning, or distributing any part of it in any form without
permission. You are supporting writers and allowing Penguin to continue
to publish books for every reader.

Most Portfolio books are available at a discount when purchased in quantity
for sales promotions or corporate use. Special editions, which include personalized
covers, excerpts, and corporate imprints, can be created when purchased in
large quantities. For more information, please call (212) 572-2232 or e-mail
specialmarkets@penguinrandomhouse.com. Your local bookstore can also assist
with discounted bulk purchases using the Penguin Random House corporate
Business-to-Business program. For assistance in locating a participating retailer,
e-mail B2B@penguinrandomhouse.com.

Portions of this book were previously published in different form as
"The Hijacking of the *Brillante Virtuoso*" on bloomberg.com in 2017.

Insert photo credits may be found on page 249.

LIBRARY OF CONGRESS CATALOGING-IN-PUBLICATION DATA
Names: Campbell, Matthew (Reporter), author. | Chellel, Kit, author.
Title: Dead in the water : a true story of hijacking, murder, and a global
maritime conspiracy / Matthew Campbell and Kit Chellel.
Description: [New York] : Portfolio/Penguin, [2022] |
Includes bibliographical references and index.
Identifiers: LCCN 2021050064 (print) | LCCN 2021050065 (ebook) |
ISBN 9780593329238 (hardcover) | ISBN 9780593329245 (ebook)
Subjects: LCSH: Hijacking of ships. | Piracy. | Tankers.
Classification: LCC HV6433.785 .C36 2022 (print) | LCC HV6433.785 (ebook) |
DDC 364.16/4—dc23/eng/20211015
LC record available at https://lccn.loc.gov/2021050064
LC ebook record available at https://lccn.loc.gov/2021050065

Printed in the United States of America
1 3 5 7 9 10 8 6 4 2

Book design by Daniel Lagin

For our families

CONTENTS

INTRODUCTION

The oceans make the modern economy possible, providing the most convenient and affordable means to move the things we buy, sell, build, burn, eat, wear, and throw away. On any given day, sneakers stitched together in Cambodian sweatshops are packed into forty-foot containers, then winched by dockside cranes into ships bound for Europe, where they will line the shelves of big-box stores. Oil sucked from a 150-million-year-old deposit beneath the Saudi desert travels the aquatic highway of the Suez Canal, ultimately filling the tanks of Ford sedans in New Jersey. Iron ore gouged from the red earth of Western Australia is loaded into cavernous bulk carriers and shipped to China, where it's forged into the steel that frames Shanghai skyscrapers.

Without seaborne trade, there would be no smartphones, and no glass of red wine with dinner. Without tankers to distribute it cheaply and efficiently, there would be no economic way to extract much of the natural gas that heats our homes, nor the fuel that allows us to fly off on vacations and business trips. The evolution of the shipping business to enable this commerce is one of the most remarkable achievements of capitalism, a symphony of technical and financial innovations that have drastically reduced the cost, and increased the reliability, of long-distance trade.

Yet the industry's success has also, curiously, led it to become largely invisible. The world's greatest cities—London, New York, Tokyo—were once dominated by their ports, their streets crowded with the sailors and dock-workers who made them run. But as ever-larger vessels required ever-larger quays, and robotic cranes replaced longshoremen's brawn, the ports moved away, to obscure locales like Felixstowe and Port Elizabeth. Eventually the sailors also receded from view—some made obsolete by automation, the rest pushed out by cheaper, less demanding workers from developing countries. Even more than power lines or sewer pipes, ships slipped into the background of modern life, not so much taken for granted as barely noticed at all. As consumers, we've never before had access to such a bounty of goods, and we've never had to think so little about how they come into our possession.

The story told here centers on just one vessel, a rusting hulk of an oil tanker called the *Brillante Virtuoso*. It is the product of more than four years of reporting, drawing on tens of thousands of pages of court filings, witness testimonies, police records, military documents, emails, memos, and audio transcripts, as well as interviews with more than seventy-five people involved in the events concerned. No scenes or dialogue have been invented or embellished; all are based on the recollections or contemporaneous notes of direct participants, or drawn from the materials described above. Where the accuracy of an account is substantively disputed, the objections are described in the text or notes.

On its own, the *Brillante* was nothing special, just another useful cog in the machine of maritime trade. Yet for a decade, this unremarkable vessel has been fought over, picked apart in court, and investigated by police, naval forces, private detectives, and experts who make their living boarding ships to look for nearly invisible clues. And it still hasn't given up all its secrets. Mention its name in one of the world's maritime hubs, and as often as not you'll get a certain kind of reaction—an arched eyebrow, perhaps, or a glance over a shoulder to see who might be listening. More than once during our research, we were warned of risks to our safety if we continued to investigate, and many of the sources we consulted asked not to be identified, fearing for their own well-being. Their anxiety was understandable. For years, the *Brillante* has been leaving a churn of ruined lives in its wake. At least one person involved has been murdered. Others have been threatened, kidnapped, or forced to flee their homes in terror.

This book is about the hidden system that powers international commerce, and, more particularly, about what can happen on its chaotic fringes. The shipping industry has the unique attribute of being utterly integrated with the world economy while existing apart from it, benefiting from its infrastructure while ignoring many of its rules. It's sometimes said that the seas are lawless, and that's true: far from shore, on a decrepit trawler or a juddering ore carrier, there are certainly no police, and often no consequences. But the most audacious crimes can occur where the maritime world intersects with the more orderly terrestrial one—enabled by the complexities of twenty-first-century finance and, perhaps most of all, the collective indifference of a global populace that wants what it wants, wants it now, and doesn't want to know the human cost.

DEAD IN THE WATER

CHAPTER 1

A LUCKY LAND

n the middle of a spring night in 2011, Cynthia Mockett woke to the sound of gunshots. The rattle of automatic rifle fire was something she'd learned to tolerate over the years. But this sounded close, just outside her bedroom. Cynthia was sixty-four years old, a small, forceful woman with silvery hair and intense eyes. Her husband, David, was still asleep as she slid out of bed and crept over to the window. She could see the outlines of the old city of Aden laid out before her, its neat white buildings clinging to the rocky slopes of an extinct volcano, illuminated by the lights of the harbor beyond.

The villa that she and David had rented for several years in Yemen was situated a few blocks back from the ocean in Mualla, a district built by the British for colonial officials and soldiers, half a century before. As she knelt at the window, Cynthia breathed in the acrid smell of burning tires. Below her, crowds of young men were running through the darkness, yelling and shooting out streetlights, the muzzles of their rifles flashing with each report. It wasn't clear if they were pursuing or being pursued. Suddenly, she heard David's voice, bellowing at her from across the room. "What the bloody hell are you doing, Cynth? Get away from there!" She climbed back in bed and lay awake until the sky began to lighten, listening to the gunfire and, farther away, the claps of artillery echoing off the hillsides.

A little before eight o'clock, Cynthia opened the villa's cast-iron gates and David eased his Lexus sport-utility vehicle into the pitted street, giving her a wave as he set out for his office near the Aden port. She looked around as he drove off. Children were playing amid the broken glass and vendors were hawking fruit, like nothing had happened the night before. At first Cynthia felt foolish, as if she'd imagined it all. But she couldn't escape a feeling of unease. David had lived and worked in Yemen for more than a decade, a period in which Cynthia had shuttled regularly between the Arabian Peninsula and their home in England. Never an easy place, Aden had been noticeably disintegrating for months. They'd begun to talk about David's plans for retirement, and spending more time with their grandchildren. Maybe now was the moment, Cynthia thought, for him to move back permanently.

The Mocketts had spent most of their forty-three years together in hot, dangerous places. They met when Cynthia was fifteen, living in a small town in Devon, a pastoral county in southwest England that's also home to Europe's largest naval base. He was a year younger, the friend of a cousin, and introduced himself by wolf-whistling in her direction. "Cheeky devil," she said to herself. Later, he turned up at her bedroom window, refusing to leave until she agreed to go to the movies with him. Just before Christmas 1968, David put on a tie and Cynthia her best dress, and they hitched a ride to the registry office in a relative's delivery van, sitting atop a pile of cabbages on their way to be married. David was a strapping six feet four, with a thunderous laugh and a way of dominating any room he walked into. In black-and-white photographs from the time, he looks like a young Sean Connery, broad-shouldered with a thick brow. His father worked for the Admiralty, the government department responsible for the Royal Navy, and he'd lived as a child in Sri Lanka and Gibraltar, gaining a taste for adventure that never left him. Cynthia thought he was the most exciting man she'd ever met. She still thought so four decades later, after he'd lost most of his hair and thickened around the middle.

As a sailor in the merchant navy, David went to sea for months at a time, which was hard on Cynthia, even if she knew the life she'd married into. It was unusual, especially in the 1970s, but David would invite her to join him on voyages whenever he could. She sailed with him once on a cargo ship carrying iron ore from India to Japan, spending much of the trip cleaning rust-colored dust out of their cabin. Some of the crew objected to the presence of a woman on board, but Cynthia didn't much care. She had a quiet manner that masked a steely streak. She laughed easily, even at the bawdy humor of the young sailors, who treated her as a kind of surrogate mother. When the captain wasn't on the bridge, David liked to let her steer the ship.

Money got tight when the Mocketts' two daughters, Sarah and Rachael, were born, and in 1977 David took the offer of a well-paid job on land, as a port superintendent in Jeddah, Saudi Arabia, in the midst of the oil boom. By then he'd earned a master mariner's certificate, qualifying him to skipper a vessel. Though he went ashore before being given his own command, he was still known thereafter as Captain Mockett.

Initially, Cynthia and the girls lived with him in a secure development for Westerners, insulated from the conservative strictures being enforced by Saudi religious police. But after a few years, Cynthia suspected she'd go mad with boredom if she had to spend many more days drinking gin and tonics with the other wives inside the walls of the compound. And she wanted their daughters to have a proper British education. She and the girls moved back to Devon, into a rambling stone cottage that everyone called the Vicarage. David stayed in the Middle East. He loved the people, and the rugged beauty of the coasts. Besides, the pay was good, and maintaining the Vicarage wasn't cheap. When he was back in England, he would relax with a jigsaw puzzle and tell Cynthia about his adventures, like the time the Saudi king's camels escaped and rampaged through the port. Some of them had to be retrieved thirty miles away.

In 1998, David took a position as a marine surveyor in Yemen. Surveyors play a vital, unsung role in seaborne trade, providing independent analyses of marine mishaps, helping to pinpoint their cause and informing decisions on compensation. It would be Mockett's job to inspect vessels and cargo passing through Yemeni waters, on behalf of the various merchants, traders, bankers, shipowners, and insurance companies who required his services. One day he might cast his expert eye over a tanker with engine trouble carrying oil from Kuwait to Texas; the next a damaged consignment of steel rebar bound for Rotterdam. Even in an age of largely automated container vessels and real-time satellite navigation, such incidents occurred at sea constantly, and with a shortage of skilled surveyors in the region there was good money to be made.

Yet moving to the poorest nation in the Middle East was a daunting proposition. Then as now, Yemen could make a strong claim to being the least governable place on earth. And many have tried to govern it, since the country sits on an important geopolitical choke point between Saudi Arabia and the Horn of Africa, abutting the main shipping route from Asia to Europe. The Ottoman Turks came in the sixteenth century, trying to bribe the local sheikhs into loyalty, only to be beaten back again and again by fierce highland tribes. One Turkish official described mountains that "pierce the clouds, a place where there was only pain." Legend has it that Ottoman troops had to be chained to their ships to force them into service in Yemen's battlegrounds.

Next came the British, who set their sights on Aden as a way station for ships sailing to and from the Indian colonies. In 1837, an attack on a British-flagged vessel provided a pretext for the East India Company to seize what was then a fishing village. British investment helped bring a degree of prosperity to southern Yemen, especially after the Suez Canal opened up the trade route through Egypt, and Aden became one of the most important ports in the Empire, a gateway between East and West. Colonial administrators installed a clocktower known as "Little Ben," a statue of Queen Victoria, and a Western-style bureaucracy. Once again, though, the region's inhabitants vigorously asserted their independence. Aden was so rough that it became a punishment posting for army regiments that had fallen into disgrace. A Scottish officer stationed there in the 1850s complained about the prickly heat, the howling of wild dogs, and an "aspect of desolation which pervades the place."

In the 1960s, as the British were being driven out by militants armed with grenades and machine guns, Egyptian troops were embroiled in a bloody campaign in the north of Yemen, in what Egypt's president Gamal Abdel Nasser called "my Vietnam." After the British left, a Kremlin-backed socialist regime took control of the south, which nearly came apart in a bloody civil conflict in the 1980s. Russians stationed in Aden were forced to flee the slaughter, ignominiously, on the royal yacht *Britannia*, which had been sailing nearby. Even fellow Marxists found the violence excessive. "When are you people going to stop killing each other?" Cuban leader Fidel Castro grumbled to a local counterpart.

By the time David Mockett settled there in the late 1990s, Yemen's southern and northern halves were united under a lavishly corrupt military ruler called Ali Abdullah Saleh. The country was still roiling and chaotic, overflowing with Russian firearms, aggressive tribal militias, and, increasingly, Islamic extremists. The president's security forces offered a haven to jihadis returning from Afghanistan, including associates of Osama Bin Laden and his growing Al Qaeda network, even as Saleh tried to persuade the outside world that he was a willing partner, deserving of foreign aid. Traveling outside the major cities often required an armed escort from police who, along with roughly three-quarters of the male population, spent every late afternoon chewing qat, a mildly narcotic leaf that produces a high said to be somewhere between a strong cup of coffee and a line of cocaine.

Despite it all, Mockett was intoxicated by Yemen. He'd tried a spell in Dubai and hated it. It was like living in Disneyland, he told friends. In Yemen, he found the Arabia of *One Thousand and One Nights*, untainted by money and modernity, home to some of the oldest continuously inhabited cities on earth. In the northern capital, Sana'a, thousands of stained-glass windows twinkled like jewels above qat sellers working by lamplight. In Hadhramaut, mud palaces painted in pastel shades were carved out of desert cliffs, unchanged since the time of the Romans, who called Yemen "Arabia Felix," the lucky land, a fertile territory where camel caravans stopped to rest and relax.

Mockett thought Yemen's dangers were mostly hype. As long as you're respectful, he told Cynthia, it's perfectly safe. He was quite happy eating breakfast on the street with regular Yemenis, using his hands as they did and making small talk in his limited Arabic. On long drives through sun-blasted mountain ranges, he and Cynthia could hear the echoing shouts of herdsmen communicating across valleys. Cynthia thought they sounded angry. "They're just talking to each other," David said. "That's the way they do it." Those peaks had a harsh beauty that appealed to him, just as they had to the interwar explorer Freya Stark, who wondered at "the high-shouldered mountains of Yemen . . . smoldering and dusky, as if the black volcanic points were coated with desert sand, and the red sandstones subdued by ashes of volcanoes."

Not even a brush with death could change his mind about his adopted home. It happened in March 2002. At the time Mockett was living in Hodeida, a port town up the coast from Aden. Returning from work one evening, he was locking his car when he noticed two men on a motorbike, stopped outside the front of his house. One of them had turned to face Mockett, raising an object to his shoulder that looked very much like a rifle. Before he could fully comprehend what was happening, Mockett heard a crack, and then felt a searing pain in his neck. "Naturally, I clapped my hand to the area and then, to developing horror, saw blood!" he wrote in a report for the police. "I dropped my keys and the phone and clipboard and RAN."

It turned out the bullet had ricocheted off Mockett's car and passed through his neck, just missing an artery. Like a good surveyor, he made sure he collected the round, as evidence, before calling a friend to drive him to the hospital. He told Cynthia about the shooting over the phone, a few days after it happened. They were in the middle of doing a crossword together—David in his Yemeni villa, Cynthia at the Vicarage, when he interrupted. "Cynth, I've been shot," he said curtly. She was shocked, although she tried not to show it; her immediate response was "How did you manage that?" Mockett never found out who targeted him or why. The local cops told him, improbably, that he'd been hit by a stray bullet fired in celebration from a nearby wedding. Later, Cynthia would come to suspect that a local businessman was behind the attempt on her husband's life, perhaps someone who'd lost money because David refused to participate in a cargo scam.

Dozens of visitors came to see the injured surveyor in hospital, including the regional governor, which Mockett took as evidence that most Yemenis wanted him around. He took the bloodstained bullet home as a souvenir and added the incident to his repertoire of stories. Whenever he told it, he mock-lamented that the doctors had done such a good job that he didn't even have a proper scar to show off, just a tiny pale dash. "No badge of honor!" he complained.

Mockett decided to stay in Yemen, later relocating to Aden, the country's primary port. As a former outpost of the Empire, it could offer comforts that were hard to find elsewhere. There was a decent hotel, the Sheraton, which had a metal detector in the lobby and a sign saying "NO GUNS OR DAGGERS."

There was an Anglican church, a smattering of eccentric British expats to hang out with, and even places where they could order beer. It was Yemen's most outward-looking city, a place where people from all over the country could let their hair down, relatively speaking. Once their daughters were grown, Cynthia never turned down a chance to visit and spend some time with her husband. She'd envisaged her 2011 trip as a vacation, though the nocturnal gunfire punctured any notion that it would be a carefree break. Not much of a holiday, she thought the next morning, as she surveyed the damage outside their villa.

In the days that followed, street protests broke out all over Aden. It was the dawn of the Arab Spring, a wave of demonstrations against oppressive regimes that had spread from Tunisia across the region. President Saleh's government was as corrupt and unscrupulous as its neighbors, and money from the country's few oil fields, which he'd previously used to placate would-be opponents, was running out. Yemeni security forces responded to calls for change by attacking unarmed protesters with tear gas, rubber bullets, and live ammunition, killing hundreds, while Saleh's image—slick hair and a prototypical despot's mustache—looked on reproachfully from billboards and murals.

One morning, the Yemeni woman the Mocketts employed as a house-keeper and cook approached Cynthia. "You need to go home, madam," she said. Cynthia nodded. "No, not on your own. You need to go home with Mr. David." Cynthia went to a meeting of expats at the Anglican church, where many of those present suggested the same thing. "I think I'll wait," she told them. Shortly afterward, the vicar fled.

But when Cynthia tried to talk to David about the situation, he told her that people were being hysterical. He refused to hire a driver or bodyguard and continued driving himself to work as usual. If there was a protest blocking the road, he simply took another route. Following his instructions, Cynthia stayed inside during the day, keeping toward the center of the house, where she passed the time reading and knitting. Otherwise, she would join him as he pored over maritime reports in his office by the port. The Yemeni employees there called her "Mrs. David."

There were things about her husband's professional life that had always been mysterious to Cynthia. She suspected he was holding information back, to stop her worrying about his safety. Every week, he would take her down to watch ships come and go at Steamer Point, where Queen Elizabeth had once disembarked. Aden's port had faded considerably since its British days—the paint on the oil pipes fueling the ships was peeling, and rubbish was strewn around in shoulder-high piles—but there was always something to see. There were hulking tankers and container ships the size of floating towns, jostling with motorboats and slender-sailed Arab dhows. There was sometimes a half-submerged wreck in the harbor, the ragged carcass of an earlier "casualty," as people in the maritime trade called broken vessels. David always watched the tugboats off-loading passengers. Cynthia often felt he was looking for something or someone, but if he was, he kept it to himself.

Anxiety was growing in Aden's tiny expatriate community. The Mocketts had hosted a security meeting with staff from the British embassy at the villa, and the UK government had advised citizens to leave Yemen as soon as possible. David and Cynthia bought a rolling airline ticket in case they needed to get out in a hurry; at the end of each day, it automatically renewed for the next available flight. One of their friends had mentioned a slightly outlandish fallback: if shelling closed the airport, they might be able to load the remaining foreigners into a dhow and sail across the Gulf of Aden to East Africa.

By April, Al Qaeda militants were fighting government troops for control of a town called Zinjibar, just sixty kilometers to Aden's east. Daily life in the port continued, punctuated by the occasional burst of gunfire. The area's warring factions were using the collapse of law and order to settle old scores. Cynthia's trip was scheduled to end that month, and she and David made use of their rolling ticket to return to Devon. "I won't be back until this is sorted," she explained to their housekeeper.

David, however, seemed more concerned about the tax man than the civil unrest. He'd once been hit with a hefty bill for spending too many days in England, missing out on the lower rate for those who met the criteria for residing abroad. The mistake had wiped out their savings. "I will never be caught out like that again," he told friends, even when they pleaded with him not to return to Yemen. He wasn't going to let a bit of local trouble stop him from working, and his wife knew better than to try to change his mind.

Mockett flew back to Aden in May, promising Cynthia he would be home in August, in time for a niece's wedding. He found the city even more unstable. The police had melted away, and outlying districts were being patrolled by masked men with guns riding pickup trucks. A July 2011 report in *The Economist* summed up the deteriorating security situation, describing a collision of Islamists, armed southern separatists, and government-backed assassins: "The south is a dangerous mess where the writ of the government in Sana'a now barely runs."

By then, Mockett's next big job had sailed through the Suez Canal and was cruising through the Red Sea toward Aden at a steady twelve knots. Painted in white letters on a blunt, flat bow was the vessel's name:

Brillante Virtuoso.

CHAPTER 2

THE GATE OF TEARS

In more than a decade at sea, Allan Marquez had seen the world—and it looked, for the most part, like the inside of a ship. The forty-year-old Filipino sailor had been born in a small town in Batangas, a coastal province south of Manila, on a plain of modest farms worked by sprawling, hard-to-feed families. But for the luckier and more adventurous among the men of Batangas, there was another option, more lucrative if hardly less difficult. Becoming a seafarer, as they're known in the Philippines, meant first attending a training college and then finding an assignment from one of Manila's manning agencies, lightly regulated companies that source crews for shipowners they're unlikely ever to meet. Marquez went through the training program as a young man. He knew that what came next wouldn't be easy. A seafarer was expected to live away from his family for as long as ten months every year, time spent isolated on vessels with cramped quarters, bad food, and, sometimes, abusive, dictatorial superiors. But he would also earn money— not much by the standards of developed countries, but multiples of what would be feasible at home. After building up some experience and rising in rank, the sailor would be able to afford to put his parents into a concrete house, instead of one made from wood and thatch, and send his children to a competently run private school instead of relying on the Philippines' underfunded public system.

Marquez, who had a square jaw, powerful hands, and wispy, slightly thinning hair, had been part of the invisible army of seafarers that powers the global economy for most of his adult life. Seafarers are responsible for the movement of virtually every product the modern world desires: shoes, cars, oil, food, and everything in between, accounting for over 80 percent of all worldwide trade in physical merchandise. The scale of the industry is astonishing, a direct result of the drastic expansion of international trade that began after the Second World War and has continued, with scant interruptions, ever since.

The merciless economic realities of the shipping industry largely explain why, by the beginning of this century, the bulk of its laborers came from just a few low-income countries: India and Indonesia and, especially, the Philippines. Filipinos tend to be favored above all others by shipowners because of their good English, as well as their willingness to work long hours, ask few impertinent questions, and accept low wages. At least 200,000 people working at sea hail from the Southeast Asian archipelago—often serving as primary breadwinners for large extended families.

Marquez came aboard the *Brillante Virtuoso* in January 2011, with a contracted salary of just $465 for a forty-eight-hour week, plus another $139.50 for "fixed overtime" of one hundred hours a month. Everyone else on board the tanker was Filipino, too. The master, or captain, was Noe Gonzaga, a fifty-seven-year-old with a dignified air and a grandfatherly smile. The task of keeping it running efficiently, and therefore profitably, fell to Nestor Tabares, fifty-four, who as chief engineer had dominion over the engine room and other mechanical systems. He had been serving on the *Brillante* since early the previous year and knew the ship intimately. All told, there were twenty-six men on board, and apart from brief shore leaves, they would work, eat, and sleep together for months, forming a sealed mini-society that's been compared to living in a monastery, or even a prison—an example of what the sociologist Erving Goffman called a "total institution," but one in near-constant motion.

More than 11,000 oil tankers ply the sea-lanes, ranging from modest barges to so-called VLCCs, or very large crude carriers, as long as the Chrysler Building is tall. The tankers share the ocean with another 5,300 container ships, the greatest of which are even larger than the biggest tankers, with capacity for tens of thousands of standardized steel boxes. The large-scale adoption of the shipping container in the 1960s revolutionized the industry, drastically reducing the time and money required to move products across vast distances. Along with larger tankers, such ships catalyzed explosive growth: in 2019, the total volume of goods loaded onto ships worldwide, oil included, exceeded 11 billion metric tons, more than four times the figure in 1970.

The *Brillante Virtuoso* was owned by a company called Suez Fortune Investments, which was domiciled in the Pacific tax haven of the Marshall Islands. In June 2011, about five months after Marquez joined the crew, the *Brillante* was hired by a Cypriot logistics firm to pick up just over 141,000 metric tons of fuel oil from Kerch, a faded industrial port on Ukraine's Crimean peninsula. Worth nearly $100 million, the cargo needed to be delivered to consumers in eastern China, two oceans away. The *Brillante* was nearly twenty years old, built in South Korea in 1992, a veteran compared with many ships at sea and near the end of its working life. But the job it was hired to perform was one of the oldest in the business. Tankers began carrying oil from the Black Sea to Asia more than a hundred years ago, when the British entrepreneur Marcus Samuel sent a vessel called the *Murex* from present-day Georgia through the Suez Canal and on to Singapore. A decade and a half after the *Murex*'s 1892 sailing proved it was feasible to carry oil halfway around the world in the hull of a ship, Samuel's London-based trading company, which had grown dramatically through its mastery of the tanker trade, merged with a competitor from the Netherlands to create an entity that would long outlive him: Royal Dutch Shell.

The *Brillante* set out for China on June 23, easing gently away from the splintered wharves and rusting, Soviet-era trawlers of Kerch's harbor. The helmsman set a course that would take the vessel toward the Mediterranean and beyond. Soon Marquez and the twenty-five other men on board settled into a dull regularity, with long shifts on the bridge, in the engine room, or attending to odd jobs like painting or scrubbing, punctuated by breaks watching action movies on laptops or sneaking cigarettes on the rear deck. Marquez was expected to pitch in with whichever tasks needed doing: maintaining a lookout on the bridge, chipping rust off the superstructure, ensuring that the lifeboats and other safety equipment were in usable condition, or anything else his superiors told him to do. It was hard, tedious work, and Marquez was sometimes so tired by the end of his shift that he could barely stand. The ragged condition of the *Brillante* didn't help. The ship threw off thick, noxious exhaust fumes, and the air-conditioning sometimes broke down, forcing the crew to sleep on deck rather than in their sweltering cabins. Whenever it got especially difficult, Marquez reminded himself of the sole reason he was at sea. His family was counting on the money he sent home, income that gave them a far more comfortable life than many of their compatriots. Thanks to his earnings, they had a foothold in the Philippines' middle class, and his duty now was to make sure they didn't slip off it.

In any case, such hardships weren't a surprise. As Marquez and the others had learned through bitter experience, few shipowners cared much for their comfort, or even their safety. Indeed, the entire modern shipping industry had been structured to interpose layer upon corporate layer between the men who profited from owning ships and those who labored on them. When something went wrong, if there was a fatal accident or the crew ran out of food, it was easy for shipowners to claim ignorance and diffuse responsibility. What mattered was getting the cargo, whatever it might be, to its destination quickly, cheaply, and in reasonable condition. Everything else was secondary at best.

A couple of days out from Kerch, an amateur photographer captured the *Brillante* as it passed through the Bosporus, the narrow waterway that cleaves the metropolis of Istanbul into its European and Asian halves. Although it was considerably smaller than the largest supertankers, the vessel was nonetheless impressive. Nearly as long as three football fields and with a deadweight, or carrying capacity, of 150,000 tons, it was shaped like a giant letter L that had been knocked over onto its side. The upright part of the L was the accommodation block, housing the bridge and crew cabins, all stacked atop an engine room the size of a large house. Every other inch of its hull was devoted to the *Brillante*'s sole economic function: carrying oil, and lots of it, separated into twelve tanks to stop it from sloshing around and destabilizing the ship, connected by a thick band of pipework that ran the length of the forest-green deck. As the tanker steamed through Istanbul, it sat heavily in the water, with its lower hull completely submerged—an obvious indication, to even a casual observer, that it was fully loaded.

Once the crew passed through the Bosporus, there would be several days in the Mediterranean, including a stop on the Greek island of Chios to take on fuel and supplies, then a journey through the Suez Canal into the Red Sea, skirting around the Arabian Peninsula at the Gulf of Aden before hitting the open ocean and powering toward India, Singapore, and finally China. But in the stretch of water beyond the Suez, the men on the *Brillante* knew that their cargo's obvious value would be a liability. Where they were headed, there would be more than just photographers watching.

The Gulf of Aden is near the top of any list of the world's most important waterways. Bound by Yemen in the north and the Horn of Africa in the south, it's shaped like a jagged rectangle, opening on its eastern side into the Indian Ocean. As the sole route between that body of water and the Red Sea—and thus the Suez—transiting the Gulf is the only way for ships to travel from Europe to Asia, or vice versa, without making a detour of several thousand nautical miles around South Africa. Apart from the Strait of Malacca, the slender passage between Malaysia and Indonesia, no single shipping lane is more crucial to global commerce.

Something happened to sailors as they approached the Gulf of Aden, a phenomenon that Marquez had seen, and felt himself, again and again. Tempers got shorter. Captains became more demanding. The amount of work to be done, rarely less than exhausting, grew even more intense. The reason was simple: At the time of the *Brillante*'s voyage, the Gulf was an intensely dangerous place. Somalia had been essentially a failed state since the collapse of its central government in the early 1990s, creating a uniquely hospitable environment for warlords, Islamic extremists, and pirates. There were more than 170 attacks on ships in the waters surrounding the country in 2010, despite deployments of naval vessels by the United States, European Union, and other world powers to deal with the ongoing crisis. In the six months before the *Brillante* chugged into the Gulf, pirate incidents were being reported every couple of days. Often occurring hundreds of miles from shore, the raids were becoming increasingly audacious, with large motherships serving as command-and-control centers and supply depots for high-speed skiffs.

The goal of such attacks was to make money by holding ships and crews for ransom, not to kill or maim the people on board—unless they got in the way, of course. But Marquez had heard the stories, traded on ships' decks and in Manila bars, about what a successful raid could mean for sailors like those on the *Brillante*. The case of the *Maersk Alabama*, the cargo vessel whose captain was rescued by US Navy SEALs in 2009—later immortalized, with the help of Tom Hanks, in the film *Captain Phillips*—was far from typical. More often the crews of captured ships could expect to be held hostage for weeks or months as ransoms were negotiated. In the meantime, they might be confined to a remote Somali anchorage, vulnerable to disease, malnutrition, and abuse or even torture by their captors. Short of sinking, it was one of the worst fates that could befall a sailor.

One of the goals of naval operations in the High Risk Area, as the region where Somali pirates operated was called, was to establish a kind of safety net over the worst-affected zone, to ensure that no vessel in distress was ever too far from assistance. Even so, the distances involved meant that during the decisive phase of an attack—the attempted boarding, with pirates attempting to scale the sides of a tanker or freighter using boarding ladders and grappling hooks—crews were likely to be on their own, with backup potentially hours away. As a result, the shipping industry had developed a set of tactics that commercial vessels could use to render themselves less appealing targets, and to give them some ability, if necessary, to fight off attackers.

The passage that marks the boundary between the placid Red Sea and the Gulf of Aden is known as the Bab el-Mandeb—the Gate of Tears—named by long-ago mariners for the dangers of navigating it. As the *Brillante* steamed toward its entrance, Marquez got to work putting the usual measures into place. With several other crewmen, he attached coils of razor wire to the white railings that marked the perimeter of the tanker's deck, using steel ties to secure them in place every few feet. He helped test the fire hoses that had been distributed up and down the ship, ready to knock a boarding party out of their skiffs, or off the hull if it came to that. The crew prepared a "citadel," stocking a room with food, water, and medicine, a place to barricade themselves and await rescue if pirates did somehow make it aboard. They had also placed a dummy in coveralls on the stern, a sort of nautical scarecrow intended to give the appearance of a man perpetually on watch.

There was one final safeguard, which made Marquez feel a bit better about the *Brillante*'s chances of making it through the Gulf of Aden unmolested. As the piracy situation worsened, some vessels had begun carrying teams of guards on board, usually ex-soldiers looking for a way to cash in on their skills. They had a reputation for being the gold standard of shipborne security measures: even in the most frenetic periods of pirate activity, virtually no vessels carrying armed guards had been successfully captured. But they were also expensive, in an industry that prioritized cutting costs wherever possible, and Suez Fortune, the *Brillante*'s owner, had never hired a security team for the tanker's previous journeys through the Gulf. This time, however, the company had decided to spring for one. The plan was to rendezvous with them near Aden, on the morning of July 6, after the *Brillante* had already been in the area for the better part of a day. Until then, Marquez and the rest of the crew would have to hope the precautions they'd taken would be enough.

Everyone on the *Brillante* knew the risks they were running as they neared the rendezvous point on the afternoon of July 5. One of the officers had scrawled an all-caps reminder on the navigation chart: BE VIGILANT PIRATED AREAS. During the afternoon watch, the bridge crew nervously debated just how aggressive, and well armed, any pirates might be, their conversations picked up by the *Brillante*'s voyage data recorder, the nautical equivalent of an airliner's black box. "I heard from the other vessels that fifty-caliber guns were used," one sailor said. Another chimed in, accurately, that they could have rocket-propelled grenades. On the other hand, they might be easy to scare off once the security team was on board, the first crewman speculated. "I heard from other vessels that once the pirates get shot at, they retreat." He added a nervous joke. Maybe, he said, the *Brillante* crew should show them they were unafraid and announce: "Hello pirates, we are here, waiting for you!"

Marquez was assigned to the evening watch, from 8:00 p.m. to midnight. He arrived at about 7:45 to begin his shift. His superior, Second Officer Roberto Artezuela, came onto the bridge a few minutes later. Not long afterward Noe Gonzaga, the ship's captain, gave the order to "finish with engines." The rumble of the *Brillante*'s powerful motors soon came to a stop, and the vessel quieted, the men suddenly able to hear the sound of breakers sloshing against the hull. For the rest of the night the ship would drift, pitching gently up and down with the waves. Gonzaga had ordered Tabares, the chief engineer, to keep the engines "on short notice," meaning they would require as long as twenty minutes to restart.

Marquez had a commanding view from his perch on the bridge, high above the deck. He could see a couple of other ships in the distance, strings of lights out toward the horizon. His job was to keep a careful lookout for danger, shuttling with a pair of binoculars between the bridge itself and the bridge wings—narrow outdoor decks that extended on either side—stopping occasionally to look at what was being picked up on the *Brillante*'s radar. To pass the time, the men on watch chatted about the usual distractions, sports and movies. Like millions of their countrymen, they were fans of the champion Filipino fighter Manny Pacquiao. They were also partial to action flicks in the Jean-Claude Van Damme mold. At one point, Gonzaga and the helmsman compared which cinemas they liked to visit back home. Occasionally the radio crackled to life, often with naval ships liaising with commercial vessels in the area to check their positions and plans for the rest of their passage—nothing that the crew of the *Brillante* needed to worry about. A bit before 11:00 p.m., Gonzaga decided to call it a night, leaving orders that he be contacted immediately if a suspicious vessel appeared.

Just under an hour later, Marquez was nearing the end of his watch and looking forward to returning to his cabin to get some sleep when he noticed a blip on the radar. "I have a target on the port side," he called out. Something was headed for the *Brillante*, and it was moving fast.

CHAPTER 3

INTRUDERS

Allan Marquez raised his binoculars to get a better look at whatever was coming toward the *Brillante*. He spotted it off the port bow, a streamlined silhouette emerging from the darkness ahead of the ship. It was a small wooden boat with an outboard engine and red, white, and blue stripes painted on the side. The boat slowed down noticeably as it came closer, illuminated by the *Brillante*'s deck lights. The men inside, Marquez thought, seemed to be looking at the forward section of the hull, as if to read the name that was painted in white capital letters just behind the anchor.

A couple of minutes later the boat was moving again, powering toward the *Brillante*'s stern. Roberto Artezuela, the second officer, told Marquez to go down and investigate. He took a walkie-talkie and walked down the stairs of the accommodation block, emerging on the deck just a stone's throw from where the visitors to the ship were floating. There were seven men in all, Marquez saw, armed with assault rifles with long, curved magazines. All but one, the man driving the boat, were wearing camouflage uniforms. Their faces were covered by what looked like medical masks. Marquez's mind raced through the possibilities of who they might be. It was certainly possible they were pirates; on the other hand, they might be some sort of naval patrol, conducting a mission. He had no way to be sure.

Seeing he was in earshot, one of the men shouted at Marquez in English, asking to be let on board. That was not a decision for a low-ranking seaman to make, and Marquez, who'd been relaying what he was seeing by radio to the bridge, needed to ask for instructions.

"Bridge, bridge," he called up in Tagalog, the primary language of the Philippines.

"Go ahead."

"The persons on the boat are requesting to lower the pilot ladder," Marquez said, referring to a piece of equipment, made of thick rope and wooden slats, carried by every commercial ship to allow someone to climb from a smaller boat onto the deck.

"No, no, don't lower, I'll call the captain," his crewmate replied.

A moment passed. "Allan, ask them if they are the security."

Marquez called down to the boat and radioed the answer up to the bridge. There, one of the crew had contacted Captain Gonzaga, who was still in his cabin. "Allan asked, sir, and they said they are security," the crewman said. The captain's order quickly came back. "Okay, Allan, lower the pilot ladder."

Looking down at the masked men bobbing around in the darkness, Marquez wasn't sure he'd heard correctly. He asked the bridge twice to repeat the instructions. Letting them on board so quickly didn't make any sense to him. The *Brillante* crew had just spent hours hardening their vessel against intruders, and every antipiracy handbook emphasized the importance of not letting unexpected visitors onto a ship without careful verification of who they were—by hauling up their passports in a bag to be inspected, for example, and checking their identities with someone trusted onshore. Those were basic procedures, expected to be observed even in far less dangerous times and places than the dead of night in the Gulf of Aden. Nor did the men in the boat match the description of the security team that Marquez knew the *Brillante* was expecting. It was supposed to have three members, not seven, and they weren't scheduled to arrive until the next morning. The last time Marquez had been on a ship that carried guards, they'd arrived with their weapons in a sealed box, which was then stowed securely on the bridge—not with Kalashnikovs slung around their shoulders.

But an order was an order, especially when it came from the captain. The pilot ladder was heavy. Marquez managed with some difficulty to maneuver it over the coils of lacerating razor wire that he'd strung around the deck himself, just a few days earlier. He dropped the ladder down, and moments later, six of the men climbed up from their boat and onto the *Brillante*.

It took just a few moments for Marquez to realize that his captain had made a terrible mistake. Seconds after coming on deck, the apparent leader of the group demanded Marquez's radio, leveling his gun to leave no doubt as to who was now in charge. The sailor handed it over. A strange, numb sensation spread through his body as it reacted to what his mind was still struggling to process. The thing that all seafarers dread, that they'd read and joked nervously about and seen in movies, was happening. To him.

Overhead, the bridge crew were trying to raise Marquez for an update. "Deck, bridge. Deck, bridge. Deck, bridge," his radio squawked. "Allan, come in." But Marquez couldn't respond. He knew he had no choice but to accede to the man's next order: to take him and the others to see the captain. With a gun pressed into his back, Marquez led the group onto a staircase leading up the accommodation block to the bridge. He kept his eyes forward, afraid to turn around. When they reached Gonzaga's cabin, Marquez got his first good look at the men he'd let on board. The leader was wearing a red-and-white keffiyeh scarf and, in addition to his rifle, carried a pistol in a holster. The camouflage he wore was desert brown; oddly, he wasn't wearing shoes. The others were dressed similarly.

Marquez knocked on Gonzaga's door, and the captain promptly opened it. "They have a gun in my back and took my walkie-talkie," he said to Gonzaga in Tagalog. If Gonzaga was afraid, he didn't show it. He told Marquez to stay calm and to gather the rest of the crew in the TV room, two decks away— one of the few spaces on the *Brillante* set aside for recreation. Following his instructions, Marquez went door-to-door, rousing his sleeping crewmates and telling them where to go.

A little after midnight, everyone was gathered in the TV room along with the six intruders who'd boarded the *Brillante*. The gunmen hadn't identified themselves or explained what they wanted, and Marquez could only guess at their intentions as he watched them counting off the crew, making sure all twenty-six were accounted for. They soon split up. Two left with Captain Gonzaga, and two with the chief engineer, Nestor Tabares. The remaining pair stayed with the rest of the ship's personnel, standing guard just outside the TV room. They closed the door, leaving the group sealed inside. Marquez put his ear to its surface, trying to hear what was being said in the hallway, but couldn't make anything out.

What seemed like hours went by. No one dared leave, not even to use the bathroom. Marquez sat silently wondering what was happening elsewhere on the ship. Just after 1:00 a.m. the main engine rumbled to life, which wasn't a good sign. Sailors in the Gulf of Aden knew that pirate attacks often ended with the ship and crew being taken to Somalia—about ten hours' sailing from the *Brillante*'s position. In Somalia, captured crews waited, sometimes for a very long time, while a shipowner or, more likely, the owner's insurance company, negotiated a ransom. One particularly unfortunate group of sailors was held for more than four years in a remote town, four hundred kilometers from Mogadishu, before a bounty was paid. Three of them died during the hijack or in captivity; the rest survived by eating rats. As Marquez and the others locked in the TV room worried about their fates, a more immediate terror took hold. At 1:30 a.m. there was a clatter of gunshots. Some of them assumed the worst: that Gonzaga and Tabares had been murdered. But they remained where they were, fearful that if they tried to leave, the next fusillade could be aimed at them.

At about 2:30 a.m., the throbbing hum of the engine stopped. The *Brillante* was no longer moving, though no one knew why. Then came the sound of an explosion, a boom resonating from deep in the bowels of the ship. Minutes later, smoke began billowing into the TV room through an air-conditioning unit. Somewhere, a fire had begun—an alarming development on any vessel, but terrifying on one carrying more than 100,000 tons of oil.

Soon the lights went out. Up to that point the sailors had tried to stay quiet, keeping their fears mostly to themselves. Suddenly the room was alive with the sound of panicked voices. Though they were still frightened of the intruders who'd taken control of their ship, the men decided that if they didn't do something, they would likely die in there. One of them slowly opened the door, only to discover that the hallway was empty. At some point, their guards had taken off.

The sailors formed themselves into a line to make their way to the bridge, where they might be able to determine what was happening. Marquez took a position in the middle, keeping his hands on his head in case the gunmen reappeared. The electricity had gone out throughout the ship, forcing the crew to navigate by the faint glow of emergency lights. As Marquez and the others were climbing through a stairwell, those went out, too. A few of the men had flashlights, which illuminated the reflective arrows showing the way to the bridge. Later, Marquez would recall the eerie silence, all of the ship's machinery suddenly stilled, and how exposed and vulnerable he felt as they drifted in the sea.

The bridge was pitch-dark as they entered. Marquez stayed low to the floor, scared that the *Brillante*'s attackers, if they were still around, might open fire if they saw or heard the sailors moving. Like the pirates who were guarding the TV room, however, the ones on the bridge seemed to be gone. The only person there was Gonzaga, his hands bound in front of his body with a cable tie. One of the crew cut it open. "Water, water," someone called out, and a sailor passed the captain a bottle. Collecting himself, a visibly shaken Gonzaga tried to explain to the crew what had happened. One of them "kept aiming his gun at me and kept asking for money," he said. "I kept telling them we do not have anything valuable."

The men still didn't know where their attackers had gone, or what exactly had happened. "Everybody just sit down," one of the sailors urged. "They might spray us with bullets." But the *Brillante* was still on fire, and even if the pirates had fled the ship, the lives of the crew were very much at risk. Standing on the darkened bridge they counted off, to make sure everyone was safe, and immediately realized that Tabares was absent. No one had seen the chief engineer since the attackers had escorted him away from the TV room, hours before. Gonzaga sent two men down through the accommodation block to look for him. He wasn't in his cabin. In the engine room, the next likeliest place for Tabares to be, the smoke was too thick for them to enter, and they soon turned back. Meanwhile, the fire was clearly intensifying. From the windows of the bridge, Marquez could see smoke pouring from the hull into the night sky. An acrid, chemical stench was rising from deep within the ship, the smell of flames consuming the contents of what was, in effect, a floating industrial facility.

The tanker had a carbon dioxide system that could suppress even an out-of-control blaze by depriving it of the oxygen it needed to sustain itself. But if Tabares was indeed in the engine room, and had managed to stay alive amid the smoke, turning on the system would likely suffocate him. And even if they somehow contained the fire, the crew had no way of knowing if gunmen were still hiding somewhere on board.

As he stared up at the black plume pulsing into the night sky, Marquez made some mental calculations about what might happen in the next few hours. He could feel his temples pulsing from the adrenaline. If the twenty-six men on the *Brillante* were going to make it through the night alive, they would need help.

At that moment, about thirty-five miles to the south, the USS *Philippine Sea* was patrolling its sector of the Gulf of Aden, on the lookout for pirates. The cruiser was an imposing sight. With a top speed of more than thirty knots, it had a full suite of advanced sensors and weaponry: high-powered search and targeting radars, antiaircraft and antiship missiles, ultra-accurate Phalanx cannons capable of directing a lethal hail of metal at incoming threats, and a pair of Seahawk helicopters that could operate well ahead of the ship itself.

Early on the morning of July 6, it also had a crew that was hungry for action. For several weeks the *Philippine Sea* had been assigned to the Combined Maritime Forces, a twenty-five-country coalition patrolling the dangerous waters off East Africa. Its job was to disrupt pirate attacks and, if possible, to detain the men who perpetrated them, perhaps even transferring them for prosecution on land. The roughly three hundred men and women on board had trained again and again for different scenarios, from intercepting a pirate skiff with a helicopter to boarding suspicious vessels with a tactical team, searching for weapons or other hints of criminal activity. But the pirates had proven frustratingly elusive. The sheer size of the Gulf of Aden, and the vast number of vessels that traversed it, meant the odds were usually in their favor. By the time the *Philippine Sea* received word of an attack, it was often too late.

This time, however, seemed like it might be different. Just after 3:00 a.m., the first transmission came into the *Philippine Sea*'s Combat Information Center, a darkened room located deep inside the heavily armored heart of the ship. There, a team of a dozen or so sailors and officers had access to all the information being collected by the radar and communication systems, which was displayed overhead on huge, glowing screens.

The message arrived over the very high frequency radio, as an open distress call to anyone in the area. "Coalition warship, coalition warship, this is *Brillante Virtuoso*. We are under attack," a Filipino-accented voice said.

An operator on the *Philippine Sea* responded twelve seconds later. "This is Coalition Five-Eight," she said—a reference to the cruiser's hull number, CG-58. "What is your position? Over."

The *Brillante* sailor relayed it. "We have pirate on board, pirate on board," the crewman went on. "And please we need immediate assistance . . . please hurry. We are in distress . . . we are on fire also, ma'am. We are already blackout." The bridge was in chaos. Its audio recorder picked up several voices yelling in Tagalog, along with the sounds of men rushing around and several of the ship's alarms going off at once. A few of the crew huddled around the radio so they could hear the Navy's reply: "*Brillante Virtuoso*, this is warship five-eight. We are en route to your position and at our best speed, over."

On the flight deck at the *Philippine Sea*'s stern, two pilots climbed into a gray Seahawk, crammed with sensors and armed with a door-mounted machine gun, and began to spin its rotors. A moment later they lifted the helicopter sharply and, once clear of the cruiser, pointed its nose downward as it roared toward the *Brillante*. A commander sent a message to other military ships in the area to instruct them on what would happen next. "PRIORITY FIRST OF ALL IS TO ENSURE THE SAFETY OF THE CREW," it read. "AND THEN TO ESTABLISH, USING OTHER CLOSE BY UNITS AND INDEPENDENT DEPLOYERS AS REQUIRED, WHETHER THE SPS"— suspected pirates—"HAVE DEFINITELY LEFT THE SHIP, IF THEY ARE

STILL IN THE AREA AND WHETHER THERE IS A POSSIBLE MOTH-
ERSHIP IN THE AREA."

Wherever the pirates were, they were no longer on the *Brillante Virtuoso*. Marquez could be reasonably sure of that. In their desperation to be rescued, the crew fired flare after flare from the bridge, illuminating the length of the tanker and the surrounding ocean for a few seconds in incandescent red. There was no sign of the masked men or their skiff. Even if pirates were lurking out of sight, the crew had no option but to focus on their own survival. The situation on the *Brillante* was worsening by the minute. Toward the stern they could see flames licking the side of the funnel, alarmingly close to the bridge. Around 3:30 a.m., with the *Philippine Sea* still miles away, Gonzaga decided it was time to abandon ship. The crew's passports and other important documents were kept in the captain's cabin, and Marquez was sent there to retrieve them. It was inky black inside the accommodation block, and Marquez could find his way forward only with a flashlight. He made his way gingerly to Gonzaga's quarters, returning to the bridge clutching the passports. A short time later he emerged onto the main deck with a life jacket he'd picked up from his own cabin.

There were two large lifeboats on the *Brillante*, bright orange dinghies with hard roofs and small engines that were designed to survive on the open ocean, at least for a time. The crew gathered near the starboard one, counting off again to make sure everyone had made it. All were present, with the exception of Tabares. The chief engineer was still missing. He could have been shot or gone overboard; they had no idea. He's probably in the engine room, hiding, someone suggested. But there was no more time to wait. The fire was moving too quickly. Gonzaga would later remember the heat on his skin as the crew prepared the lifeboat, and hearing ominous cracking noises as the blaze began to consume the interior structure of the tanker.

Marquez helped lower the lifeboat slowly into the water alongside the *Brillante*. He climbed down the pilot ladder to get in, cutting his hands as he moved past the razor wire that still ringed the perimeter of the deck. Then, he released the lines that still connected the lifeboat to the ship. Once everyone was aboard, a helmsman took control of the engine, maneuvering to get as far away as possible.

As the crew evacuated they heard the distinct sound of a helicopter's rotors, growing louder. They looked up to see the Seahawk overhead, hovering above their burning vessel. An airman on board reported seeing a large explosion, which he guessed came from somewhere above the engine room. It wasn't clear how much longer the tanker would survive, and naval commanders were beginning to worry about the possibility of an oil spill.

The hulking outline of the *Philippine Sea* appeared on the horizon just as the first crack of morning light split the sea and the sky. But the *Brillante*'s crew wasn't permitted to approach the warship that had come to rescue them. For understandable reasons, the Navy preferred not to allow unfamiliar craft to come anywhere near its vessels. Instead, it deployed a pair of inflatable boats, one carrying a heavily armed tactical team, in case the pirates were found, and the other to ferry the sailors in small groups from their lifeboat.

While that operation was under way, the helicopter crew spotted something through their infrared camera: one man standing on the *Brillante*'s deck, waving a flashlight to try to get their attention. It was Tabares, the chief engineer, apparently unharmed. The flames were too intense for the Seahawk to attempt a rescue, but an inflatable boat could get close enough. Just after dawn, Tabares, wearing an orange life jacket, leaped off the *Brillante* and into the water, where two US sailors grabbed him and hauled him up.

The rescued crewmen were taken to the *Philippine Sea*'s gym, where they were given fresh clothes and food and checked out by naval medics. No pirates had been spotted by the cruiser or any other military vessels in the area. Once the *Brillante*'s crew had been attended to, Tagalog speakers on board the *Philippine Sea* began conducting interviews with the Filipino sailors, asking them to recount precisely what had happened. Captain Gonzaga told naval personnel that the pirates insisted there was $100,000 in cash on board the *Brillante* and demanded he hand the money over. They told him they would take the tanker to Somalia, Gonzaga said.

Tabares then explained what he'd done after being separated from the rest of the crew. Two of the pirates had marched him down to the engine room and ordered him to get it running. While their attention was elsewhere, Tabares recounted, he decided to frustrate their plans to reach Somalia by sabotaging the engine, starting and stopping a key component several times until a release of steam stopped it from functioning. After this daring act, the chief engineer said he ran to the citadel, the secure room the crew had stocked with supplies for waiting out an attack, and kept the door locked until he was sure he was safe. He recalled hearing two explosions as he fled, but couldn't say what had caused them.

Soon, Marquez and the other sailors shifted from shocked exhaustion to giddy relief, laughing as they went over the details of their escape again and again. Beyond mere survival, there was another reason to rejoice: the men figured their ordeal might mean a free trip home. Hours earlier, they feared they were about to die; now they might get precious, unexpected time with their families. Soon they were posing for a picture with some of the Navy sailors, burly midwestern types with blond hair and thick, muscular necks. The slight Filipinos, some wearing the paper-thin white jumpsuits they'd been given to replace their wet clothes, smiled from ear to ear.

Morning had broken over the Gulf of Aden. The *Brillante* drifted nearby, still on fire with not a soul on board, a naval helicopter flying loops overhead. From a distance the ship looked almost peaceful, the only sign of distress the thick plumes of smoke that continued to pour into a sky that turned from slate gray to powdery blue as the sun rose higher.

CHAPTER 4

DISTRESS SIGNALS

A supertanker in trouble is a singular event. It requires the attention of naval fleets, coast guards, international marine agencies, and governments across the immediate region, as well as in the homelands of its crew. That's not to mention those with a financial interest: the shipowners, cargo owners, bankers, and insurers backing the voyage, and a diffuse crowd of brokers, lawyers, traders, agents, and investors from London to New York, Dubai, and Singapore.

If the *Brillante Virtuoso* sank to the sandy bottom of the Gulf of Aden, the financial blow would be substantial. Most obviously, a vessel with a nominal value of $55 million would be lost. The $100 million of oil stored in its hull would also have to be recovered in an expensive underwater operation, or else secured to stop it from spilling out and fouling the coastlines of the Gulf with a million barrels of black sludge, the cleanup of which might run into the billions. Equally worrying, if the events on the *Brillante* signaled a new tactic—if Somali pirates were willing to blow up ships traveling along one of the world's busiest maritime highways—that was the kind of problem global leaders would need to address.

At 3:06 a.m., three minutes after the *Brillante* crew made radio contact with the USS *Philippine Sea*, someone on the tanker's bridge pressed a concealed button, triggering a distress signal. Vessels over a certain size are required by antipiracy regulations to have security systems capable of sending real-time data to shore, enabling a rapid response to an incident. The moment the *Brillante*'s Ship Security Reporting System (SSRS) was activated, it automatically generated messages that were delivered to various government and private-sector organizations. The alerts included the vessel's name, position, speed, and status: "MV *Brillante Virtuoso*, IMO 9014822, Liberian flag at posn 1229N 04445E crse 140, 0.5 kts."

Within seconds, one such message arrived at the office of United Kingdom Maritime Trade Operations, or UKMTO, in Dubai. To this day, the UK retains an outsize role in marine affairs, a legacy of when the Royal Navy patrolled an empire on which the sun never set. Even as Britain's influence waned after the Second World War, much of the legal and administrative machinery of modern shipping remained in British hands. In the 2000s, with piracy escalating into a severe problem, the UKMTO was made responsible for connecting military forces with the merchant ships they were supposed to protect, keeping everyone communicating during a crisis.

Petty Officer Bob Boosey got a call summoning him to the UKMTO operations room just after 3:00 a.m. "We've got an incident," the official on watch told him. Boosey, a Royal Navy lifer, lived in an outbuilding within the pale walls of the British Embassy compound in Dubai's diplomatic district. It was a short walk, and he hustled over without stopping to change into his white uniform. Boosey was surprised to be called in the dead of night. In his years tracking piracy, he'd never known Somali raiders to attack after dark, when boarding a ship was far more challenging. But he had little time to dwell on the thought.

Inside the dimly lit operations room, about a dozen computer screens relayed nautical data, including three large wall monitors showing UKMTO's zone of responsibility: roughly four million square miles of ocean, stretching from the mouth of the Suez Canal down to Kenya and eastward to the Indian coast. The pirate-infested High Risk Area was outlined in red, with the *Brillante Virtuoso* displayed as a dot squarely inside the danger zone. Pinned against another wall were printed images of other ships that had fallen victim to piracy that week, a reminder of the importance of Boosey's mission.

Boosey had dealt with numerous hijackings in his career, including the

2009 *Maersk Alabama* incident that inspired *Captain Phillips*. UKMTO personnel were amused to see their portrayal in the film, which depicted a smartly dressed young cadet communicating with the eponymous captain from what looked like a space-age communications hub. "Chances are it's just fishermen," the UKMTO cadet said in the scene. "They're not here to fish," replied Phillips.

In fact, back in 2009 the agency had operated from less impressive premises: a converted apartment in a Dubai tower block. Staff would come to work in shorts and T-shirts, so as not to alert the other residents to what was happening inside. They moved to the safety of the British Embassy after being warned that the criminal gangs behind Somali piracy were operating in Dubai and might consider the UKMTO enough of a nuisance to pay a visit.

After sitting down at his workstation, Boosey began to coordinate with all the naval forces in the region, including US and British installations in Bahrain and allied vessels deployed around the Middle East. Officers were firing questions at him through Mercury Chat, a shared military messaging system. Boosey zoomed in on the *Brillante*'s icon on his wall monitor to bring up its profile. "TO ALL: BRILLIANTE VIRTUOSO, flag Liberian, owner Marshall Islands, crew 26 all Filipino," he wrote in a Mercury message at 3:55 a.m. That one transmission encapsulated a set of challenges typical of the fragmented nature of modern shipping. The tanker was owned by a corporate entity in a Pacific tax haven—the Marshall Islands—which was in turn owned by a Greek family based in Piraeus, just outside Athens. It sailed under the flag of tiny Liberia, which augments its finances by selling cheap, hassle-free registrations to about one in ten of the world's commercial vessels. Not that its regulators actually resided in that impoverished West African nation; by historical quirk, the Liberian registry was run by Israeli-American entrepreneurs operating out of a headquarters in Dulles, Virginia. Meanwhile, the oil the tanker was carrying was owned by a trading firm based in Switzerland and Monaco.

The *Brillante*'s patchwork of relationships wasn't unusually complicated by industry standards. It was the by-product of a system that had evolved over the previous six decades to eliminate financial and regulatory friction at every opportunity, driving the price of transporting goods as low as possible.

Operating with minimally paid crews and subject to almost no meaningful taxation, by the early years of the twenty-first century giant cargo ships had become so efficient that it cost only about $2,000 to get a container of gadgets from Shenzhen to one of the dozen or so major US ports. For better and worse, this remarkable fact had transformed the lives of hundreds of millions of people—from European and American consumers, who gained access to unimagined bounties of cheap stuff, to workers in countries like China and Vietnam, given a ticket into the middle class by newly profitable export industries.

Yet the intricacies of this process are hidden from the people who benefit from it, and sometimes even from those charged with policing the oceans. It's standard practice for vessels to be legally owned by brass-plate companies set up in far-flung tax shelters, of which the Marshall Islands is one of many. Even maritime insiders often find it difficult to determine who a ship actually belongs to, behind whatever entity, usually with a meaninglessly generic name, is listed on an official document. This lack of transparency allows for substantial cost cutting, for example by placing vessels' earnings far beyond the reach of major tax authorities—as well as regulatory evasion. In the offshore legal netherworld that tankers and container ships inhabit, responsibility for things like safety and crew welfare can be passed around in an endless shell game.

For one thing, the location where a vessel is owned often bears no relation to the country where it's officially registered, or "flagged." Technically, the applicable law on any ship is determined by the ensign flying on its deck. In the early twentieth century, most shipowners paid to register under the jurisdiction of major marine powers like Britain and the United States, benefiting from their legal regimes and military protection. But eventually, entrepreneurial officials in countries like Panama realized they could raise revenue by offering what's now called a flag of convenience. By registering their vessels in these places, owners could avoid developed-world rules on wages, working hours, and union membership, while also being subject to fewer inspections and a more relaxed attitude to regulation.

The practice got a running start during Prohibition, when American cruise liners were able to serve booze to passengers by flagging themselves as

Panamanian, and became increasingly common after the Second World War. Today, Panama, the Marshall Islands, and Liberia serve as the ostensible homes of more than a third of the global merchant fleet, and there are even flags of convenience available from places like Mongolia and Bolivia, land-locked countries with no actual maritime industries to speak of. As one chronicler put it, flags of convenience represent "free enterprise at its freest," with governments competing to provide shipowners with the most laissez-faire environments in which to domicile their assets.

In the UKMTO office in Dubai, it fell to Bob Boosey to untangle this knot of ownership and responsibility in order to get the approvals required to rescue the *Brillante*'s crew and secure the vessel, hopefully before it ended up on the seafloor. Boosey contacted people in London, the Marshall Islands, Liberia—via its registry headquarters in Virginia—and the Philippines. He was also communicating with a Greek firm called Central Mare, which the *Brillante*'s owners had hired to operate the tanker day-to-day, making sure it was fully crewed, supplied, and documented.

At approximately 6:00 a.m. Dubai time, a Central Mare employee whom Boosey had tracked down hurried to the firm's office in Athens and emailed over a crew list, allowing Boosey to check that all personnel were accounted for. Boosey replied with a situation update, passing on that the *Brillante* had lost engine power and was "DIW": dead in the water.

Thanks to the rescue operation by the USS *Philippine Sea*, the crew were safe, and the pirates had apparently vanished. UKMTO and other agencies now needed to do something about the ship full of toxic, flammable liquid that was drifting, abandoned and ablaze, a dozen or so miles off the coast of Yemen. Boosey had been trying for several hours to raise the Yemeni Coast Guard, without success. Then, as the dawn broke, he received a message that help had arrived.

"Two Panamanian flagged tugs are alongside the stricken vessel," the battle watch officer on the *Philippine Sea* reported, carrying a salvage team sent by the *Brillante*'s owners. In every major port and waterway, there are salvage companies waiting to respond to distress calls, serving as something like a private emergency service for the open ocean. In return for the difficult and dangerous work of putting out a fire, plugging a leak, or towing an immobilized ship to safety, salvors have the right to claim a portion of the value of what they save—often around 10 percent, though the most challenging jobs can earn them far more. With so much oil on board, the *Brillante* would be a major prize for this team, who'd come with impressive speed from nearby Aden.

As Boosey continued working the phones, news of the tanker's situation was rippling outward, reaching everyone who had money riding on its voyage. In Limassol, Cyprus, at an office wedged between a fruit market and a Mercedes-Benz showroom, Evgeny Sokolov arrived to an email explaining that the *Brillante* was on fire. Essentially a middleman, Sokolov worked for a company called Solal Shipping, whose business was to find seaborne transport and manage logistics for clients looking to move their goods from shore to shore. In this case, the client was Holt Global, an international oil trading firm, which had engaged Solal to arrange the shipment of a cargo from Ukraine to eastern China. In mid-June Solal had made a deal to charter the *Brillante*, agreeing to a fee of about $3.2 million for the safe delivery of the oil. Almost from the start, the relationship had been a frustrating one. Sokolov had repeatedly emailed the *Brillante*'s managers and agents to protest over unscheduled stops and delays and to express concern about the cargo's temperature. If it wasn't kept warm enough, there was a risk it could congeal inside the hull.

Solal's employees had been especially dismayed to learn that the *Brillante* was going to stop near Aden to rendezvous with its security team, "totally ignoring safety procedures" that emphasized moving as quickly as possible through dangerous waters. One of Sokolov's colleagues had even threatened legal action, writing that "needless to say, our patience in this matter is now more than exhausted." Now, Solal and Holt had a much bigger problem.

Around midday on July 6, 2011, a London-based crisis communications agency engaged by Central Mare issued a statement revealing what had happened to the *Brillante*. "It is understood that the pirates fired RPG"—a rocket-propelled grenade—"into the accommodation area which started a fire. As a result the pirates abandoned their efforts to take control of the ship and left the scene and the Master ordered evacuation of all crew members," the statement announced. "All 26 crew members are now safely on board a U.S. Naval forces vessel that has arrived at the scene. The *Brillante Virtuoso* is presently safely adrift and two (2) tugs have arrived from Aden and having secured the vessel, are proceeding with fire fighting measures."

The story was picked up by the news agency Bloomberg, and published with the headline: "MILLION-BARREL TANKER ON FIRE OFF YEMEN AFTER GRENADE ATTACK." The article quoted maritime-security expert Jakob Larsen, who explained that "pirates go for targets of opportunity, and if they see a ship and it's clear they have a chance, they will go for it regardless of size." Reuters and the Associated Press also covered the incident, which warranted a mention the next day in a subcommittee hearing at the US House of Representatives, cited as an example of the continuing threat posed by pirates.

The voyage of the *Brillante Virtuoso* had reached a stage all too familiar to those who do business at sea. In maritime trade, events can quickly spiral from unfortunate, to dire, to worse. The owners of the oil in the *Brillante*'s hull were staring at a potentially ruinous loss, as were the proprietors of the ship itself, which was about to be transformed from a tanker worth tens of millions of dollars into a pile of charred scrap metal. The tugs sent from Aden were cooling the hull with firehoses and might be capable of preventing disaster, but their crews wouldn't be willing to risk their necks to save the *Brillante*, and the valuable cargo on board, unless they were confident they were going to get paid.

Fortunately for all parties involved, the shipping industry has long been able to call on an organization created specifically to deal with this type of crisis. It is one of the world's largest and oldest financial markets, and it can be found among cobbled alleyways and bustling pubs deep within the most ancient quarter of London. The market's entire purpose is to absorb the kind of catastrophic loss that the rest of us learn about on the news. Faced with disaster daily, the men and women—though for more than three hundred years, it's mostly been men—who run this market have developed a nonchalant, almost scornful attitude to danger.

CHAPTER 5

A BRAVER WORLD

Phil Norwood hadn't been in the office long when an insurance broker strolled into his cubicle. "We've had a tanker attacked," the man announced. Norwood sighed—another one—then grabbed a pen and scrawled out the vessel's name on the front of an empty file: "Brillante Virtuoso."

Norwood was a tall Englishman with the ruffled demeanor of a not-so-serious schoolboy. He worked as a claims manager for the marine arm of Zurich Insurance Group, which was housed in a building with a gloomy, faux-gothic façade, one among several towers clustered around Lloyd's of London, the world's leading insurance market. Months earlier, another broker from the same firm as the one now standing beside Norwood's desk had brought the *Brillante* business to Lloyd's, where a group of insurers, including Zurich, had agreed to cover the $100 million of oil it would soon be carrying. Now, as the broker shared what he knew about the attack, Norwood listened intently, scribbling notes on a pad. It was far too soon for any claim to be made on the policy, but Norwood had much to do. There were attorneys to be informed and funds to be made available. He picked up the phone to call some colleagues. "This is going to be a biggie," he warned them.

The first thing to know about Lloyd's is that it doesn't, in fact, sell insurance, and it never has. The name instead refers to an umbrella organization for hundreds of "members"—a mix of corporations and wealthy individuals—who actually provide policies, which are then said to have been sold at Lloyd's. The next thing to know about Lloyd's is that it is everywhere. If you take a train to work, there is a good chance that train was insured at Lloyd's. The *Titanic* was insured at Lloyd's. When Black residents of Montgomery, Alabama, boycotted segregated buses in the 1950s, Lloyd's was the only place they could find to insure their substitute carpool system. After 9/11, Lloyd's members paid out billions of dollars to airlines, businesses in crisis, and the relatives of those killed in the attacks. If you were to compile a list of the worst catastrophes of the last century, virtually all of them would, at some point, have ended up as claims at Lloyd's, to be assessed and valued by Englishmen in bespoke suits who represent billions upon billions of dollars in capital.

Lloyd's does have a physical home, a spectacular high-rise on London's Lime Street. Designed to display its pipes, ducts, and other internal systems on the outside, the building resembles nothing so much as a towering oil rig, beached in one of the most historic parts of the British capital. (As an aside, anyone planning to build an actual oil rig would likely insure it at Lloyd's.) Broadly speaking, Lloyd's is a marketplace. It's a forum where those seeking protection for life's riskiest endeavors can meet those willing to take on the risk, in return for a fee, or premium. Lloyd's members aren't generally interested in anything so prosaic as insuring the family car. Instead, they specialize in what no one else will insure: the biggest, the most unusual, the hardest to analyze. Without Lloyd's to cover them, many of the assets the global economy depends on couldn't exist.

Imagine, for example, a new communications satellite intended to give internet access to parts of the world not yet reached by fiber optic cable. No bank would be willing to lend the sums required to build and launch this satellite into space, where a single misfire could incinerate the entire investment, unless it had some certainty of being repaid. That's where Lloyd's comes in. There, a broker is appointed for the project, and then shops it around to Lloyd's members, who come together in one or more "syndicates" to insure it. Each member of a syndicate takes on a piece of the liability, as much as the individual insurer can afford to lose. After all the financial exposure has been divvied up, the satellite qualifies for a bank loan, the bank knows that it will still be paid back if the satellite goes down in flames, and the insurers at Lloyd's get a few million dollars in premiums. Those premiums, combined with the income from tens of thousands of other policies, give Lloyd's members the financial clout to pay up if the worst occurs. And the rest of the world keeps on turning, oblivious to the deals being made in the curious-looking tower at One Lime Street.

Lloyd's is the place where "storms and fires and floods and earthquakes, and every possible man-made calamity are systematically reduced to manageable routine," Godfrey Hodgson, the author of one of the few histories of the insular market, wrote in 1984. "These perils are chopped up and spread around and shared out so that instead of being an unbearable risk for a few, they are a small risk for many, and thus lose their terror." Or, as the organization's chief executive officer put it in a recent brochure: "Lloyd's helps to create a braver world." There are other insurance markets, but none that are so important, and none that accept so diverse a range of risks. Lloyd's members are willing to apply its basic model to pretty much anything with economic value that could be diminished by an unexpected event. Dolly Parton's breasts were insured at Lloyd's, as were Bruce Springsteen's voice, David Beckham's legs, and a distinctive mustache belonging to a famous Australian cricketer. But the market's bread and butter has always been ships.

Lloyd's began life as a coffeehouse run by Edward Lloyd, the son of a stocking knitter, in the late seventeenth century, only a few hundred yards from its modern home. At the time, coffeehouses were fashionable, sometimes raucous places for London merchants to conduct business. Over the subsequent decades, Lloyd's attracted a varied crowd of traders, speculators, gamblers, and con artists, as well as businessmen who funded lucrative sea voyages—and those willing to insure them. (As Lloyd's acknowledged in a 2020 apology for its role in the trade, many of those journeys were to transport African slaves.) Edward Lloyd recognized the importance of reliable information and realized that if he provided his customers with the latest maritime news, they would have more reason to stay on the premises. That insight led him to create a journal called *Lloyd's List* to record the comings and goings of ships. It's still published today, making it one of the world's oldest continuously running periodicals.

The earliest surviving marine insurance policy, predating even Lloyd's, gives an insight into the hazards sailors faced in the early modern era. The insurers of the *Tiger*, a vessel undertaking a journey to Greece to purchase currants and wine in 1613, pledged to bear the financial impacts of "men of warr, fyer, enemyes, piratts, rovers, theeves, Jettezons, letters of marte & countermarte, arests, restreynts & deteynments of Kings and princes and all other persons, barratry of the Master & mariners, and of all other perills, losses and misfortunes whatsoever they may be." The same language remained in use in contracts, only modestly updated, well into the twentieth century. In that time, Lloyd's evolved from a sandy-floored coffeehouse into a financial institution of global significance, still hewing to its maritime heritage. When the first automobile policy was sold at Lloyd's, in 1904, the documentation described the unfamiliar conveyance as a "ship navigating on land." The market still boasts an impressive collection of nautical artifacts, on display at the Lime Street building, that includes a combined fork-knife given to Admiral Horatio Nelson after he lost his arm fighting the Spanish in 1797.

During the long history of Lloyd's the shipping business has changed drastically, of course. The vessels insured have grown steadily larger and more technologically advanced, evolving from treasure-laden galleons to huge, satellite-guided container ships. Letters of marte (or marque)—official documents authorizing attacks on merchants, given to state-sanctioned pirates, or "privateers," like Sir Francis Drake—have ceased to be much of a problem. But the sea remains as dangerous as ever.

Most Lloyd's member firms have offices a short walk from Lime Street, so that the insurance industry dominates the area between the Tower of London and the Bank of England. One of them, Talbot Underwriting, is located about a half mile away, and around the same time that Phil Norwood was learning of the attack on the *Brillante Virtuoso*, a Talbot employee named Paul Cunningham was taking in the same news. Talbot Underwriting was part of a syndicate of "hull" insurers—Lloyd's members who were covering the ship itself, separately from the oil on board. Cargo ships often require several types of insurance at once, to protect against any foreseeable problem. Syndicate 1183, the typically cheerless name given to Talbot's group, were the "war risks insurers," meaning they were responsible for compensating the shipowner in the event of a mishap of the man-made variety. War risks policies pay out more often than the name might suggest. They certainly cover infrequent situations like the Tanker War, the 1980s conflict in which Iran and Iraq attacked commercial vessels in the Persian Gulf. But they also apply to piracy, as well as more routine "vandalism, sabotage and malicious mischief," in the words of the *Brillante*'s policy.

Years later, Cunningham couldn't recall precisely when he first heard about the *Brillante* incident, but there's a good chance he saw one of the early transmissions from the Lloyd's Marine Intelligence Unit. The Lloyd's market has long benefited from an extensive network of overseas agents, shipping specialists who keep an eye on happenings in faraway ports, on the principle that a well-informed insurer has an edge over competitors. On the morning of July 6, several hours after salvage tugs had arrived beside the vessel, the MIU sent a bulletin that read: "Crude oil tanker *Brillante Virtuoso* (80569 gt, built 1992), 26 crew members, was attacked by pirates and on fire in lat 12 29N, long 44 45E at 0300, local time, today. Understand the fire has been extinguished. All the crew are accounted for and in the vicinity of the vessel in a liferaft."

If the *Brillante* sank, or was damaged beyond repair, Syndicate 1183 and its partners were liable to pay its owner roughly $80 million, which covered the value of the ship and associated loans, as well as lost earnings. Still, since Talbot's parent company, Validus Holdings, had assets worth several billion dollars, the matter wasn't yet serious enough to worry Cunningham. Like Norwood at Zurich Insurance Group, who was pushing through paperwork on the *Brillante* in his cubicle a dozen blocks away, Cunningham began the process of checking in with Talbot's attorneys and the other members of the syndicate to prepare for what might happen next.

An amiable character with a toothy grin and gelled hair, Cunningham was in some ways a typical Lloyd's man. Until the COVID-19 pandemic disrupted habits that had endured for centuries, business in London's insurance district was done face-to-face, preferably over a lunch meeting that might stretch long into a well-refreshed afternoon. A clubbable personality was essential, and the uniform stubbornly formal. Before 2007, anyone seen on the floor of Lloyd's without a jacket and tie risked being thrown out. When the dress code was finally relaxed, there was grumbling among the more traditionally minded members. "It's the beginning of the end," one told *The Sunday Telegraph*. "It's nearly as bad as when they let women in." (Women were fully admitted to Lloyd's only in the 1970s, over bitter opposition from some.)

For decades, Lloyd's had a reputation for being a bastion of the upper and upper middle classes. It didn't quite attract the best and brightest, who were more likely to end up as lawyers or politicians, but served as a refuge for those who came from the right sort of background and attended the right schools, though they might not have dazzled the world academically. It provided "an interesting life with congenial society, a good income and financial security, and departure at a gentlemanly hour," Godfrey Hodgson wrote. Packed into pubs at 2:00 p.m. on a weekday, silk handkerchiefs folded neatly into their suit pockets, the old boys of Lloyd's could seem like something from another era. Long after the rest of London's financial industry had converged toward international standards of workplace conduct, the market remained a deeply retrograde environment for women. Member firms competed to hire the most attractive assistants, who were rated for "shagability." As late as the 1990s, male workers on the Lloyd's floor put up a cash prize to be claimed by anyone who managed to have sex there during working hours.

Unsurprisingly, working practices at Lloyd's could also seem almost willfully old-fashioned. In the 1980s and 1990s, deregulation and computerization transformed banking and trading in London, vaulting the city into direct competition with New York for the title of the world's premier financial hub. The Lloyd's crowd liked the lack of rules, but wasn't quite as ready to embrace technology. The *Brillante*'s hull insurance contract, for instance, was placed at the market in late 2010 in a style that Edward Lloyd himself would have recognized.

The central feature of the Lloyd's building is the Underwriting Room, a vast trading floor at the base of an atrium that rises fourteen stories. The Room, as everyone calls it, takes up most of the ground level, and during the trading day is full of insurers sitting in little wooden booths, waiting for business to find them. The broker working for the owner of the *Brillante* would have sat down next to the Talbot syndicate representative and provided a piece of paper, or "slip," detailing the coverage he wanted, along with a file, perhaps sixty pages deep, that contained information about the vessel and its planned voyages. After some discussion of the merits of the contract and its likely risks—an exchange taking normally around twenty minutes and certainly no more than thirty—the satisfied Talbot man would have stamped the slip, initialed it with a fountain pen, and written out the percentage of the liability that his employer was willing to take. The broker would have continued in this manner until he'd filled the slip with "underwriters," so called because they write their names one under the other. And thus, on the floor of Lloyd's of London, an insurance contract is born.

It might seem surprising that any financial institution would commit itself to a multimillion-dollar liability after so little deliberation, but that's how business is done at Lloyd's, and always has been. The entire market is built on trust. Its Latin motto, *"Uberrima Fides,"* means "utmost good faith," an implicit promise not to mislead, reinforced by familiarity. The Talbot underwriter would have dealt with the broker many times before, probably shared a beer or three with him, and would certainly do business with him again.

That trust extends to the ultimate users of the market, the customers, who can be confident that Lloyd's members will pay claims quickly and efficiently, no matter how large they might be. After an earthquake leveled most of San Francisco in 1906, a prominent Lloyd's underwriter, Cuthbert Heath, told agents to "pay all of our policyholders in full, irrespective of the terms of their policies," an injunction that became something of a guiding principle. Because risks are spread among so many members, and because most policies never need to pay out, the system works, sufficiently well to have kept Lloyd's as the world's preeminent insurance market for more than two hundred years.

The amount of money that now passes through Lloyd's is difficult to fathom. Every year its members collect 35 billion pounds, or roughly $49 billion, in premiums. That's just what customers pay to be insured. The value of the reserves held against those contracts is many times greater. On average, about 30,000 pounds ($41,800) is paid out in claims every minute. Lloyd's underwriters also buy their own insurance, called reinsurance, through

Lloyd's, so they can claim unexpected losses back from even bigger syndicates. If the reinsurers need insurance, guess where they go?

For all its stuffiness, Lloyd's has remained dynamic enough to survive scandals, brushes with bankruptcy, and vigorous global competition. The market rewards those brave enough to take a risk. With enough canny decisions, the men sitting in the underwriting booths can earn great fortunes for themselves, as well as the syndicates they represent. Ian Posgate, the top underwriter of the 1970s, earned the nickname "Goldfinger" for the scale of his profits. During the Vietnam War, when ships traveling through the Mekong Delta had to navigate Viet Cong rockets, Posgate hiked his prices and signed his name next to any slip put in front of him. Wars could be lucrative for Lloyd's, he recognized, as long as customers absorbed the cost of the extra risk. Provided the premiums kept flowing, Lloyd's would keep on doing business the way it had always been done.

No wonder, then, that the hijacking of the *Brillante Virtuoso* barely registered. It meant a busy day for a handful of individual managers, nothing out of the ordinary. The whole purpose of the market was to absorb bad news and soften the blow with a big check. Shipping disasters, while regrettable for those involved, are "just marvelous free advertising" for Lloyd's, as former chairman Sir Peter Green once observed.

Back at Zurich's offices, Phil Norwood spent the afternoon filling in forms. His most pressing task was to deal with the salvage crew floating alongside the *Brillante*, off the Yemeni coast. The cargo insurers, including Zurich, would foot the bill for the salvage effort, since they had the most to gain if the tanker's oil was recovered and sold. Norwood prepared a document on Lloyd's-headed paper authorizing the salvors to proceed and promising that the syndicate would compensate them if, and only if, they were successful. Then he put his *Brillante* folder on top of a pile of a dozen or so other piracy cases he was dealing with that day, locked the stack of papers inside a filing cabinet, and moved on to the next order of business.

The entire ground floor of Lloyd's is arranged around a mahogany frame that rises, like a pulpit, toward the sunlight streaming down through the barrel-vaulted glass roof. Hanging inside the wooden frame is the Lutine Bell. In 1799 the HMS *Lutine*, a thirty-two-gun Royal Navy frigate, sank off the coast of the Netherlands while carrying a million pounds' worth of silver and gold. The treasure was never found. But almost sixty years later, the ship's bell was salvaged from the ocean floor and put on display in the Lloyd's Underwriting Room, where for the next century it was rung to announce the fate of overdue vessels: once for a loss, twice for safe.

Nowadays, because of its age, the Lutine Bell only sounds on ceremonial occasions. But its companion at the center of the Room, a huge leatherbound ledger known as the Loss Book, is still in routine use. Since 1774, Loss Books have recorded every sinking of a ship insured by the Lloyd's market, a comprehensive record of nearly 250 years of maritime calamity in every corner of the world. On July 5, 2011, the Head Waiter—a functionary dressed in a midnight-blue tailcoat and trained in comportment and calligraphy—used a quill pen and inkpot to write out the most recent entry in looping cursive. The *Aries*, an American boat with a displacement of ninety-eight tons, had sunk at latitude 56 46.36N, longitude 167 20.45W, off the coast of Alaska.

But the page for Wednesday, July 6, was left blank. The *Brillante Virtuoso* wasn't lost yet, and until its fate was clear, nothing would be noted in the Loss Book and no money would be disbursed. There were still any number of circumstances that would affect the final tally of who would be paid and how much. Phil Norwood, Paul Cunningham, and the rest of the human apparatus of the Lloyd's market were poised to put its risk-absorbing machine into action. But first, they needed to get someone onto the tanker to see what they were dealing with.

CHAPTER 6

THE TALLEST MAN IN YEMEN

On the afternoon of July 9, 2011, David Mockett was at his office, in a utilitarian Aden commercial block called Ma'alla Plaza, when an email from a sender he didn't know pinged into his inbox. Mockett kept an eccentric schedule by Western standards, starting work early and then heading home for lunch and a nap before returning around 4:30 p.m. for a few more hours at his desk. By then the worst of the searing heat had drained away, and Yemenis had settled into their afternoon ritual of chewing qat, the mildly narcotic leaf most local men consumed daily. He used the lull to go through his correspondence: reports on maritime trends, rumors of the latest political intrigues in Sana'a, the Yemeni capital, and updates from his wife Cynthia on life in England with their daughters and grandchildren.

This message, under the subject line "Brillante Virtuoso," was from a fellow Brit named Stuart Wallace. Wallace explained that he worked for a well-known marine services firm in London, Noble Denton, that had been hired by the insurers of the *Brillante Virtuoso*. He'd been given Mockett's contact by a mutual acquaintance. "David," Wallace wrote, "we . . . have been instructed to act in the case of above vessel, currently at anchor off Aden following an act of piracy. At this time intentions for the vessel and the exact scope of our requirements are being defined, however we may have a requirement for a damage survey to be undertaken." He wanted to know if Mockett might be available.

Mockett received requests like this frequently. Over his years in Yemen, he had earned a reputation as one of the top maritime experts in the country, relied upon by a long list of clients in London and other financial hubs. As a surveyor, an important part of his job was to evaluate the damage from wrecks or other marine incidents, providing information that would help reconstruct how they'd occurred—and therefore what, or who, might have caused them. It was an essential role for keeping the wheels of one of the world's most important industries turning. Although the insurers at Lloyd's generally paid claims in full, reports from surveyors like Mockett were a crucial part of the process, allowing everyone involved to declare they'd done their due diligence. Without them, the money machine didn't work.

Mockett sent back his reply to Wallace's email: he was "available and able to attend should you so require." He was pleased to get the request. Mockett made a reasonable living, and his expenses in Aden were modest; even a comparatively luxurious life in Yemen was cheap. But between maintaining the seven-bedroom home he and Cynthia kept in Devon and saving for the retirement he hoped to begin soon, every job mattered. Working on a case as complex as the *Brillante* would be a good way to make some extra cash before he went back to England for his usual summer holiday—"a very good earner," as he put it in a message to Cynthia.

Mockett checked with some local contacts and reported to Wallace that the tanker was about twenty-five miles offshore, advising him to make sure it stayed there. Bringing the ship into Yemeni waters would mean submitting to the jurisdiction of the country's unpredictable, corrupt authorities, a situation that was best avoided. Mockett's next task would be to figure out how to get on board. The ship's owner would probably soon file a claim on his insurance, exposing the companies that had underwritten the vessel and its petroleum cargo to a combined loss of well over $100 million. That process couldn't really advance until survey reports were complete. Nor, if they were so inclined, could the insurers deny the claim without solid evidence of what had happened. Wallace—and the Lloyd's market—needed Mockett to get started straight away.

For most Westerners, finding a way onto an abandoned oil tanker off the coast of Yemen, especially with the country on the brink of political collapse, would have been a daunting task. Not for David Mockett. Everyone in the Yemeni shipping industry seemed to know "Mr. David," both because of his physical presence—some of his local friends, whom he generally towered over, called him "the tallest man in Yemen"—and because his job brought him into contact with so many people and companies. The sea lanes off the Yemeni coast are some of the most important in the world, and its harbors remained busy despite deepening political turmoil. An able surveyor like Mockett was seldom short of work, compiling evidence to adjudicate the disputes that popped up every day as goods were shipped from port to port. He might be called to evaluate whether a shipment of oil had been contaminated by seawater, or to inspect the damage caused by a freighter that had crashed into its dock, determining if the port operator was demanding fair compensation or trying to use the accident to cover the upgrade of a whole pier. Offshore, there were shipboard fires and groundings on sandbars, as well as the occasional collision.

Armed with a notebook and digital camera, Mockett would set out to the site of whatever event he'd been hired to investigate, sometimes in the company of his deputy, a young Sri Lankan man he'd begun to think of as his protégé. After taking hundreds of photos and interviewing witnesses, he would retire to his office to write out a report and send it to his clients. That was usually the end of it, although the more contentious cases might end up in court, where Mockett could be called to give testimony. A surveyor's first-hand account of conditions on a stricken vessel was invaluable evidence.

Over the years Mockett had grown alert to the possibilities for mischief in the maritime-accident business. After a fire on a ship loaded with grain, the captain might wrongly accuse the shipowner of failing to maintain firefighting gear, while a negligent shipowner might try to pin the blaze on the crew. Meanwhile, the owners of both the vessel and the grain would have an incentive to exaggerate the damage on their insurance claims. It wasn't unheard of for the men with money at stake to bribe a surveyor to see things their way, or, if that didn't work, to attempt a more threatening approach. But they'd learned that with Mockett it wasn't even worth trying. Earlier in his career, when he served as a port superintendent in Saudi Arabia, Mockett would periodically get requests to let some ship jump the queue of vessels waiting outside Jeddah's congested harbor in exchange for a bit of under-the-table cash. He always refused, politely telling the shipping agent or importer that they would need to wait their turn.

He'd carried the same attitude into his work as a surveyor. In Yemen, Mockett was known for doing things fastidiously by the book, sometimes to the point of annoying local partners who wanted him more squarely on their side. They would plead with him to be more flexible, to no avail. As he would explain to anyone who challenged his approach, Mockett believed that the role of a surveyor was to determine the facts, avoiding assumptions and never making inferences beyond what those facts could support. He sometimes repeated a favorite mantra, a twist on a quote purportedly uttered by the British prime minister Harold Macmillan: "Evidence, dear boy, evidence."

The crisply precise report he sent to Yemeni police after he was shot in 2002 provided an example of how he saw the world. After a detailed description of everything he remembered about his assailants, who fled on a motorbike, Mockett wrote that he didn't "know what make of motorbike was used. I only saw them for two or three seconds—perhaps four at the outside. I did not recognize either of them and doubt if I would again. The driver, I simply did not see at all." Evidence, dear boy.

The *Brillante*, Mockett learned, was quickly becoming the focus of a complex multinational undertaking. Salvage tugs were shuttling back and forth from Aden's harbor to the tanker, picking up men and supplies for a weeks-long operation. Some of the personnel had been urgently flown in from Greece, an indication of the importance of the job to the *Brillante*'s owners. Most were there to perform tasks that fell into two main categories: to make sure the vessel could be towed without sinking to a safe location, either for repairs or scrapping; and to prepare for the off-loading of its oil, which still had a paper value in the millions. Others were needed to provide security, ensuring that there would be no repeat of the kind of attack that had brought them all to Aden in the first place.

On Monday, July 11, Mockett got in touch with a burly diver named Vassilios Vergos, whose permission he would need to get onto the *Brillante*. One of a tight-knit group of seafaring Greeks based in Yemen, Vergos had an unusual biography. As a young man he'd served in the Underwater Demolition Unit, an elite special-forces element of the Hellenic Navy. He was so fluent in the water that some of his colleagues thought he swam more like a fish than a human. After leaving the military Vergos had put his diving skills to work in the private sector, helping dislodge grounded ships and repair damaged hulls around the Aegean, before relocating part time to Aden to open a branch of his company, Poseidon Salvage. Equipped with rickety tugs and a floating crane, Poseidon's business was to respond to accidents in the vicinity of the Yemeni coast. Vergos had been speedily hired by the *Brillante*'s owner to salvage the ship, and it was now his jurisdiction. Although they were both among the tiny number of Westerners in the city, Mockett didn't know Vergos, who tended to keep to himself. He didn't even have an apartment. Instead Vergos slept on one of Poseidon's boats, venturing onto land only when necessary.

In their initial conversation, Mockett told Vergos that he needed to inspect the *Brillante* right away. But the Greek wasn't very accommodating. He hadn't received "instructions" to allow a survey, he told Mockett, and would have to get back to him. Later that day, Mockett wrote to Wallace to inform him that he'd tried Vergos again and been unable to connect to his mobile phone. The salvor had apparently left port without him, which presented a significant problem. Monsoon winds were whipping the Gulf of Aden into heavy swells, and Mockett couldn't just hire any boat to take him offshore. Heading out in one that was too small or poorly maintained was risky. All the tugs at the Aden port authority were spoken for. "Sense of humor is fading fast," Mockett told his client.

In the meantime, conditions in Aden were deteriorating by the day. Electricity, rarely a significant problem before, was becoming unreliable as the government unraveled, forcing Mockett to find ways to work around extended blackouts, and oil shortages meant that there were hours-long waits to fill up at gas stations. Using a mobile phone was getting trickier. Yemen's strongman president, Ali Abdullah Saleh, had imposed onerous restrictions on one of the main cellular networks after its owners began supporting the Arab Spring–inspired opposition. That left subscribers like Mockett unable to call internationally or dial local landlines. It was even difficult to mail packages overseas. In 2010 British and Emirati authorities had intercepted two sophisticated bombs, hidden inside printer cartridges, that had been sent from Yemen in parcels addressed to Jewish sites in Chicago. As a result, couriers in Aden would no longer accept anything but documents for delivery abroad.

As he waited to get onto the *Brillante*, Mockett commiserated about the assignment, and the rising challenges of operating in Aden, with some of the other expats who remained in the city—a motley, largely British group who still preferred its difficulties to a more conventional life elsewhere. There was Roy Facey, a port consultant and former sea captain from Cornwall, who'd lived in Aden with only brief interruptions since the late 1980s—when it was the capital of a Marxist state so repressive that speaking to a foreigner could attract the attention of the secret police. Roger Stokes was a quiet, workaholic lawyer from the north of England, whose only apparent hobby was producing detailed drawings of flashy sports cars, but who drove with the caution of a small-town grandmother. Another shipping expert, Nigel Chevriot, was a living link to Aden's colonial past: he'd actually been born in the city, before the end of British rule.

Together they'd found ways to sand off the harder edges of the place, ferrying back creature comforts like cheese and chocolate from trips to Dubai or London and tapping each other's networks to sort out the bureaucratic complications they all confronted from time to time. They also took comfort in good food and particularly drink, which wasn't easy to find in a devoutly Islamic country. Improbably enough, Aden's dining options included a passable Chinese restaurant, Ching Sing, which somehow managed to serve cold Heineken and paint-stripping African gin along with spring rolls and fat steamed crabs. Mockett ate there frequently, gathering with whoever else was around at one of its wobbly tables, which were topped with sherbet-orange tablecloths a long way from their last laundering. Foreign shipping hands still came through the city periodically, and they could count on an invitation to join Mockett for dinner. After a drink or two he would get to telling self-deprecating war stories, bursting after the punch line into a booming laugh that filled the restaurant.

Some of the guests were mystified as to why Mockett had stayed in Yemen for so long, and what he found so magnetic about the hot, dusty, and increasingly dangerous country. But occasionally they got glimpses of the personal warmth that he always cited as one of the things that kept him there—how seemingly menacing interactions could, with the right amount of patience and an open mind, end with a kind of cross-cultural intimacy. On one occasion, Mockett and a marine expert visiting from Dubai were driving along the coast when the visitor suggested they stop to take some pictures. It was a spectacular, cloudless day, and they pulled over to capture the rocky shoreline. Soon a beat-up car pulled over and three Yemeni men stepped out. They were dressed in traditional fashion, with long skirts called *futa* topped with belts that also held imposing, curved daggers in wooden scabbards.

"Are you American?" one of them asked—not a question one wanted to hear in a minimally governed part of the Middle East. Mockett indicated that they were British. They all shook hands. Mockett's companion pointed at the handgun one of the Yemenis was carrying, and then to the small scar on the surveyor's neck, the only remnant of his shooting. That turned out to be hardly impressive by the standards of the Yemeni men. One of them lifted his *futa*: a substantial chunk of his leg was missing. Everyone laughed, and soon the Britons and Yemenis were posing for pictures together, and joking around with the Kalashnikov rifle that the locals had in the trunk of their car.

No one seemed to want to help Mockett get onto the *Brillante*. While ship-owners and salvors aren't always accommodating of surveyors hired by insurance companies, he found their reluctance to assist him a little bit unusual. He wasn't some high-seas rubbernecker trying to ogle the aftermath of a pirate attack. A surveyor's report was an essential step in handling a major marine casualty, and if the owner wanted to get his money, they needed to let Mockett do his work.

Wallace encouraged Mockett to keep trying to find a way on board, even if it resulted in a substantial bill for the insurers. "We believe that your attendance on the vessel is of great importance," he wrote in an email—particularly to compile a photographic record of the condition of the ship. Wallace had been told the blaze that consumed the *Brillante* was the result of the pirates' firing rocket-propelled grenades; he said it was critical for Mockett to examine the precise location where the RPG rounds entered. Wallace also needed to get a sense of how much damage the vessel had sustained to inform an assessment of whether there was any point in trying to repair it.

On July 12, Mockett's luck changed. He'd contacted a local shipping firm that was assisting the *Brillante*'s owner, and they told him they would arrange a boat out. Mockett would be welcomed on board the vessel and would be free to inspect it as long as he stayed out of the way of Vergos and the other salvors. That afternoon, Mockett made the ten-minute drive from his office to Aden's waterfront. He wouldn't be traveling in luxury. His transportation was a rickety fishing trawler, with rivulets of rust running down its hull and heavily used nets piled on deck. But it looked sturdy enough, and when Mockett climbed aboard, he was glad to find that the *Brillante*'s chief engineer, Nestor Tabares, would be sharing the ride. Tabares had been helping with the salvage effort, and talking to him would be valuable.

Mockett was relieved to be finally setting out. He knew that Wallace and a long chain of others, sitting behind desks in London's financial district, needed a report from him as soon as possible. It was late in the day when the trawler finally churned away from Aden's harbor and into open water. The skipper knew the waters of the Gulf of Aden intimately, and he scanned the horizon as he steered, keeping a watchful eye on the monsoon winds.

CHAPTER 7

EVIDENCE, DEAR BOY

Dusk was approaching as Mockett neared the *Brillante*, the trawler captain slowing his engines for a gentle landing from the tanker's stern. An uninterrupted dome of clouds had formed, and from the surveyor's vantage point the water of the Gulf of Aden was nearly the same steely shade as the sky above. In the flat, dull light, the *Brillante*'s jet-black hull stood out sharply in the vastness. The sea undulated gently; the foul weather Mockett had feared was, for the moment, some way off.

It would hardly take an elite surveyor to understand that something calamitous had occurred on the *Brillante*, even from a distance. The ship's funnel had been scorched to its tip, evidence that flames had climbed from the lower levels to some of the highest points on board. The white paint on the exterior of the accommodation block was blistered from heat, and thick bands of soot streaked upward from the deck. A group of salvage vessels with canary-yellow deckhouses was tied up along the starboard side, a third of the way down the hull: a flotilla from Vassilios Vergos's Poseidon Salvage. The trawler captain brought his boat in next to one of them, and Vergos's men helped lash them together. Mockett stepped off, already evaluating the condition of the *Brillante* before he'd even stepped on board, noting which parts of the ship he wanted to give particular attention to in his inspection. He wouldn't be doing it alone. Another surveyor had been sent from Greece, hired by the *Brillante*'s owner to produce a parallel report. Such duplication was unusual, though not unheard of in a situation like this one. While the survey-ors and other specialists hired to evaluate a maritime incident—fire experts, marine engineers, and so on—present themselves as impartial, in complex cases insurers and shipowners may prefer to have opinions from people they've directly paid, in the event that they end up on opposite sides of a legal dispute.

The real work would have to wait for morning. Mockett needed plenty of light to survey the ship, and there was little point getting started so close to sunset. He would spend the night on Poseidon's floating crane, a battered barge with a deck so rusty that it looked as if it had been painted an alarming shade of burnt red. One of Vergos's subordinates, a balding Greek who introduced himself as Dimitrios, laid out a bed for Mockett and invited him to join the boss for dinner. Though he had the paunchy belly of a man in late middle age, Vergos was powerfully built, with thickly muscular arms and a barreled chest. Yet Mockett noticed that he seemed to have trouble walking, particularly when going up or down. Years before, Vergos had gotten the bends, the de-bilitating illness that can occur when a diver ascends too quickly from deep water. He survived the decompression sickness but was left with a lifelong limp—and a short temper. He could be brusque, as he was when Mockett first asked to board the *Brillante*, and was quick to raise his voice at his employees when they displeased him.

Over dinner, Vergos and Mockett chatted about their families. Dimi-trios, who spoke better English than the other Greeks, stepped in to translate when needed and tried to answer some of Mockett's initial questions. Slight and bespectacled, he stood out next to the other members of the Poseidon crew: brawny, weather-beaten men who, in another era, might have passed for pirates themselves. Mockett couldn't help but wonder how someone like Dimitrios had ended up in the Gulf of Aden.

Mockett rose early the next morning and clambered up a ladder from one of Poseidon's boats onto the tanker's deck. Hard-hatted salvage crewmen were milling around, mostly Bangladeshi workers employed by Vergos, and he tried to give them plenty of space. As Mockett walked, he could feel a faint crunch beneath his feet: the heat of the blaze had turned the deck's surface into a rough canvas of ash and paint chips that splintered with each step. His clients in London wanted a detailed photographic record, and Mockett stopped every few moments to take pictures with his digital camera: of the razor wire looping along the exterior railings, of rusting barrels strewn about and flare cartridges left by the *Brillante*'s fleeing crew. Looking up at the T-shaped accommodation block looming over the hull, he photographed walkways and ladders, as well as pipes, vents, winches, and cables, some discolored by flame, others by almost twenty years of exposure to salty air.

When he entered the accommodation block, Mockett realized the damage he'd seen so far was nothing compared with the state of the *Brillante*'s interior. One of the main corridors resembled the bottom of a well-used barbecue, coated with char from floor to ceiling. The Greek surveyor had made the mistake of wearing chinos and a white shirt, and as he and Mockett moved through the ship, his clothes were gradually covered with bands of grease and soot. In one area they examined, the fire had thrown a steel doorframe entirely clear of the bulkhead where it had been embedded. Near the galley, Mockett found rows of blackened dishes still on their shelves and took a photo of a scorched cheese grater, so warped by the heat it had turned concave. Along another passageway, the wall panels had been deformed into funhouse shapes, and protruded inward in pregnant bulges. On the bridge, at the top of the accommodation block, there was a maze of tangled metal that was almost impossible for the surveyors to navigate. Most of the windows had been blown out, and as the *Brillante* bobbed up and down, shards of glass almost three-quarters of an inch thick crashed intermittently to the deck below.

Mockett was eager to identify the source of the fire, or at least to narrow down the possibilities. To do that, he would have to enter the lower levels of the *Brillante*, where the engine and other critical systems were housed. It was stiflingly hot as Mockett made his way down, as though the corridors were still warm from the touch of the flames. By the engine room, Mockett saw that the broad console that controlled the machinery had been burned completely, and all that remained of the chair where its operator would have sat was a spindly metal frame. He could make it only partway into the engine room itself, a cavernous space threaded with catwalks and stepped ladders. He paused to take a photo at the top of one that, on a functioning ship, would have brought him down toward the base of the chamber. Instead, it descended into a consuming darkness: everything below it was flooded with oily water from firefighting. It was too dangerous to go farther.

Mockett had done what he needed to. He returned to the deck, then climbed back down the ladder onto Poseidon's floating crane, filthy and sweating in the summer heat. The fishing captain was standing by to take him and the shipowner's surveyor back to shore, and after a gruff goodbye from Vergos they boarded his trawler. Mockett kept taking photos as they made a slow, full loop around the *Brillante*, documenting the condition of its exterior. Soon they were on a course for Aden, and Mockett watched from the boat's stern as the tanker got smaller and smaller, until it was just a black smudge on the horizon. The trawler crew had prepared a lunch of sandwiches, salad, and small, flat fried fish, about the size of a palm, which Mockett didn't recognize. Eager for a decent meal, he tucked in with gusto.

During the trip back, Mockett contemplated what he'd seen. He'd concluded that the blaze probably began in the vicinity of the *Brillante*'s engine control room; almost all the spaces above it had been destroyed, while the damage farther down was much less severe. Beyond that assessment, he couldn't quite make sense of it. The insurers had been told that the pirates had fired rocket-propelled grenades, and Stuart Wallace, Mockett's client in London, had instructed him to locate and assess the damage from the RPGs. But there was none. Among all the debris and destruction, Mockett could find no sign of even a single RPG strike. Nor had he discovered evidence of the pirates' having shot up the vessel with guns, which its captain, Noe Gonzaga, had described in his statement after the attack. Nor, as Mockett told Wallace in an email, were there indications that they had detonated hand-thrown grenades, which had also been posited as a cause of the fire. Mockett was a long way from being able to say what exactly had happened to the *Brillante* the night it was boarded. He did know that if he was going to find out, he had a lot more work to do.

The return to Aden didn't go as expected. A small tender was supposed to meet the fishing boat outside the harbor and ferry the two surveyors to shore, but it didn't show up. From the trawler, Mockett played an extended game of phone tag with port officials and local shipping firms to get it sent out. At first, he was told port traffic was on hold because there was a warship in the harbor. Mockett noted wryly that it must have been a submarine, because he couldn't see any naval vessels nearby. It turned out, after a few calls, that the man who was supposed to be driving the boat was still at home. Unaccustomed to such mix-ups, the Greek surveyor was furious, but Mockett had enough local experience not to be surprised. Things rarely went to plan in Yemen, though they usually worked out in the end. Eventually the tender appeared, and Mockett scrambled over a series of winches and greasy cables to climb inside for the brief trip to shore. Shortly afterward he was in his car, heading back to his house for a shower—though not before pulling into a gas station that appeared, despite the fuel shortages that had been frustrating local drivers, to be in full operation. To Mockett's delight, an attendant filled his Lexus's tank to the brim.

Later that day, Mockett drove to the Mercure Hotel, one of Aden's few decent hostelries. The Greek surveyor was there with a British lawyer named Russell Rawlings, who'd flown in to conduct interviews with the *Brillante*'s crew. Mockett wanted to know what Rawlings had learned, and to discuss his own findings with fellow professionals. It was evening by the time their meeting wrapped up, and everyone was ready for dinner. Mockett still couldn't call landlines from his mobile phone, so he had a friend book them a table at Ching Sing, the Chinese restaurant beloved by Aden expats. Both of his companions seemed friendly. They paid for dinner, and Rawlings even offered to gift Mockett the remains of a bottle of Bell's whisky—not an easy commodity to come by on the Arabian Peninsula—which he accepted eagerly.

Later that week Mockett sent a note to his wife Cynthia in England, filling her in on the assignment. He'd made a habit of writing her long, detailed messages—letters, in his younger days, now replaced with emails—that contained exhaustive descriptions of what he was working on as well as everything else he'd been up to. Mockett knew how much Cynthia appreciated them. Between his years working at sea and assignments in Saudi Arabia and Yemen, the two had spent the bulk of their marriage living in different places, and the correspondence allowed them both to feel like they were fully present in each other's lives.

"My darling Cynth," he began. "The trip out to the ship was very interesting, but very tiring, as you can well imagine." He was eager to know what his clients would make of his report; he told Cynthia that he would blind-copy her on the memo. "I don't think that I will have to go out again," he said, "but you never can tell." Another trip would take a toll on his wardrobe. Mockett recounted how his Yemeni housekeeper, "God bless her, came yesterday and tried to clean up the clothes that I had had on." They were so dirty from the vessel that "one set had to be thrown away and I think that one pair of the cargo pants will have to be downgraded to gardening or dirty jobs trousers."

He moved on to other topics. The weather was poor—the hot summer winds had come through, blowing down trees and scattering dust all over Aden. A local kid had pilfered some fruit from a tree in the yard. "I had to laugh at the cheek of it," Mockett wrote, then added that the housekeeper "said that she will sort the lad out." He ran through a series of breezy replies to news Cynthia had related in earlier messages: the replacement of a local priest, a planned trip to Leeds, the disappointing state of the cucumbers she'd tried to grow—"what a pity," Mockett remarked. They would see each other in just a few weeks. "I am looking forward to the gentle summer Sundays walking and watching cricket," he wrote.

But before he could go on vacation, Mockett needed to complete the *Brillante* job, which was turning out to be more complex than expected. When he came into a tricky assignment, Mockett sometimes chatted about it with friends in the local shipping community, tapping their experience to help him think through a particularly vexing investigation. One of them was Roy Facey, the Cornwall-born port consultant. Cheerful and energetic, with a snow-white beard, Facey had taken to Yemen just as enthusiastically as Mockett. In the afternoons, he could often be found pounding up the slopes of Shamsan Mountain, the five-hundred-meter peak that abuts Aden's city center, and he had a wide network of Yemeni friends, many of whom he'd met through his work as an infrastructure adviser for the city's port authority.

Mockett valued his opinion: like him, Facey had years of experience of all that could go wrong at sea. Not long after he returned from the *Brillante*, Mockett invited Facey to his office, where they talked about the case over tea. Mockett had taken almost 250 photographs on board, and he clicked through them on his laptop as Facey looked on, narrating what he'd seen. What he'd been able to learn so far about the attack, Mockett informed his friend, had left him with even more questions.

Even the most basic facts of the *Brillante*'s voyage seemed odd. Every commercial captain knew that the best defense against pirates was speed; a ship moving slowly, or worse, not moving at all, presented much too easy a target. But Gonzaga, the *Brillante*'s master, had left the vessel to drift in a dangerous area, with no ability to quickly flee if a threat appeared. Similarly, elementary antipiracy procedures—protocols with which a mariner of Gonzaga's experience would be intimately familiar—called for taking every precaution before letting unfamiliar visitors onto a vessel. Yet the pirates who attacked the *Brillante* had apparently been able to deceive the crew into letting them on board without firing a shot.

The source of the fire was another mystery. Mockett had spoken at length to the tanker's chief engineer, Nestor Tabares, during their trip out to the *Brillante* on the fishing trawler. Tabares told Mockett he was asleep when the pirates came aboard and was woken by shouting. He said the intruders had threatened him and forced him into the engine room, where they shot out the windows with a handgun, but Tabares hadn't seen any grenades and couldn't explain how the fire began. While Mockett didn't have any firm theories of his own about what had happened, he told Facey that he couldn't take the existing story at face value.

Mockett wasn't the only person in Aden who was beginning to have doubts about the *Brillante* attack. Although much of the government no longer really functioned, Yemen's Maritime Affairs Authority was also conducting an inquiry into the *Brillante*'s fate, eager to understand whether the incident signaled an increased threat of piracy in the area. Its investigators had interviewed the tanker's crew, and some of Mockett's local contacts passed a summary of their view on to him, which he then relayed to Wallace in London. "I am informed the MAA are very suspicious about the entire incident," he wrote in an email. Mockett then sent another message hours later, keeping his client apprised of what he was hearing: "The MAA interviewer has advised that he cannot come up with a satisfactory conclusion as to what transpired on the vessel with regards to the fire."

As the *Brillante* casualty made its way through the complex machinery of the Lloyd's market, more and more people—the ship's owner, of course, but also salvors, insurers, lawyers, and a host of further experts—had an interest in what Mockett was finding out. The progress of the insurance claim had financial implications for all of them. Wallace's company, Noble Denton, was compiling Mockett's reports into more official form for further circulation in London, relaying his difficulties proving out the initial accounts of the attack. "There are no hull punctures from rocket propelled grenades, evidence of a grenade explosion was not seen and there were no readily identifiable bullet holes," Wallace wrote in one memo. "No further reports as [to] the actions of the alleged boarders have been received. There is no detail as to how they were persuaded to leave the vessel." Several days later he sent another, including Mockett's report that Yemeni investigators were growing suspicious. "Captain David Mockett is continuing to monitor the situation from his base in Aden," Wallace concluded.

Mockett kept working the case, though it was growing even more difficult for him to operate. The gasoline shortages were getting worse, he wrote to one of Wallace's colleagues, and "we make the minimal number of journeys to conserve fuel." The situation in the streets was also becoming less predictable, and Mockett was trying to stay home in the evenings. "We don't go in after dark," he said, "as roads get blocked by youths on a haphazard basis."

On Wednesday, July 20, 2011, the day after he sent that email, Mockett drove as usual to his office in Ma'alla Plaza after breakfast. The summer heat was beginning to crest as he arrived at his parking spot just outside, with a gusty wind providing scant relief from temperatures that topped 90 degrees Fahrenheit. He spent the morning working on his computer, pausing toward lunchtime for a call to catch up with one of his local friends. Not long after that conversation ended, he got up to leave. Mockett preferred to have lunch at home, where he would sit down to a substantial meal—often treats like sausages or pork chops, which were taboo in Yemen but he or Cynthia rarely had trouble smuggling through the airport. Even the customs agents knew

"Mr. David," and didn't mind if he bent the rules now and then; the celebrity of being the tallest man in Yemen had its perks.

Mockett walked out of his office, down the hall, and past the reception booth in the lobby. The building's long-forgotten architect had tried to combine crude modernism with Islamic motifs, and Mockett passed under an Ottoman-style arch, rendered in thick concrete, as he entered the bright light of the parking lot. He climbed behind the wheel of his Lexus and turned the key, easing the vehicle past a low metal fence and onto the street. He'd only been driving for a few moments when the bomb that had been carefully placed beneath his seat exploded.

CHAPTER 8

SHOCK WAVES

R oy Facey was in a board meeting at the Aden port authority, on the bank
of the busy channel separating the city's harbor from the open sea, when
the boom rumbled across the short distance from Mockett's office. Over
Facey's decades in Yemen, where he'd remained through periods of political
instability, terrorism, and civil conflict, he had heard a few explosions. This
one was loud, and close by—certainly within a mile or two.

The group had been coming to the end of a discussion of staffing at the
Aden container terminal, and stopped their conversation as they listened for
further blasts. They decided to conclude the meeting a few minutes early, in
case something serious was going on, and Facey rose for the short walk back
to his desk. There he checked his text messages, and saw that one had come
in from another of Aden's longtime British expats, a friend of both Facey's
and Mockett's. The man was passing on information about the explosion he'd
just heard: There had been a car bomb in the city center. The news wasn't good.

At the scene, the mutual friend had recognized the car, stopped in the
middle of a street. A thick billow of smoke rose from the Lexus into the afternoon sky, as a crowd of Yemeni men jostled toward it, shouting and holding up their cellphones to take pictures. The street was thick with pedestrians
at that time of day, but none of them appeared to have been harmed despite
the obvious power of the blast. The windows and windshield had been blown

apart, and the car's interior had been reduced to a snarl of twisted steel. The subsequent fire had consumed everything that wasn't metal: the upholstery had disappeared, as had the vehicle's tires. It rested on the asphalt on its naked wheels. A tall figure lay on the ground by the driver's seat, blackened grotesquely. One arm was extended and bent at the wrist, as though reaching for a gear stick.

Word was soon spreading around Aden, passed from table to table in cafés and emailed between air-conditioned offices around the port—a Westerner had been killed. Al-Arabiya, a Dubai-based TV network, picked up the news, and it quickly reached foreign missions in Yemen's capital, Sana'a. A couple of hours after the bombing, a diplomat in the British Embassy sent a message to colleagues summarizing what they'd been able to learn. "We have just had news," the diplomat said, "that a British national, David Mockett . . . was killed by a car bomb at 1330 local time today." Few other details were available. "The body is currently at a local hospital. I'll send more info as I get it."

The email was circulated at the Foreign & Commonwealth Office, the UK equivalent of the US State Department. Senior officials were informed, and the FCO's Counter-Terrorism Department looped in. A teleconference was set up to discuss the bombing and potential plans to send British investigators to Yemen. With the culprits likely to be found among the myriad Islamic militant groups operating in the country, the detectives would be drawn from SO15, the terrorism unit within London's Metropolitan Police. But no one was sure such a deployment would be feasible. After all, the conditions apparently responsible for Mockett's murder also made Yemen extremely hazardous for visiting law enforcement.

The government in Sana'a certainly seemed to think that a jihadist group was to blame, even if none had yet claimed responsibility. After a meeting with Yemeni bureaucrats, an FCO official reported to London that the country's interior minister believed the bombing would prove to be a terrorist attack, like others in the past. That was a reasonable inference, but the British government had few avenues for verifying it. It had no consulate in Aden, leaving it reliant on Facey and others in the dwindling band of foreign residents to relay what was happening there. In Sana'a, its diplomats and spies were limited in their ability to operate beyond the walls of their embassy. In 2010 the UK ambassador, Tim Torlot, had been targeted by a suicide bomber while driving through the capital. Though he escaped unharmed, British officials were permitted to visit only certain parts of the city. Much of the rest of Yemen was essentially off-limits.

With so little information to go on, the FCO decided to put out only a brief statement about the explosion, confirming the identity of the victim and expressing the government's condolences. An FCO staffer suggested including a reference to the British government's official warning to its citizens against remaining in Yemen, but a more senior official overruled the idea; he thought it would imply that the government was blaming Mockett for his own death. The announcement would go out later in the day. First, someone would have to tell his family.

Cynthia Mockett was at the kitchen sink, washing the dishes from lunch, when she saw a police car roll up the driveway of the Vicarage. As it approached the house the driver stopped, pulling into a three-point turn to go back the way he'd come. He must have been looking for a different address, Cynthia thought. But then he parked, and a moment later there was a knock on the door. "Mrs. Mockett, may I come in please?" the policeman asked. She invited him into the living room at the front of the house, a space ringed with photos of David, Cynthia, and their children and grandchildren. The officer opened by asking Cynthia to sit down. As he began to speak, she felt a shard of dread rise through her body, sharpening with each word. "I have to tell you that your husband's car has been blown up," the man said. "Is he all right?" Cynthia asked. The look on the officer's face had already provided the answer.

Cynthia would remember what happened next as a period of almost dissociated shock. Some part of her refused to integrate the information. She'd spoken to her husband on the phone just a few days before, and he'd signed off as he always did, garrulous and confident: "Love you, sweetheart. Look after yourself." Soon he was coming home for the rest of the summer, an extended vacation of afternoons in the garden and family dinners. That the same man—the constant pole of Cynthia's life since she was a teenager, with whom she'd gone to sea, raised a family, planned a retirement—could be gone made no sense to her. It was beyond her ability to process.

Gradually, Cynthia emerged into what she realized was her new reality. Her first impulse was to call her daughters, both of whom lived nearby. They came to her immediately, and collapsed into tears as they entered the home where they were raised, triggering in Cynthia an instinct more powerful than her own grief. All she could think to do was to hold them in her arms, cradling and gently rocking them as she had when they were children. The news was filtering out into the neighborhood, and people streamed toward the Mocketts' house, offering to help however they could. "What are we going to do without this big man?" one of their longtime friends asked Cynthia, his voice breaking. She had no idea how to answer.

In Aden, Roy Facey was attempting to make sense of what had just happened. After the bombing he spent much of the day in his office, fielding calls and emails from both Yemenis and foreigners who were horrified by the news of Mockett's death and anxious to learn more. As one of only a handful of Westerners still in Aden, Facey had become a crucial source of information for anyone with an interest in the place, and he tried to respond to all of them, thanking them for their condolences and passing on what little he knew about the attack. With dusk approaching, he decided to take a break; some of the other expats were meeting for drinks, hoping to soothe their raw nerves with a gin and tonic or two. Facey drove over and parked his car, asking a neighborhood man to keep a close eye on the vehicle in exchange for some cash. There was almost certainly nothing to worry about, Facey thought, but it couldn't hurt to be careful.

Before he went to bed, Facey opened his laptop to compose an email to his regular distribution list, a diverse group of shipping hands, diplomats, academics, and others who followed developments in Yemen. "Dear All . . . the report today will be short," he wrote, leading with the event that many of them already knew about. "Besides this, other news on the city seems irrelevant," he continued. "The shipping and port agency community is deeply upset, as many of them relied on David for his professional expertise and the honesty of his reporting." Over the previous hours, Facey had "been inundated with phone calls from Yemeni friends expressing their shock and concern and sorrow that such a thing should happen in Aden. Both from those who knew David, of whom there are many, and those who did not know him."

Facey had found the local reaction genuinely moving. As public order weakened, life for many of Aden's citizens had become increasingly precarious. Those who'd been fortunate enough to keep their loved ones safe were still affected by Yemen's economic collapse, which put even middle-class residents at risk of sliding into poverty. Even with their city falling apart around them, many of the Adenis whom Facey spoke with seemed devastated by Mockett's murder, deeply upset that someone they'd welcomed into their community could meet such an end. Who could possibly have wished harm to Mr. David?

Mockett's local friends wanted to demonstrate their dismay, and a couple of days later there was a sort of memorial vigil for him in the center of the city. Cynthia had emailed some photographs of her husband, and someone printed his blown-up portrait to carry on a sign as the group marched. The mood was angry, but it struck Facey more as a general venting of emotion than a protest against a particular culprit. Whoever was responsible for Mockett's death, he thought, was a long way from public view.

Conscious of the popular mood, the Aden police force had opened what it said would be a thorough investigation. It was hard for Facey to know how seriously to take that pledge. Law enforcement in Yemen was riddled with corruption, and even honest cops might not have access to modern investigative practices. After Al Qaeda's 2000 suicide attack on the USS *Cole*, an American destroyer on a refueling stop in Aden, FBI agents had descended on the city, finding that their local counterparts were unfamiliar with routine techniques, like how to gather DNA samples. Even fingerprinting wasn't uniformly practiced. After a bombing, there was typically little effort to secure the scene to collect evidence; instead, the authorities seemed to pride themselves on how quickly they could clean up the wreckage and get traffic moving again. But in this case the police appeared at least to be going through the motions, taking possession of Mockett's burned-out car for forensic analysis and reviewing surveillance footage for clues about who might have planted the explosives.

They also spoke to Facey and asked him to prepare a report on Mockett's background to help guide their investigation. He agreed, although some Yemeni friends told him to be cautious about what he included. Following their advice, Facey tried to stick to basic biography, avoiding anything that could be interpreted as an accusation. In the memo he produced, he ran through Mockett's daily routines and explained that he "surveyed ships and their cargoes," work for which he'd been hired by "many of the large traders." The job entailed some risks, Facey said: "making damage assessments can lead to disputes," and "threats [had] been made" against other surveyors in the past. On the subject of the *Brillante Virtuoso*, he kept his comments spare. "I discussed this case with him the morning before he was attacked," Facey wrote, noting that "the reason for the piracy attack is not known." He did, however, mention one line of inquiry that Mockett was pursuing before his death: "David did not think that they"—the pirates—"were Somali." Facey had a friend translate his report into Arabic and passed it to the police on July 23. Afterward he went back to his normal routine, commuting from his apartment to his office at the port authority. He was being more cautious than usual, varying his routes to and from work in line with advice from the FCO. But things didn't seem so bad that he needed to get on a plane.

At about 1:30 a.m. on July 25, Facey's phone rang, waking him. Groggy with sleep, he picked up. He recognized the Scottish accent of the woman on the line: a senior diplomat at the British Embassy in Sana'a whom he knew from his dealings with the mission. She had an urgent message to deliver. Facey, she said tersely, had come up as a "potential target," and he needed to leave Yemen as soon as possible. She refused to discuss the specifics of the threat or how the British government had come to know about it. All she would say was that, for the moment, Facey shouldn't leave home. Someone would be in touch soon to discuss arrangements for getting him out of the country. Facey was surprised. In all his time in Yemen he'd never felt unsafe; he'd always hoped that if a threat to him did emerge, one of his local contacts would warn him well before it became a problem. But he certainly wasn't going to argue with the diplomat, and he followed her advice, remaining in his apartment throughout the next day and night. Embassy officials called again and again to check in, making sure nothing had happened to him.

Facey had stayed home for more than thirty-six hours when a pair of SUVs roared to a stop outside his building. The neighborhood kids playing outside stopped to stare as a group of thickly built American men stepped out. They were wearing civilian clothes, but their military bearing would have been obvious even without the pistols they carried on their belts. The men fanned out from their vehicles and toward Facey's door, looking carefully up and down the street. None of them identified themselves to him, though it wasn't difficult to guess who they were. The US had been stepping up a campaign of drone strikes against Al Qaeda–linked militant groups in Yemen, and small groups of American special forces personnel and military contractors were on the ground. Facey's embassy handlers had told him to expect the team, and he took a seat in the back of one of the SUVs, taking a long final look at his apartment building as he climbed in. The driver pulled away, and soon the vehicle was speeding through the city to a hotel where Facey had been instructed to remain until his flight out.

The security team took him to the airport early the next morning. It was still half dark when his plane took off, the twinkling lights of the country Facey had called home for more than twenty years falling away below the fuselage. He would never return.

CHAPTER 9

AN UPSTANDING CONSTABLE

Richard Veale had been in enough conference rooms in the City, London's ancient financial district, to know they all looked the same: polished-wood table, swivel chairs, passable coffee in brushed metal pitchers. The middle-aged white men who stared back at him in those rooms tended to look the same, too, all starched collars and expertly knotted ties. But at this meeting, in the summer of 2009, the crowd was a little different. The thirty or so attorneys, insurance executives, and other professionals who'd come to hear Veale speak were all involved in shipping in one way or another, and they were there to talk about pirates.

A private investigator specializing in financial fraud, Veale had been invited to a London law office to give a presentation about an expensive problem for the maritime world. Freeing the increasing numbers of vessels being hijacked by Somali pirates was costing shipowners and insurers a great deal of money. One group of researchers estimated that, during the most intense periods of piracy, outlays for ransoms accrued at a rate of more than $400 million a year—a huge sum even for a market as well capitalized as Lloyd's. This included the payments themselves, plus the expense of negotiating them and delivering the cash, often in private jets or helicopters.

And while the insurers were able to pass a large chunk of their losses to clients in the form of higher premiums, the attacks presented a more fundamental threat to the business models of everyone involved. The modern evolution of shipping had been, in large part, about predictability: ironing out the uncertainties of the sea in order to all but guarantee that products would arrive where and when they were supposed to, and for an affordable price. The Gulf of Aden was vital to many of those journeys, and pirates operating there had severely undermined the confidence that the industry depended upon. The men gathered in the conference room waiting for Richard Veale to start talking were looking for novel solutions. And Veale believed he had some.

Veale's ideas had nothing to do with protecting vessels. That wasn't his area of expertise. Although he'd spent much of his career in the Metropolitan Police, Veale had never carried a gun, and with a stout frame and a round, gentle face, it would have been hard to mistake him for one of the ex-soldiers who'd reinvented themselves as marine mercenaries, employed to scare off would-be hijackers. What Veale understood was money, and the creative means that criminals used to move it around the world. He'd learned over the years that no matter where they were from or what line of business they were in, lawbreakers tended to share one overriding desire: to get their funds into safe, legitimate assets, preferably in Western countries with strong protections for private property. The Somalis who ransomed ships for a living were no different, he told the men gathered in the conference room. They might wear mesh shorts and dirty tank tops and be armed with rusty Russian assault rifles, but they represented the sharp end of a sophisticated criminal enterprise, funded by a network of internationally connected financiers.

"In all probability," Veale said, "ransom payments are finding their way into financial systems outside Somalia." Specifically, the money that insurers and shipowners paid, in cash, was being magicked into bank accounts in Dubai, moving from there into the global financial system and investments like real estate and restaurants, some of them a long way from the Horn of Africa.

That flow of funds represented a vulnerability that Veale was proposing to exploit. "We're not talking about trying to seize money from guys with guns," he said. "We're talking about frustrating their financial ambitions." There was an obvious place to start. Pirates tended to be sloppy when it came to information security. Often they used the phones or computers on board captured ships. In one project he worked on, Veale traced their calls and emails to addresses in Minnesota and the English Midlands, nodes in an international money-laundering network. "We can lawfully intercept those communications," he explained. After all, a shipowner hardly needed a warrant to monitor his own computers. With better surveillance, investigators could map connections between pirates at sea and their backers and enablers onshore, building a picture of where the cash might be going.

That information could be handed over to the police and used in civil claims against anyone identified as an accessory to the process—people with businesses and reputations to lose. Even if a London lawsuit didn't present much of a deterrent to an actual Somali pirate, Veale argued, for a banker in the United Arab Emirates or an accounting firm in the US, it certainly could. "What you really want to do is terrify this middle strata of corrupt professionals," he said. "If you remove them you've got no one to help the pirates move money." And without confidence that they could enjoy their gains, the people who organized maritime attacks might shift their investments to activities that didn't disrupt international commerce.

The group listened attentively as Veale gave his presentation. But to his surprise, their reaction was mixed. Everyone seemed to agree that the shipping industry needed to come up with a more effective response to piracy. But some of the attendees were reluctant to consider such an aggressive approach. If insurers went after the criminals' money, one of them asked Veale, wouldn't there be a risk that the criminals could come after the insurers? Veale found the question strange. Wasn't the whole point to stop the bad guys?

As a child in the 1960s, Veale never wanted to be anything other than a cop. When he was a toddler, a great-aunt bought him a miniature police uniform, and it quickly became his favorite outfit. One night soon after, he noticed a policeman walking by his family's flat in the Docklands, a working-class stretch of East London that received substantial Luftwaffe attention during the war. "Go on, salute him," his mother urged. Veale did, and the officer promptly saluted back. He never forgot the moment, an idealized image of an upstanding constable protecting his neighborhood. East London had its share of villains—the Kray twins, arguably Britain's most notorious gangsters, operated a criminal empire there until their arrest in 1968—and to Veale it was clear that the police were what stood between families like his own and the crooks, keeping ordinary people from harm. He wanted to enlist as a cadet in the Metropolitan Police when he was just fifteen, and was rejected because of poor eyesight. (At the time the Met, as the London force is known, didn't want new cadets who needed glasses.) But three years later, Veale received a letter asking if he was still interested in becoming an officer. He sent his response immediately—an enthusiastic yes.

His first posting, in 1978, was to Canon Row, an ornate brick police station with jurisdiction over many of London's best-known landmarks, including the Houses of Parliament and Downing Street. Veale would be a probationary constable, a bobby on the beat, walking the streets in the Met's distinctive domed helmet, a dark blue uniform with silver buttons, and black boots that he polished to a high sheen. His only weapon in case of trouble would be a wooden truncheon; then, as now, British police were only rarely armed.

Much of the work in Canon Row's precinct was routine—helping tourists who'd been pickpocketed, responding to car break-ins, and the like. Yet for a working-class kid, the access that being an officer there afforded was mind-blowing, like having a backstage pass to some of the most famous places in the world. They included Buckingham Palace—or Buck House, as the cops called it—where Veale helped investigate the 1982 break-in by Michael Fagan, the mentally ill intruder who made it as far as the Queen's bedroom before being apprehended.

Veale's ambitions went well beyond chasing burglars and pickpockets, and a few years after he joined the force he put in for the sergeant's exam—and then forgot he'd registered. When a superior reminded him that the test was coming up, he had only a couple of months to study material that usually took officers a year to master. If Veale was going to pass, he knew he was going to have to be systematic. He booked two weeks of holiday to do nothing but study. First, he went over exams for the previous five years, comparing them with recent legislation and discarding any questions based on laws that had changed. The more he scrutinized, the more he could see patterns.

The questions that came up again and again were drawn from a few sections of the General Orders, the procedural bible that governed the operations of the Met. Veale figured that if he studied those passages intensely, he would be fine. After several all-nighters, he could recite them word for word. He passed easily.

It turned out that being a uniformed sergeant wasn't much of an upgrade. At his new post, a station responsible for the boutiques and nightclubs of Mayfair and Soho, Veale spent most of his time behind a desk, dealing with the paperwork created by cops who were closer to the action. He wanted desperately to be back on the front line cracking cases—the more complicated the better. Fortunately, his superiors seemed to like him, and bit by bit Veale convinced them to let him take on more demanding investigative work. After a couple of years, he shifted to doing it full-time. He proved to be an able detective. Veale and his team worked to bust up a major car-theft ring, eventually tracing the vehicles to the docks in Bristol, where they were sealed in crates awaiting export. And he interviewed suspects for Operation Circus, a delicate inquiry into sex trafficking of minors. Veale's studious manner sometimes threw people off. Once, when he was going door-to-door looking for witnesses, someone called the police to report that there was a man who looked like an accountant bothering people in the neighborhood, pretending to be a detective.

But after a decade with the Met, Veale wasn't sure it was where he wanted to spend the rest of his career. Some of his hesitation stemmed from a sense that the force was becoming much more political than when he'd joined. Margaret Thatcher, who led Britain throughout the 1980s, had gone out of her way to appeal to officers, raising their pay and favoring a gloves-off approach to policing. In turn many cops became bombastic supporters of the Conservative prime minister, a development that Veale, who'd always considered himself left of center, found uncomfortable. He was even more disturbed by her government's use of the police against striking coal miners, escalating one of the most convulsive social conflicts of the era. Veale had been raised among factory workers and longshoremen, union men all, and deploying officers against picket lines felt to him like a perversion of the powers of law enforcement.

His restlessness was also motivated by a more pragmatic consideration. Like everyone who lived in London, he could see that the place was changing. The sooty, decrepit city of Veale's childhood was disappearing, morphing into a cosmopolitan hub for international business. When he'd gone to school near Canary Wharf, the district's main quays—the West and East India docks, once thronged with vessels bound for the Caribbean and the British-ruled subcontinent—were all but abandoned, ghostly monuments to a country's fading grandeur. Now a gleaming new financial district was under construction there, to be populated with banks attracted by Thatcher's laissez-faire approach to financial regulation. It was obvious that this new city offered plenty of opportunities for those with the right skills, and Veale, whatever his political sympathies, was pretty sure he had at least some of them. By joining the Met he'd fulfilled his childhood dream. Now it was time to make some money.

After he left the police, Veale took a series of private-sector jobs, work that took him as far afield as Russia—ground zero, in the 1990s, for Western companies getting mixed up in situations that might require delicate investigation to resolve. He'd never traveled much, and Veale was energized by the openness he experienced wherever he went. Barriers to people, ideas, and money were collapsing everywhere, creating a truly global economy. Yet this unprecedented internationalization seemed, if anything, to be making London even more central, the only place where nearly everyone felt comfortable parking themselves or their assets. The city—and, more specifically, the City—had become an essential nexus, connecting Western institutions to the fortunes being made in what the bankers had started to call emerging markets. Soon, ex-Soviet oligarchs would be suing each other over soured mergers in the English courts, while Central Asian mining companies tried to raise money on London's capital markets and African politicians shifted their assets into British-domiciled banks.

Eventually, Veale decided to start a company to take advantage of the trends he was observing. European Business Information Services, or EBIS, which he founded in 1997, would undertake deep-dive investigations on behalf of lawyers or other clients, focusing on inquiries that required substantial amounts of technological know-how. London's rise had radically expanded the demand for such services, yet many of the ex-cops who populated the investigative business had little knowledge of international finance, or even of the internet. Veale, who'd found he was a natural at online research, pitched himself as a high-tech alternative, able to reliably determine the financial connections between parties to a lawsuit or trace the location of assets someone wanted frozen. He slowly built a stable of clients, one profitable enough to allow him to move into and then expand a spacious home in a prosperous village—a long way, physically and financially, from the serried lanes of the Docklands.

Police work had a way of drawing Veale back, though. One day he caught up over coffee with an old boss from the Met, who mentioned that he and his team were struggling with a knotty asset-tracing problem. An ex-employee had stolen a substantial amount of money from the force, and the police had been unable to recover the cash. Such a case wouldn't normally tie up a senior commander and a squad of elite detectives, but this was far from a typical workplace matter. The former staffer was an accountant assigned to undercover operations, including programs for surveilling the Irish Republican Army and other radical groups. In particular, he'd been in charge of a secret fund used to pay for reconnaissance aircraft the Met used to snoop on suspected IRA hideouts.

Veale thought he could help the team working the case, and his ex-superior invited him to an unmarked Met office to talk to them. As an example of the power of the new investigative tools available online, Veale offered to perform a demonstration. The aerial surveillance program was so off-books that the model type and registration numbers of the police aircraft, and the names of the corporate entities that owned them, were known to only a few investigators. Veale bet the team he could find the planes, and after his initial briefing, he asked to use one of their computers.

He consulted Jane's, the private-sector database for aerospace information, and identified a twin-engine turboprop that he thought was likeliest to be the one employed by the police. Then he pulled up the UK's civil-aviation registry, which had a list of all aircraft of that type operating in the country.

The records indicated that most belonged to conventional government agencies. But a small number of the planes, Veale told the detectives, "stood out like bulldogs' bollocks." Their ostensibly private owner was a partnership, rather than a limited company, which could leave the people behind it personally liable in the event of an accident. "No businessman in their right mind would own an aircraft in a nonlimited structure," Veale said. "They are your aircraft." The cops bought him a drink—and then asked what else he could do.

Veale began taking contract work for the Met and other British law-enforcement agencies, training officers on cybersecurity and recovering stolen funds. The real money was in private-sector assignments, though, and they occupied most of Veale's attention. Over time, more of those jobs came from the shipping industry. It was growing rapidly in the 2000s as the volume of international trade swelled, and in some ways the business was ideally suited to Veale's skills. Shipowners and a fleet of enablers, most of them in London, had spent half a century making their world harder to understand, hiding maritime tycoons' true identities—and their tax and regulatory obligations—within nesting dolls of shell companies. Compared with other sectors, it was remarkably accommodating to such obfuscations. A bank that wanted to finance the construction of an office tower, for example, would do extensive due diligence on the borrower, compiling detailed "know your customer" documentation to comply with mandates from financial regulators. But the insurers who covered ships and voyages at Lloyd's might have little idea who was ultimately behind the corporate entities they protected. The result was that when something went wrong—a major collision, for example, or a suspected fraud—they were often operating in the dark. All of that meant opportunity for an investigator like Veale.

Yet his proposals to deter Somali pirates by going after their financiers' money met with only limited success. The shipping industry seemed to be more interested in talking about piracy than confronting it. But the presentation Veale gave on the subject in 2009 did make him better known within Lloyd's, and the constellation of insurers and law firms that orbited around it. One of the people he pitched was Paul Cunningham, the personable claims manager from Talbot Underwriting. Cunningham was responsible for guiding insurance cases through the Lloyd's system, verifying whether a shipowner's loss was covered, ensuring that they followed the procedures correctly, and, all being in order, paying out their money. Serious complications were rare; like other Lloyd's underwriters, Talbot usually erred on the side of cutting checks. But once in a while, a case crossed Cunningham's desk that gave him pause.

He and Veale kept in touch, and in the late summer of 2011 he gave the investigator a call. Talbot was the lead underwriter for an oil tanker that had been hijacked in the Gulf of Aden, Cunningham explained. The circumstances were not typical. The crew's accounts of the incident didn't match the physical condition of the vessel, and the pirates had behaved in a way completely contrary to their financial interests, all but destroying the ship instead of holding it for ransom. Even more unusual, the surveyor hired by the insurers to investigate had been murdered not long after getting started, for reasons no one could be sure of. Before paying out on the claim, Cunningham said, Talbot wanted to know more—about the ship, its owner, and what happened on its final voyage. Would Veale be willing to take it on?

CHAPTER 10

FOR THOSE IN PERIL ON THE SEA

About a week after her husband's death, Cynthia Mockett heard someone knock on the door of the Vicarage, their home in Devon. It was a police sergeant in uniform, there to take a statement. She invited him into the living room, where David's image remained constant in her life, thanks to the framed photographs of him all around: some as a handsome young sailor, others smiling with a glass of wine in the garden, or posing with an arm around their daughters. The officer seemed apologetic that he couldn't do more for Cynthia. The Devon and Cornwall Police obviously had no jurisdiction in Yemen, and the British government had decided it was too dangerous to send detectives there to conduct a proper investigation. The police were doing their best in difficult circumstances, he explained, and they needed her help.

Cynthia was exhausted. She'd spent the week acting as a focal point for her entire family's grief, receiving condolences from all over the world. The bureaucracy of loss also fell to her. Retrieving David's body had proved difficult. Officials in Aden had been reluctant to facilitate the repatriation until a friend of the Mocketts' persuaded the boss of a local shipping company to foot the bill. And there were so many financial matters to settle, including his life insurance policy. She wasn't entirely confident that it covered death overseas by car bomb.

To add to the pressure on Cynthia, the British media had taken an interest in what happened to David, and reporters had been showing up at the house. A Briton apparently blown up by terrorists made for a compelling tabloid story. One newspaper published a quote in Cynthia's name, saying she feared the blast was so powerful that there would be no body to bury. Either the statement was fabricated, or the reporter had spoken to someone else: she never gave the interview and never said anything remotely to that effect.

But despite Cynthia's weariness, she was keen to help the police if she could, so she gathered herself and offered the sergeant a cup of tea. She was under no illusions about how difficult it would be for the British police to tease the truth out of Yemen. As she'd learned in her years visiting Aden, it could be a confounding place. "Yemen is a world of relationships, not institutions," wrote Ginny Hill, an analyst and journalist who covered the country for more than a decade. Partly for reasons of self-preservation, "each version of events that is revealed to you depends on the speaker's assessment of your connections and suspected affiliations."

When it came to investigating Mockett's death, the identity of the person making the inquiries would be critically important. Were they a Saleh loyalist, linked by shadowy financial ties to the president's family? Or were they connected to another of the dynastic clans jostling for position in the aftermath of the Arab Spring? Perhaps the questioner was an honest local detective, or a jihadist double agent who'd fought allied forces in Iraq. The answer could be different each time. A Westerner ignorant of Yemen's power structures might not get a meaningful response at all. "There are many versions of the same moment, and each of them is somehow valid," Hill wrote.

After taking notes of Cynthia's account of her last conversations with David, the sergeant asked about the details of his final job: the *Brillante Virtuoso*. The police wanted to explore any avenue that might have led him unwittingly into conflict. Cynthia explained that most of Mockett's professional materials were held at his office in Aden, and agreed to call the young Sri Lankan surveyor that David had taken under his wing there.

When he answered the phone, Mockett's protégé sounded terrified. "Madam, the file has been stolen," he said. In the days since Mockett's murder, he told Cynthia, someone had slipped into the office and rifled through his things. Whoever it was had taken Mockett's diary, as well as his entire dossier on the *Brillante*. The surveyor seemed worried about his phone being bugged. "I have got to be very, very careful what I say," he said. "What do I do, madam?" Cynthia had met the man several times, and always thought he was an excellent choice as David's understudy. She could think of only one thing to say. "Do what he's taught you to do," she said. "You have to do what you think is right."

In the City of London, the insurance market was also absorbing the news of Mockett's death. While there was no direct evidence that the crime was connected to the *Brillante*, the murder of a key participant in the claims process added to a sense that it might not be an ordinary piracy case. Greater than usual scrutiny seemed to be justified. To better understand the incident, a law firm working for the insurers that covered the *Brillante*'s hull commissioned a report from a piracy expert, a former soldier who'd helped negotiate ransoms for kidnapped sailors. The expert concluded, based on the limited information available, that it was unlikely to have been Somali pirates who boarded the tanker. Like Bob Boosey, the Royal Navy officer who was roused from his Dubai bedroom on the night of the attack, he pointed out that Somali gangs didn't generally strike after dark, and that they usually attempted to ransom crews. Why walk away from a multimillion-dollar bounty without taking a single hostage? There were other baffling inconsistencies. According to the crew's statements, the pirates seemed to be wearing uniforms, and their rifles were clean. Somali teams, by contrast, tended to appear in ragged clothes and carry poorly maintained AK-47s.

What this meant for the Lloyd's market wasn't exactly clear. For the purposes of the insurance policy, it didn't really matter what type of bandits had burned the *Brillante*. Whether they were Somali pirates or opportunistic Yemeni militiamen, the hull insurers, led by Talbot Underwriting, were still facing a loss of $80 million or more. But the companies weren't ready to part with the money just yet—not until they cleared up some of their questions. In internal communications, Lloyd's players started referring to an "alleged pirate attack."

The firms that covered the $100 million of oil in the *Brillante*'s hull—led by RSA Group and Zurich, two of the world's biggest insurance providers—also had concerns. In addition to that potential loss, they were on the hook for the cost of the operation to salvage whatever was left of the ship and its cargo. That was already looking like it would run into the tens of millions. The sums at stake motivated them to begin their own probe into what happened on the night of the assault.

All these inquiries were taking place separately, without much communication between the different Lloyd's factions. Traditionally, all the executives, lawyers, and investigators involved in a casualty would get together in a "market meeting," held at the Lloyd's building, to update the different syndicates about the progress of a claim. However, in recent years, lawyers had begun expressing concerns that these meetings could be viewed as anticompetitive, potentially breaching laws against cartel activity. So the *Brillante*'s hull and cargo insurers met separately and didn't share much with each other apart from cursory information. If they wanted to glean anything more, insurance executives would have to rely on the Lloyd's gossip mill: quiet conversations in the Underwriting Room, beside the Lutine Bell, or in the pubs around Lime Street.

Cynthia Mockett knew nothing about the deliberations in London. No one from any of the insurance interests her husband represented had even contacted her to offer condolences. All she had were her family and friends, who tried to form a protective shield for Cynthia and her daughters. There was a small comfort, she thought, in how much the people around her wanted to help.

David Mockett's funeral was held on a cool, sunny August day at Our Lady of Lourdes in Plympton, a few miles from the Vicarage. A crowd of people packed into the little white church, under a low slate roof. Some had flown in from the Middle East to say goodbye. Cynthia walked down the aisle with two of her grandchildren at her side, one holding each of her hands, to take her seat in the front row.

The Bishop of Plymouth started the service with the words of an old seafarer's hymn. According to maritime lore, it had been written by a nineteenth-century clergyman after he survived a severe storm in the Mediterranean.

Eternal Father, strong to save,
Whose arm doth bound the restless wave,
Who bidd'st the mighty ocean deep
Its own appointed limits keep;
Oh, hear us when we cry to Thee,
For those in peril on the sea!

The grandchildren came to the front to read prayers, asking the Lord for peace in Yemen and for the fighting and killing to stop. They prayed for their granddad, and for those who had gone before him, to find peace and happiness in the beyond. The emotion was too much for one of them, and his father had to help him finish.

Charles Dawson, one of the Mockett family's closest friends, read the eulogy. Dawson spoke of Mockett's birth on the Isle of Sheppey, off England's southeast coast, "surrounded by the sea, as he was to be for much of his life." He talked about Mockett's time in the merchant navy, the ships he had served on—the *Cornish City*, the *Elena*, the *Victoria City*, and the *Welsh City*—and how Cynthia had been the first wife allowed to join her husband on some of those vessels.

Dawson described meeting Mockett in the 1980s, when the former sailor was a port official in Saudi Arabia. There, a stream of captains, agents, and officials came to him each day with their problems. "David," he recalled, "listened carefully, promised little, and then, when a gap in visitors appeared, made all the phone calls and fixed everything in a quiet yet commanding way." Dawson finished the eulogy with words from another close friend: "David Mockett was a very good friend, a thoughtful, kind, amusing, and wonderful family man, who gave freely of his time to others, particularly those in need, and to good causes. David was a magnificent man and we all miss him terribly."

There was no burial. Mockett's coffin had to be taken away immediately after the service and given to the local coroner, who would conduct an autopsy. Cynthia made a point, on the way out, of shaking hands with everyone in the church. Then they all drove to Boringdon Hall, a local manor house and hotel, for a buffet meal and a collection for the Royal National Lifeboat

Institution, the UK's coastal rescue service. David had been a paying member, with voting rights and a subscription to *Lifeboat* magazine.

Once that was over, Cynthia returned to the Vicarage with a handful of friends. She laid out all the wreaths she'd received in the garden, so many that the white flowers carpeted the lawn. Roger Stokes, the shy Aden lawyer who liked to sketch sports cars, was there. He asked for some of David's employment paperwork to bring back with him to Yemen. Mockett was owed a significant amount of back pay, and Stokes thought he could help. Eventually the group got to discussing the small vigil that had been held in Aden after Mockett's death, and how sad and angry people in the city had seemed. It didn't make sense for anyone, even Al Qaeda, to assassinate her husband, Cynthia thought. Surely a terrorist group would have claimed responsibility, or broadcast some kind of grisly message.

After holding herself together through the memorial and buffet, Cynthia could feel her strength starting to ebb. One of David's friends, who worked as a Lloyd's representative in Yemen, noticed her flagging and offered to take her to the local pub for dinner. The George was a seventeenth-century former coaching house selling pies, burgers, and battered fish with fat fries—just what Cynthia needed.

After they arrived, the conversation soon turned to the *Brillante Virtuoso*, a subject that her companion knew a little bit about. "I'm not sure I should be saying this," he said as they sat down with their drinks. From what he'd heard, he continued, the *Brillante* was "not the first ship that's gone down like this."

Cynthia stared back at him. "What do you mean?" she asked.

"Same place, same owner, and same salvage crew," the Lloyd's man replied. "This has happened before."

CHAPTER 11

NO CURE, NO PAY

B y late August, seven weeks after its fires were doused, salvors had towed the *Brillante* to a position off the coast of the United Arab Emirates, about twenty miles from Ajman, a sleepy city near Dubai. The tanker was still full of oil, and its owner had decided to unload it in the heavily policed waters of the Persian Gulf rather than risk the misfortunes—both piratical and bureaucratic—that could befall a vessel closer to Yemen. It had taken nearly a month to complete the roughly 1,800-mile journey, in part because Yemeni authorities had unexpectedly seized one of the salvage boats, holding it in Aden while they demanded various fees. Then, after getting under way, the weather was so bad that a team of Greek guards sent to protect the *Brillante* found it difficult to stand up on the listing deck. Two powerful tugs were needed to pull the tanker's dead weight through the choppy seas and keep it pointed in the right direction.

Compared with Yemen, the UAE would also be a much safer place for the substantial volume of investigation that needed to occur before any insurance claims could be resolved. Fire and explosives specialists were waiting to collect evidence on the still-unexplained inferno that had gutted the *Brillante*, while Noble Denton, the firm that hired Mockett, had assigned another surveyor to inspect the vessel. Mockett had been murdered before he was able to complete his work, and the Lloyd's market still needed a comprehensive accounting of the damage. The plan was to complete all the surveys and then pump the million barrels of oil inside the *Brillante* to another tanker in a ship-to-ship transfer, or STS, a risky and complicated maneuver requiring specialized skills and equipment.

Nick Sloane had been preparing for weeks to get on board. A thickset South African salvor with thinning reddish hair and a ruddy face weathered by years at sea, Sloane had been hired to monitor and advise on the STS operation. Concluding it safely would require a keen understanding of petroleum chemistry, marine engineering, and, perhaps most important, everything that could go wrong when vessels the length of three football fields came so close together that their hulls nearly touched. At the beginning of the process, the ship with empty tanks would be sitting high in the water, well above the one being off-loaded; as the oil was pumped across their positions would reverse, requiring delicate calculations to ensure that neither was destabilized. Sloane knew that a mistake could result in a spill that could do serious environmental damage, and possibly land everyone involved in an Emirati jail.

If an STS was tricky even in the most benign circumstances, executing one on a tanker severely damaged by fire was substantially more so, and Sloane had been appointed in July to keep tabs on the preparations. He'd been on vacation with his family, beginning a week in a safari camp in Kruger National Park, when a lawyer working on the *Brillante* response called him on his mobile. How fast could he get to the Middle East? Sloane's wife knew the routine. He grabbed his things, leaving her and their children to continue their holiday, and drove straight to Johannesburg. He was on the next flight to Dubai.

In the salvage game, Sloane had grown accustomed to dropping whatever he was doing to react to a ship in distress. He'd been a young seafarer with Safmarine, a South African merchant line, when a tanker caught fire and split in two off Table Bay in 1983. Safmarine put out a call for volunteers to fight the spill, and Sloane stepped forward. The oil was contained—though not before the stern of the vessel capsized and sank—and Sloane was hooked. Over the next three decades he would take part in operations in more than thirty countries, be involved in two helicopter crashes, and miss the births of all three of his children.

Sloane found everything about the job intoxicating: the urgency, the stakes, the intellectual challenge of finding a new solution for each vessel that needed rescue. On any given day, a salvor might be eating breakfast, or playing with his kids, or in the middle of a night's sleep when his phone rang, sending him sprinting out the door with a bag of clothes and equipment that he kept packed at all times. Within hours he could be leaping from a helicopter onto a foundering freighter, mustering every ounce of seamanship he possessed to save the vessel and its cargo. There was no rush like it.

Salvage, however, is critically different from other adrenaline-junkie pursuits. Unlike, say, BASE jumping or hang gliding, serious flows of capital are involved. When a vessel runs into trouble, its insurers have an interest in preserving as much of its value as possible in order to limit what they ultimately need to pay out. Not surprisingly, Lloyd's serves as a hub of the salvage world, setting its rules, such as they are, and ironing over the inevitable disputes. The industry's standard contract is called the Lloyd's Open Form, which can be agreed over the radio between the captain of a damaged ship and the master of a tug racing to the scene. Later, the compensation the salvor receives from the ship's insurers may be determined through a Lloyd's division called the Salvage Arbitration Branch. When it works correctly, the system functions as a virtuous circle. Lloyd's insurers pay salvors handsomely to save ships and cargoes; with those profits, salvors can buy faster, more powerful tugs and hire even more skilled personnel, allowing them to be more effective rescuers the next time.

The oversight of salvage from London, however, provides only a thin layer of formality to one of the world's most cutthroat businesses. Salvors have existed virtually as long as people have been going to sea, and before the development of modern marine insurance they could be more like scavengers, taking anything of value from a wrecked vessel whether its owner consented or not. Sometimes they caused the wrecks themselves, perhaps by luring a ship onto rocks with deceptive coastal lights. While salvage is more regulated today, it's still a game played only by the toughest, most aggressive seafarers. For obvious reasons, speed is critical. Once they arrive, salvors can go to extreme lengths to secure their possession of a vessel, occasionally even ramming another company's tug to force it to back off. And while it is expressly forbidden under Lloyd's regulations, it's an open secret that some salvors, in exchange for receiving a contract or being tipped off about an accident before competitors hear of it, kick back part of their compensation to shipowners.

The monetary rewards can be enormous. The basic principle of salvage, rendered in bold capitals on every Lloyd's Open Form, is: "NO CURE—NO PAY." Under the industry's traditional rules, a salvor who fails to save a ship or cargo gets nothing—instead, as a scholar of the industry once described it, "the sea wins." (More recent changes provide for payment for preventing environmental consequences in some cases, even if a salvage fails in other respects.) A salvor who succeeds, by contrast, is entitled to a substantial proportion of the value he protects, to be shared out among his crew. In the case of a fully loaded tanker or similarly important asset, that may tally to tens of millions of dollars, and the best in the business can afford to live in rock-star luxury, at least for a time.

Sloane's successes had afforded him an enviable lifestyle, including a family home in the wine country outside of Cape Town. But it came at a cost. At any moment, the next ship in trouble was only a phone call away. And it was impossible to ever really know, as he flew toward it, what he would find on board.

The sun was still low in the sky as Sloane arrived on one of Ajman's beaches, on a broad inlet bordered by drab office blocks. A white launch had pulled up onto the sand, its pilot sheltered beneath a flimsy canopy fixed over the cockpit. This would be Sloane's ride to the *Brillante*. He threw his rucksack over one of the gunwales and hauled himself inside. The pilot pushed away from the beach and pressed on the throttle, sending the skiff churning across the waves, the wind threatening to pick up anything on board that wasn't heavy or tied down. It took more than an hour to reach the tanker. As he climbed onto its broad deck, just as David Mockett had weeks before, Sloane could feel the heat radiating from the metal with almost tangible force: it was more than 100 degrees Fahrenheit. One of the salvage crew had set up a café umbrella to provide some relief, but compared with the scale of the *Brillante*, and the severity of the conditions, it looked absurdly inadequate.

Sloane pulled down his hat to shade his face a little, then began addressing the long checklist of tasks he had to get through. Before any cargo transfer could begin, he needed to carry out a detailed examination of the ship, assessing the prospects for pumping out its oil and keeping it stable in the process. Leaks in the pumping gear would be a problem, obviously, as would failures in the inert-gas supply, which was necessary to keep a protective, low-oxygen bubble over the payload. The oil in tankers produces flammable vapors, which can ignite into a catastrophic fire if they're not "inerted." Then there was the question of the strength of the hull. If another tanker was going to come alongside the *Brillante*, separated only by a set of rubber fenders, Sloane wanted to know that its side shell hadn't been so damaged that it might buckle under the pressure.

Sloane started working his way down the vessel from bow to stern, taking pictures and recording observations in his notebook. He'd been involved in dozens of STS operations and knew the procedures virtually by heart. But as he went about his assessment, something about this ship struck him as odd. In Sloane's experience, tankers working long transoceanic journeys tended to be kept in reasonable condition. It wasn't so much that shipowners felt a moral obligation to protect their crews—for many of them, sailors' lives were hardly a top priority. There just wasn't much margin in cutting corners. High-profile spills had provided vivid lessons in the financial and reputational consequences of mishaps: the most extreme example, BP's *Deepwater Horizon* disaster, would ultimately cost shareholders more than $65 billion. The result was that any oil company with a public profile typically wouldn't hire a tanker unless it could be assured the vessel was well maintained.

The *Brillante*, Sloane quickly realized, was different. There was rusty pipework all over the ship, and the equipment required to keep the cargo at the correct temperature—a basic stipulation of most charter contracts—didn't work. If it hadn't been attacked, and instead had reached its destination in China, Sloane wasn't sure if the *Brillante* would have been able to discharge its contents safely. He was surprised that a vessel in its condition was carrying oil at all.

After spending the night onshore, Sloane returned to the *Brillante* with a larger group, including the fire and explosives experts sent by the parties to the insurance claim. Sloane watched as they descended toward the engine room, where Mockett believed the fire on board had begun. Though the water from the salvors' hoses had been drained out, the belly of the ship was still a mess, stinking of oil and burned paint. It was hard to see much. But when they made their way to the purifier room, where in normal operation oil would be filtered for use in the main engine, one of the investigators spotted something that shouldn't have been there. There was a noticeable indentation in the steel floor of a raised walkway, about forty centimeters wide and four deep, as if a giant had punched into the plating with all his strength. On some machinery nearby, there was a series of small dents and perforations, more than twenty in total. Crouching over the crater, a British explosives specialist named Adrian Wilkinson reached into his forensic kit and pulled out a set of cotton swabs, which he soaked with acetone. Wilkinson touched each swab to the deformed metal and then bagged them separately for further analysis. He was pretty sure he knew what he was looking at.

Later, back at their hotel in Ajman, Wilkinson and another of the investigators met with a pair of agents from the US Naval Criminal Investigative Service to brief them on their findings. Traditionally, the NCIS focused on crimes committed by American sailors and ferreting out fraud in military contracts, but as hijackings multiplied, the agency had been taking a much greater interest in piracy. The near-wrecking of the *Brillante* was unusual, and the agents were trying to understand what had occurred—and to rule out any connection to terrorism. Pirates, after all, didn't typically destroy the vessels they hijacked.

Meanwhile, word was getting around the salvage teams. Sloane and some of the others working on the tanker had gathered for drinks on an outdoor terrace, where they got to talking about what the investigators had learned on board. Sloane listened as someone relayed the news. What they'd found in the bowels of the ship confirmed what David Mockett had only suspected: the early accounts of how the *Brillante* had come to be in its present condition were wrong. The fire hadn't been started by an errant grenade, or gunfire igniting a fuel tank. Instead, someone had made their way deep below deck, to perhaps the best place on the whole vessel to start a devastating blaze, and planted a bomb.

The rest of the preparations for the oil transfer didn't quite go as planned. After dark one night, the salvors received an unexpected hail on the radio. "This is the Iranian Revolutionary Guard Navy," the stern voice declared. "You are in Iranian territorial waters. You must leave." While a couple of islands in the vicinity were indeed ruled by the Islamic Republic, that was, at most, debatable. Still, Sloane thought it would be distinctly unwise to get into an argument about maritime boundaries with the Revolutionary Guard. He was relieved to learn, shortly afterward, that the *Brillante* needed to move anyway. The Emirati authorities had denied the salvors permission to perform an STS off Ajman, and they had to tow the vessel a further two hundred miles to the port of Khor Fakkan, on the other side of a peninsula that extends like a raised thumb into the Strait of Hormuz.

Once the three-day tow was complete, surveyors came on board to verify the quality of the *Brillante*'s cargo, extending sampling containers downward through small ports on the main deck. They reported that a significant quantity of water seemed to have infiltrated the oil—a bizarre finding for which there was no obvious explanation. Sloane needed to remain with the vessel for weeks to observe further tests, as well as the process of transferring the fuel. It took until October, nearly three months after Sloane had received his first call about the *Brillante*, to complete the pumping and formally return it to the custody of its Greek owners. Sloane was finally free to return to Cape Town, in time for summer in the Southern Hemisphere.

Burned out and drained of the commodity whose transport was the sole reason for its existence, the *Brillante* sat at anchor well into the new year. Before, it had been a workhorse of the global energy industry; now it was a floating heap of metal. In February 2012, a firm called Aryana Shipping bought it for scrap, paying $700,000 for a vessel that previously had an insured value more than one hundred times that amount.

Not far from Karachi, on Pakistan's Arabian Sea coast, is a place where ships go to die. The Gadani breaking yard occupies some six miles of beach, segmented into plots by small recycling outfits that are servants to capitalism in its most elemental form. The bottom drops away quickly from the shore, which means that even very large tankers and freighters can be pushed right onto the mottled sand, their bows out of the water. More than twelve thousand people are directly employed at Gadani, many of them migrants from Pakistan's least developed regions. Far from their families and paid as little as a few dollars a day, the workers sleep in dense clots of settlement just inland. They take neither weekends nor holidays.

The *Brillante* arrived at Gadani in April 2012. After it came to a stop on the beach, teams of men armed with saws and blowtorches clambered onto its decks, beginning the laborious task of taking the vessel apart from stem to stern by hand. Nothing of value would be allowed to go to waste. Of the materials on board, steel was the most important. Loaded into trucks bound for mills in Karachi, it would be rerolled and combined with other scrap, perhaps destined for new buildings in the ever-sprawling megacity. Though there was far less of it, copper would be another source of revenue, sold into a supply chain essential to meeting the world's demand for new electronics. Any wood that had somehow survived the fire would also have its use: building more of the shanties to which shipbreakers returned at the end of each day.

The Gadani yard is one of the most dangerous workplaces in the world. Despite efforts by activists to impose meaningful safety standards, fatal accidents are common, as is contamination by the many toxic chemicals that can be found in aging vessels. But the dismantling of the *Brillante* proceeded without incident. Soon, all that was left was an impression in the sand, marking where its keel had come to rest before it was cut into pieces. Any remaining evidence of what really happened on the night of July 5, 2011, vanished with it.

CHAPTER 12

HOT FROGS

N early a year after David Mockett was murdered, his widow Cynthia made the short trip to central Plymouth for a coroner's inquest into his death. The hearing would be held in a room normally reserved for local government business, within the concrete complex that housed the city council. Inside, fluorescent bulbs threw a harsh light over tables laid out in a rectangle around the small space, with attendees free to find a spot anywhere they liked.

Cynthia took a seat near the front with a few members of her family. There were also a handful of police officials and local journalists present, along with Stuart Wallace, the manager from Noble Denton who'd hired Mockett to survey the *Brillante Virtuoso*. Partly, he'd come to answer any questions the coroner might have for him. His other motives were more personal. No one from Noble Denton had contacted Cynthia in the immediate aftermath of the bombing, an oversight that Wallace felt terrible about. When he found out about it a few months later, he had sent Cynthia an apologetic note, explaining that there'd been an internal mix-up over who was supposed to reach out to her. Attending the inquest to pay his respects had seemed to Wallace like the least he could do. He was struck, as he watched Cynthia settle in, by how composed she seemed, given the grim nature of what was about to be discussed.

On average, roughly half a million British citizens die each year. Of those fatalities, only a tiny fraction, around thirty thousand, are referred to a coroner for an inquest into the cause of death. The proceedings are reserved for sudden or "unnatural" ends, or for when a person dies in the custody of the state—in a prison cell, for example. Since the 1980s, they have also been legally required for all violent deaths abroad, after a campaign inspired by the fate of Helen Smith, a British nurse who fell from a balcony in mysterious circumstances in Saudi Arabia. Coroners occupy a unique position in the legal system: part medical professional, part judge, part undertaker. As they conduct their duties, many also act as unofficial social workers or clergy members, trying to bring some solace to bereaved families.

Since his death, Cynthia had spoken to most of Mockett's friends in the shipping world. Many shared the misgivings of the Lloyd's agent who'd taken her to a local pub for dinner after the funeral. There was something suspicious about the *Brillante*, they agreed. Cynthia had provided the local police with everything that she thought might aid an investigation, including emails Mockett sent expressing doubts about how the tanker came to grief. But eleven months after she'd lost him, the whole situation remained a confusing mess. Cynthia had no answers, or even solid leads, as to why her husband had been targeted. She hoped the inquest might yield some.

Once everyone was ready, the senior coroner, Ian Arrow, took his place in a tall chair. He began the proceedings with an explanation, directed at the Mocketts, of what they were there to do. "The purpose of an inquest is to find answers to four questions," he said. "Those four questions are: who is the deceased? How, where, and when did he come by his death?" Arrow, who had auburn hair and wore a dark suit, continued in a calm, measured voice. "It's not for the coroner to find any fault, liability, or blame. There is nobody on trial here today. However, we will hear facts which, I'm sure you will appreciate, give an indication that something very unusual has happened."

First, Arrow quickly established Mockett's identity. His body had been so badly burned that it was unrecognizable. He had to be examined by a forensic dentist, who'd sent a report confirming that there were fifty-four "features of concordance" with earlier dental records, meaning there could be no reasonable doubt about who he was.

Then Arrow read out a statement about how Mockett came to be in Yemen, describing his work as a surveyor and laying out his daily routine. It had been written by Cynthia, who listened attentively as the coroner entered her words into the public record. Mockett was in good health, according to the document, though he was taking medication for high blood pressure. He normally parked his car directly in front of his office, not out of fear it could be tampered with but because he worried about theft. He never checked underneath the vehicle for explosives; at no point in Yemen had he felt he needed to, even after he was shot and wounded, in 2002, by an unidentified assailant.

Next, a forensic pathologist testified about the autopsy. The cause of Mockett's death, based on her examination, was the impact of the pressure wave from the bomb under his seat and resulting shrapnel—what she called "1a blast injuries." It was likely that Mockett died very quickly, she said, since there was no evidence in his lungs of smoke from the fire that engulfed his car after the explosion. When the pathologist concluded her testimony, Arrow turned to Cynthia. "I hope that gives you a degree of comfort," he said.

"Yes," she replied quietly.

A coroner for nearly twenty years, Arrow's style was that of a schoolteacher, encouraging his students to speak up. "Help me in this way," he often said to witnesses before asking a question. Once, in a newspaper interview, he compared his job to solving a puzzle, fitting the different pieces of a person's life together in order to learn about their death. His first case, he told the reporter, involved "a lady who was speaking with her neighbor over the garden gate. She suddenly dropped down dead."

Since the British police had been unable to send officers to Aden to conduct a full investigation, Arrow's task was significantly more challenging than usual. It turned out, however, that the UK government did have one representative on the ground in July 2011: Jonathan Tottman, a slim, silver-haired detective superintendent from the antiterrorism unit of the Metropolitan Police. He'd been dispatched on a brief trip after the bombing, with orders to find out what he could. Arrow called him up to share what he'd learned.

From Cynthia's perspective, Tottman's testimony got off to a dispiriting start. Mockett, he said shortly after being sworn in, was a "hot frog," a term used by government personnel to describe expatriates who stick to their routines despite rising danger. "There are those frogs who sit in warm water as it simmers, then boils, and stay there," Tottman explained. "It's a term of endearment." It wasn't to Cynthia. The comment made her so angry that she had to stop herself from jumping out of her seat. David had always understood the environment around him, she thought. It left such an impression on Cynthia that, years later, a friend gave her a painting of a big red amphibian sitting on a lily pad as a bitter joke.

As Tottman continued, it quickly became clear to Cynthia that no one was seriously investigating who'd killed her husband. Based in the Omani capital, Muscat, Tottman had been seconded from the Met to the Foreign & Commonwealth Office, advising Oman and Yemen on enhancing the rule of law. But his role was as much about soft power, and keeping a British eye on the regional security situation, as it was about encouraging good policing. The government of Ali Abdullah Saleh, the despot who ruled Yemen until early 2012, had shown how much it respected legal norms by gunning down peaceful protesters during the Arab Spring, even pursuing the wounded into hospitals.

Neat and well-spoken, Tottman sounded more like a diplomat than a policeman, and during his time in Aden he'd had to act like one. He had no jurisdiction there; instead, he told the coroner, the primary purpose of his trip was to "give some advice and guidance" to the Yemeni authorities. He did have a couple of advantages. The relationships he'd built at the Foreign Office, as well as a residual respect for British police left over from Aden's colonial days, gave Tottman good access to the city's law enforcement agencies. Although Yemeni cops were famously corrupt, and hadn't done any serious analysis of the bomb that killed Mockett, let alone given any indication that they had identified suspects, Tottman was careful to praise their efforts and the openness he said they'd shown him. His deployment, Tottman said, was a "very humbling experience, working with some very, very gifted Yemeni colleagues, or interlocutors as we call them, who had very few resources."

"Did the Yemenis carry out the investigation to what would be considered a normal standard out there?" Arrow asked.

"They do take a very significant interest in cases where critical allies of Yemeni nationals are murdered," Tottman replied, referring to Mockett's broad web of local friends. "This was about as good as it could have been."

In truth, Tottman's trip to Aden had been a deeply frustrating one. Although he didn't say so at the inquest, he'd been escorted from the airport by heavily armed American security personnel, who advised him that his suit and tie made him too conspicuous and were so worried about the risk of an ambush that they asked if he knew how to use an assault rifle. (Tottman declined their offer of a weapon; like many British police officers, he'd never carried a firearm in his life.) Obtaining more than cursory information was a struggle. For one thing, it wasn't clear that the Aden police knew how to conduct a forensic examination of Mockett's laptop. When Tottman asked them to allow the Met to take possession of the computer instead, his counterparts were initially open to the idea. But they were overruled by a senior police official, who sternly told Tottman that handing it over was "forbidden." There were also surreal moments. During a meeting with a general, Tottman was struck by a painting hanging behind his desk. It depicted President Saleh, proudly riding a winged horse.

But with Mockett's family and reporters watching, Tottman limited his testimony to what he thought would help them, and the coroner, understand the bombing. He explained that it was too dangerous for him to move around Aden without a full security escort, making discreet inquiries impossible. "At the time we thought any British or certainly European or white face in Aden would be a target," he said. He'd also been hindered by the fact that his visit coincided with Ramadan, a month of fasting and prayer for Muslims. To accommodate his observant Yemeni partners, Tottman had invited them to his hotel for iftar, the sunset meal to break the daily fast. It was there, he said, that he'd gathered his most useful intelligence about Mockett's death.

By then he had already discounted the initial explanation from the Yemeni government and local media—that Mockett had probably been killed by Islamic militants. "I've been dealing with terrorism in the Middle East since 2004," Tottman told Arrow, reeling off the names of some of the fundamentalist groups operating in Yemen at the time. "Had they caused the death of a British national or European, they would be on the front foot very quickly telling the world that they had killed a British person." Instead, the Yemeni police officers told him over dinner that they believed Mockett's murder was a "criminal" act.

"David had obviously upset somebody," Tottman continued. There was a "rich seam of criminal activity" in Yemen, encouraged by the absence of effective government. Some of it, Tottman said, was linked to the busy shipping lane passing through the Bab el-Mandeb strait, the maritime choke point west of Aden. The theory that Mockett had been assassinated by conventional criminals, not terrorists, was supported by the method of the attack on his car. He hadn't been caught in the wrong place at the wrong time, passing by a market or police station when a suicide bomber turned up. He'd been targeted personally.

Arrow wanted to know what else Tottman had learned about Mockett from the Aden police. "Was there anything he was doing that made him more vulnerable?" Arrow asked.

"We spoke about David's last investigation and I think, perhaps, this criminal enterprise," Tottman replied. "It seems like this was a scam, if you like, where a lot of money was being made on what the police call insurance jobs. So I suspect that this was the motivation. That David, being a man of great integrity and professionalism, wasn't going to bow to some bully boy tactics."

Tottman presented no evidence to support this theory, nor offered any details of the alleged scam. But his words carried weight. He was, as Arrow reminded those present, "our best witness" as to what happened. "Are we likely to get any more information out of Yemen?" Arrow asked.

"I don't think we are," Tottman said.

The final witness was Detective Inspector Ian Ringrose, from the major crimes unit of the Devon and Cornwall Police. His team had made a formal request to the Yemeni authorities for information about the case. They had responded in writing, and Ringrose read sections of their reply aloud. The explosive under Mockett's car had likely been TNT, weighing no more than one kilogram, the Aden police found. Officers had interviewed workers in Mockett's office building, examined surveillance camera footage, and questioned his secretary, but, Ringrose said, "nothing essential was found out."

They had no one in custody and reported that they couldn't say whether "this act was a terrorist act, or criminal murder personal dispute."

Arrow asked again if there was likely to be any more information that British police could gather from Yemen. "No, not likely," Ringrose replied.

The coroner addressed Cynthia once more. "Members of the family, you will appreciate we've conducted this inquiry at a very great distance from where it happened, and I feel I have received all the information I am going to receive touching David's death." Returning to the four questions he posed at the start of the hearing, Arrow said he was satisfied that the deceased was David Mockett, and that he had died in Yemen from injuries caused by a "relatively sophisticated device" placed underneath his vehicle.

"I shall record that he was unlawfully killed," Arrow concluded—meaning that Mockett's death was found to be the result of an illegal act, by an unknown perpetrator. It had taken less than an hour to hear all the evidence and record a verdict. Cynthia had a conclusion, in legal terms at least. But she was left with as many unanswered questions as ever about her husband's fate.

CHAPTER 13

BELOW THE SURFACE

There are many ways to sink a ship. The mightiest naval destroyer can be laid low by a single rogue wave. In a storm, if the swell is taller than a boat is long, it can flip a vessel like a tossed coin, tumbling it end over end into a vertical dive. Sailors call this pitch-poling. The long steel hull of a tanker might twist and flex as mountains of water pass underneath, causing enough stress to break it in two. A heavy cargo, such as coal, can sink a vessel and its crew simply by shifting position, unbalancing the precise naval engineering that keeps them afloat.

Then there are fires and icebergs and submerged rocks, as well as the oddities: stray missiles, hull-eating shipworms, an encounter with an inquisitive killer whale. But the simplest way to send a ship to the depths is to open the side hatches, or "scuttles," and wait for it to fill with water. Consequently, deliberately sinking a ship has become known as "scuttling." While it might seem strange that sailors would destroy their means of survival, the term exists for a reason. Sometimes wrecking a ship is the logical option.

On February 5, 1831, the Dutch naval lieutenant Jan Van Speijk was commanding a gunboat when he was blown off course. The Belgian Revolution was under way, and as the vessel veered into the hostile territory of Antwerp harbor it was stormed by rebels. A proud Dutchman, Van Speijk had always sworn he would rather die than become a Belgian. True to his word, he either threw a lit cigar at, or fired his pistol into, a barrel of gunpowder, causing an explosion large enough to kill several of the intruders, most of his crew, and himself. His ship was blown to smithereens. Van Speijk remains a national hero in the Netherlands, where there is a lighthouse named after him.

Readers of military history may be familiar with a common use of scuttling: to stop valuable assets from falling into enemy hands. After the First World War, German commanders ordered their men to sink their captive fleet at Scapa Flow rather than surrender it to the British. In the icy waters off the north of Scotland, the Germans signaled to each other using flags and searchlights, then began releasing sea valves, smashing pipes, and opening watertight doors. Fifty-two craft sank so quickly that the Royal Navy could do nothing but watch them disappear. (When Denmark was occupied by the Nazis during the next global conflict, a Danish admiral gave a similar order to his men in the port of Copenhagen. More than thirty vessels went down, along with nine sailors.)

In wartime, scuttled boats can function as a barrier. During the American Civil War, Union forces decided to fill whaling ships with rocks and deposit them on the floor of Charleston harbor, an attempt to stop the import of military supplies, and export of cotton, by the Confederacy. Sailors drilled and plugged holes in the bottom of the whalers, sailed them into position, then pulled out the corks and rowed away. A *New York Times* correspondent wrote enthusiastically of the event: "The weather was delightful . . . the water, far and near, presented a busy scene." Although this "stone fleet" blockade was partially successful in stopping Confederate trade, the northeastern whaling industry never fully recovered.

Scuttling is also a convenient way to get rid of ships that have outlived their usefulness. The seafloor is littered with the bones of old vessels sent by their owners to the great trash heap down below. Before modern environmental concerns, scuttling was a standard method of disposal, and it still happens occasionally. In 2009, for example, a decommissioned American spy ship called the *Gen. Hoyt S. Vandenberg* was stripped, cleaned, and towed to the Florida Keys. Once there, it took some explosive charges and two minutes for the 523-foot-long craft to slip beneath the waves, where it lives on as a man-made reef.

But scuttling doesn't always have a military or pragmatic purpose. It can also be used to commit one of the oldest frauds in the history of crime.

For virtually as long as there's been a shipping business, Greeks have been among its most innovative players. It's not surprising, therefore, that some Greek entrepreneurs were among the first to realize that ships can be worth more below the surface of the water than above it. In the ancient world, merchants employed a primitive form of insurance called bottomry. (The Romans knew it as *foenus nauticum*, or maritime interest.) In simple terms, a captain borrowed money for a voyage, repaying it with interest only if the passage was successful. Otherwise, the lender wrote off the loan. The ship served as collateral.

We know about this, in part, because of the Greek orator Demosthenes, who described the first documented case of maritime insurance fraud, which occurred around 360 BC. It was a tale, Demosthenes said, of "daring and villainy" to "pass all records." The perpetrators were a captain, Hegestratos, and his friend Zenothemis, who had borrowed money to haul a cargo of grain from Syracuse, in Sicily, to Athens.

Knowing their loan would be forgiven in the event of an accident, the pair took the cash and set off planning to sink their ship midvoyage. One night, some passengers heard a strange noise belowdecks and found Hegestratos boring a hole in the hull. Enraged, they pursued the captain around the vessel; in his rush to get away, Hegestratos leapt into the sea and drowned. Thus, Demosthenes noted, "as was very proper, being a bad man, [he] had a bad death." The ship was saved. Zenothemis, thinking on his feet, said that Hegestratos owed him a large sum of money and then claimed the cargo as his property. In the ensuing legal dispute, the owner of the ship hired Demosthenes to present his side in court. The result of the case, and the fate of the conniving Zenothemis, were lost to time.

Frauds like the one attempted by Hegestratos and Zenothemis may have occurred frequently. The moneylenders of antiquity seem to have been all too aware of the activities of ship-sinking conmen—"a gang of scoundrels," as Demosthenes put it in his legal arguments—operating in Piraeus, the port city outside Athens that remains Greece's maritime capital. But they didn't let the problem stop them from doing business. Instead, the financiers simply raised their prices to cover the losses.

Faced with fraud centuries later, the insurers at Lloyd's of London would do much the same thing.

Sinking a ship to claim the insurance money isn't so different from a debt-ridden bar owner lighting a match to escape his failing business, or a driver engineering a fender bender to claim whiplash and collect a payout. The trick is to make it look like an accident. Maritime insurance fraud has certain advantages, however. The rewards can be enormous, since ships are expensive, and incriminating evidence usually goes down with them. The downside is that ships have crews, which means there are a lot of potential witnesses.

Henry Greathead was a ship's carpenter whose captain steered their vessel into sandy banks between the English and French coasts in 1779. The captain blamed bad weather, but Greathead, who would go on to invent the first modern lifeboats, was no fool. He knew the ship was insured for a small fortune at Lloyd's and was carrying an "insignificant cargo" that no one would miss. The crew didn't much like the idea of being drowned for someone else's benefit, so they sent up flares and were rescued by French sailors. In Calais, Greathead refused to sign a statement supporting the captain's story. He and his crewmates got a message to the underwriters, who declined to pay.

The insurers who met at Lloyd's—at the time, still essentially a café, and a disreputable one at that—would have been wise to the many possibilities for mischief at sea. "Few industries offer such opportunities to scoundrels, and there has never been any real shortage of scoundrels to take advantage of them," Godfrey Hodgson wrote in his history of the market. Right from the start, its members were entangled with the darker side of maritime trade. From the wanted criminal who took on a new identity and signed on with a tramp ship destined for the New World, to the gentleman merchant willing to sacrifice the lives of seamen in pursuit of profit, the ocean has always accommodated all manner of sins and sinners, and many of their actions have been parsed and paid for—or not—at Lloyd's. But as the coffeehouse coalesced into something resembling the massive financial institution that it is today, insurers came to prioritize discretion when confronted with wrongdoing. Ideally, such problems could be dealt with quietly. Scandals were bad for business.

Amid the explosion of maritime trade in the Victorian era, and the lockstep growth of the Lloyd's market, the life of the sailor remained absurdly dangerous. In a given year as many as one in five British mariners might die at sea, many on ancient and overloaded ships sent out by avaricious owners with little regard for the consequences. A substantial number of them were "overinsured," with policies negotiated at Lloyd's worth far more than their actual value. These vessels were known as "coffin ships" because of the high likelihood of disaster, and not always of the natural kind.

The idea of men drowning on doomed freighters to enrich the merchant class seized the popular imagination at a time when Charles Dickens and others had ignited campaigns to improve the plight of the poor. Eventually, a British politician called Samuel Plimsoll took up the sailors' cause. A Liberal member of Parliament and philanthropist with a defiantly bushy beard, Plimsoll railed against the leaders of the British shipping industry, who responded with a high-profile campaign to discredit him, questioning his sanity and suing him for libel. Plimsoll refused to stay silent and, in July 1875, gave a speech accusing fellow MPs who were involved in marine trade of complicity in murder.

The official parliamentary reporter recorded that Plimsoll rose to his feet "with great excitement." After begging the government not to consign thousands of seafarers to an "undeserved and miserable death" through inaction, he set out the scale of the problem: "The Secretary of Lloyd's tells a friend of mine that he does not know a single ship which has been broken up voluntarily by the owners in the course of 30 years on account of its being worn out. Ships gradually pass from hand to hand, until bought by some needy and reckless speculators, who send them to sea with precious human lives."

Plimsoll was forced to apologize for his comments, but his campaign led to the Merchant Shipping Act of 1876, which required every vessel to have a mark showing its maximum level of submergence to prevent overloading: the Plimsoll Line. (The term also gave rise to a popular style of rubber-lined gym shoe.) The legislation helped, as far as it went, although it didn't take away the financial incentive for scuttling. And the Lloyd's insurers whose cash kept the shipwreckers in business escaped Plimsoll's ire—and any public reckoning.

Published in 1926, a novel called *The Death Ship*, by an author who wrote under the pseudonym B. Traven, vividly captured the continuing squalor and peril of life in the commercial fleet. In the story, an American sailor finds himself stranded without papers in Europe and is forced to take a position shoveling coal on a rust bucket called the *Yorikke*. All the members of the crew, whom Traven describes as something like indentured slaves, stateless and expendable, know the *Yorikke* will eventually be sunk so its owner can claim the insurance money. The American sailor's only hope is that he will be fortunate enough to be rescued. While the book was a work of fiction, it may have been at least partly autobiographical. B. Traven's real identity remains the subject of academic debate, but it seems likely that he served on commercial steamships under an assumed name before settling in Mexico, using the experience to inform his writing.

One reason the Lloyd's market has historically been slow to tackle maritime fraud is that there is no real financial incentive to do so. Even though it costs money to compensate owners for scuttled ships, the market has evolved to respond efficiently to marine accidents, even faked ones, by passing on the cost to someone else. When the number of casualties increases, through an outbreak of war or a spate of frauds, members raise premiums. Indeed, dangerous seas are more profitable, since they mean that customers are more likely to seek the protection of Lloyd's in the first place.

The other problem is one of enforcement. Most frauds occur in international waters, beyond the ability of terrestrial police to investigate, and the states whose flags are flown by the bulk of modern vessels—Liberia, Panama, and so on—have never looked too closely at what occurs on board. Generally, the only recourse for a party wronged by a maritime fraud is a lawsuit, often filed at London's admiralty courts, which have adjudicated nautical matters for more than five hundred years. But when scuttling cases do make it before a judge—which is rare—the results illustrate why Lloyd's insurers are so reluctant to accuse clients of sinking their own ships.

In 1973, a Greek-owned freighter called the *Michael* suffered an engine failure in rough seas off Venezuela. A salvage tug arrived, only to find that the freighter's crew had inexplicably thrown its towing cable overboard, even as the engine room began to flood. A young English lawyer named Michael Baker-Harber was dispatched by Lloyd's to nearby Curaçao to investigate. Baker-Harber, who kept a bag always packed in his office for just this sort of assignment, arrived the next morning, in time to see the sailors from the *Michael* disembark from a rescue boat.

He recognized one of them almost immediately, even though the man had recently shaved off his beard. The tall, gaunt figure walking down the gangplank was a ship's engineer named Stylianos Komiseris. Baker-Harber had sparred with him in a London courtroom months earlier over another suspected scuttling. In that case, Komiseris had spent four days in the witness box, explaining, among other things, why he had declined an offer of help from salvors. Baker-Harber could hardly forget Komiseris, who'd sworn he could only speak Greek but greeted his opponent outside court every day, in perfect English, with a cheery, "Good morning, Mr. Baker-Harber." Komiseris's testimony had caused peals of laughter in court. He'd claimed the salvors had simply misunderstood him. He wasn't saying "No, no!" when they came to his aid. What he'd actually been saying was *"Nai, nai!"*—Greek for "Yes, yes!" As the two met again, in a tropical harbor more than four thousand miles from London, the English attorney could hardly believe his eyes.

When Komiseris spotted Baker-Harber standing on the jetty, he threw up his hands and laughed nervously, exclaiming, "It's you!" Baker-Harber took some photographs to capture the moment, then pursued Komiseris to a nearby shop, where he cornered the engineer and extracted a written confession that he'd been paid $5,000 to scuttle the *Michael*. Case closed, or at least one might assume.

When the lawsuit over the *Michael*'s insurance policy came to trial, however, the shipowner's legal team didn't dispute that it had been scuttled. Instead, they argued, the cause of the sinking was "barratry," an obscure term for an offense committed by a captain or crew without an owner's knowledge. Komiseris, they said, had downed the ship to spite the owner, Nestor Pierrakos, over a long-standing personal grievance. Pierrakos was called to court to defend himself. Like many wealthy Greeks, he'd been educated at elite institutions in England, and wore a Cambridge University tie as he testified, indignantly, that he'd never do something so grubby as scuttling a ship.

The judge believed him. "No one decides to scuttle a ship lightly; there are too many risks of failure or blackmail or both," he wrote in his decision. Since barratry was covered by the *Michael*'s policy, the Lloyd's insurers were obligated to pay. By establishing a high legal bar for rejecting claims, the ruling made it even harder for the London market to fight suspected fraud. It wasn't enough for insurers to prove that a vessel had been deliberately wrecked. They also had to prove the owner was directly responsible.

Baker-Harber never saw Komiseris again. Pierrakos lost a couple more ships in unfortunate circumstances, then became an insurance broker himself.

A glut of new tankers arrived on the world market in the 1970s, the result of shipping firms trying to take advantage of surging energy prices. But thanks to a series of political and economic shocks, many of the vessels turned out not to be needed. With so much excess capacity, charter rates plummeted and shipowners were put under severe financial strain. It was "the grimmest period in post-war history" for oceangoing trade, according to the 1978 Lloyd's annual report. Not coincidentally, the same period saw an epidemic of maritime fraud.

Some have traced its origins to West Africa, where a building boom in Lagos left hundreds of ships queuing up offshore, waiting to dock. This chaotic situation, as Hodgson described it, "attracted criminals the world over and alerted them to the possibilities of marine fraud." There was cargo theft, piracy, rampant official corruption, and suspicious fires on overinsured ships. The crew of one vessel were found to have booked local hotel rooms a month before a supposedly accidental explosion stranded them off the coast.

From the Gulf of Guinea, the outbreak spread to the Middle East before arriving in Asia. In the late 1970s, so many cargo ships were going down in the South China Sea that the Lloyd's market took the unprecedented step of ordering an inquiry, to be led by the specially appointed Far Eastern Regional Investigation Team, or FERIT. In typical Lloyd's style, FERIT's report was kept confidential and was not to be shared with nonmembers, although several historians have written about its contents.

More than half of the forty-eight casualties it investigated were deemed "suspicious," while sixteen were found to be probably the result of scuttling. In all cases, the ships were older and ostensibly loaded with valuable goods: Japanese stereos or, in one instance, about half of Singapore's annual export volume of cloves. (A port official became suspicious when he noticed that the shipment lacked the distinctive odor that normally accompanied nine hundred tons of spice.) Sometimes the cargo had already been removed and sold in secret before an insurance claim was made. In a few cases it had never existed at all. The cost to the London market of the South China Sea claims alone was estimated at $100 million.

FERIT's most significant finding was that the scuttling craze was linked to organized crime groups operating out of Taiwan, Hong Kong, and Singapore. They seemed to have access to shipwrecking specialists. A welding contractor, for example, was hired to cut four half-meter holes in a vessel's hull and then seal them with metal panels that could be removed when the time came. A few of the culprits were jailed, but most disappeared before they could be captured.

The lesson, for those at Lloyd's willing to listen, was that maritime fraud was no longer the preserve of rogue merchants and desperate captains. Gangsters had already built international networks to profit from drug trafficking and human smuggling. Now they had their eyes on the vast pools of money in the global shipping industry.

The most audacious scuttling case of the twentieth century began simply enough. In January 1980, a British ship came across some lifeboats drifting off the coast of Senegal, next to an abandoned, sinking oil tanker called the *Salem*. Its Greek captain claimed there had been an explosion on board. The

British rescuers fulfilled their obligation to aid fellow mariners, although they found it odd that there were no flames coming from the stricken tanker as it went down, only the faintest trail of smoke, and that the *Salem*'s fleeing sailors had found time to load its lifeboats with packed suitcases, sandwiches, and cigarettes.

The *Salem* and its documented cargo, 190,000 tons of Kuwaiti light crude oil, were insured at Lloyd's by more than one hundred syndicates, individuals, and companies, who stood to lose $80 million as a result of its sinking. The claims men in London, though, were immediately suspicious upon learning of the ship's demise. The *Salem*'s captain had no master's certificate, the qualification required to command a ship, and was wanted by the Greek police in relation to other suspected frauds. Even more curiously, the tanker didn't leave behind an oil slick as it was swallowed by the sea. There didn't seem to have been any crude in its cargo tanks.

What emerged after police investigations in several countries was an ingenious multinational fraud, the largest ever attempted at sea up to that point. One of its prime movers was a Lebanese-American businessman named Fred Soudan, who helped engineer a complex scheme to deliver oil to South Africa in defiance of the international embargo then in place against the apartheid regime. Working with a Piraeus shipping agent named Nikolaos Mitakis, Soudan secured financing help from the South African government to purchase a tanker called the *South Sun*. Renamed the *Salem*, in December 1979 it took on its cargo of oil in Kuwait, with paperwork claiming that it was bound for Italy.

The shipment was owned by Pontoil, a small Swiss company that wasn't in on the scam. Once the *Salem* was at sea, Pontoil—unaware that anything was amiss—sold the cargo to Royal Dutch Shell for $56 million, with the energy giant planning to deliver it to France. But the tanker's crew, who had been selected by Mitakis, had no intention of taking the oil to Europe no matter who it belonged to. Shortly after leaving Kuwait, they painted over the first two letters of the name on the Salem's bow, and added an *a* at the end. As far as anyone could see, the vessel's name was *Lema*—a ruse probably intended to allow it to be confused with another tanker, the *Lima*, that was sailing a similar route.

The *Salem* was traveling via the Cape of Good Hope, rather than the Suez Canal, and as it neared Africa's southern tip, the captain, Dimitrios Georgoulis, made an unscheduled detour. Stopping at the port of Durban, he unloaded nearly all of the *Salem*'s cargo—stealing oil owned by Shell, which disappeared into South African pipelines. He then ordered the crew to fill the *Salem*'s tanks with seawater to make it appear fully laden, before sailing up the west coast of Africa and scuttling the vessel to hide the theft. In return for slipping a supertanker's worth of oil past the embargo that was hobbling its economy, the South African government paid some $32 million to Soudan and his associates.

The *Salem*'s crew—a mix of Greek officers and lower-ranking Tunisian sailors—were paid for their silence. But one of the latter objected to being bullied into compliance, and eventually walked into the British Embassy in Paris to reveal what he knew. He told investigators that the Tunisians on board had been so terrified of their Greek crewmates that they carried knives for self-defense, and feared being thrown from the *Salem*'s lifeboats if they didn't obey orders. The sailor's testimony allowed investigators to begin unraveling the entire scam, but his assistance came at a significant personal cost: he received death threats from Greece, and the Lloyd's market had to provide him with protection.

The consequences of the *Salem* fraud included a flurry of lawsuits and some minor diplomatic quarrels, as well as a few criminal cases. The underwriters who'd covered the oil denied Shell's claim for the loss, prompting the company to sue. The subsequent legal battle reached the House of Lords, at the time the UK's highest court. (Shell lost.) Mitakis and Georgoulis were jailed after a chaotic trial in Greece, along with several other *Salem* crew members. US federal prosecutors convicted Soudan on seventeen charges and secured a thirty-five-year sentence; astonishingly, he escaped from custody less than three years later, walking out of a minimum-security prison in Texas. He was never recaptured.

Many of those involved in the case were left with a lingering sense of injustice, and not only because Soudan walked free. They felt the men imprisoned in Greece and the US were fall guys, small fish, while the true architects and financiers of the conspiracy—Greek shipowners, perhaps, or Western European bankers, none of them conclusively identified—remained hidden. One investigator claimed that millions of dollars in profits from the Durban oil sale had been deposited into a Greek-owned bank account in Geneva, where he'd observed five Mercedes-Benz sedans being loaded with briefcases of cash before driving away, toward the Italian border. After that, the trail went cold.

Years later, a British lawyer involved in the *Salem* insurance dispute found himself in Piraeus. He'd heard that one of the tanker's scuttlers, a "knuckleman" who'd intimidated the crew into going along with the scam, had retired with his share and opened a bar. The lawyer couldn't resist stopping by for a coffee. Sure enough, there was the Greek sailor. As he got up to leave, the attorney caught his eye and said: "Don't forget the *Salem*." He walked out before getting a response.

The relationship between London's insurance market and the Greek shipping community is complicated. On one hand, Greece is undeniably the most successful shipping nation on earth, and a vital source of business for the marine specialists at Lloyd's. Both sides share a fondness for lunches in London's fanciest restaurants and black-tie industry dinners to celebrate their mutual successes. On the other hand, most people at Lloyd's have heard of the *Salem*, the *Michael*, and the many other scams believed to have emerged from the backstreets of Piraeus.

There are those within the London-centric world of Lloyd's who will, in private, describe Greek shipowners as bandits. In Greece, conversely, there is a feeling that a majority of reputable entrepreneurs, who pride themselves on their sense of honor, are being unfairly tarnished by the behavior of an unscrupulous minority. The Greek commercial fleet is the world's largest, and mostly operated by small, family-owned firms. There are bound to be a few bad actors. With suspicions and secrecy on both sides, it's hard to know where the truth lies.

Even when the market has tried to seek answers, investigators working for Lloyd's have faced a hostile reception in Greece and indifference back in the UK. In the 1980s, insurers were alarmed enough by the casualty rate for

Greek-owned ships, as well as other problems including disappearing cargo, to send a pair of London lawyers to Piraeus to see if they could learn more about the phenomenon—and perhaps put together a legal strategy to stop it. The preferred scuttling method at the time was arson, according to an individual familiar with the lawyers' work, who asked not to be identified because he feared that speaking openly could put him in danger. Among other things, the lawyers learned about a corrupt salvage crew that had arrived with containers of gasoline to start a fire in a vessel's engine room. The salvors and owners shared the insurance money.

But little came of the lawyers' inquiries. While their findings made clear that a sophisticated criminal network was behind the rash of damaged and sunken ships, no formal action was ever taken at Lloyd's in response. After the investigation, one of the English attorneys went on to set up a lucrative practice in Piraeus representing Greek salvage firms. The Greeks referred to him as "Saul," the Hebrew name for Paul the Apostle, who persecuted Christians before converting and joining their cause.

Over the decades, it became something of a tradition at Lloyd's to discover alarming information about the scuttling business in Greece and then do little about it. In the autumn of 2012, a British private detective who'd gone to Piraeus to investigate fraud cases returned with a document, apparently drafted by an outraged member of the Greek shipping industry, entitled: "Sex, money laundering, extortion, murder." It described the existence of a "scum market," a community of experienced fraudsters who, for the right price, could cause a shipwreck or manufacture a fictitious insurance claim. Allegedly, the players in the scum market had underworld contacts powerful enough to have judges killed. According to the report's author, they gathered regularly at wild parties, stocked with beautiful young women, at a villa in central Athens.

The document pointed a finger at prominent bankers, shipowners, and organized crime figures, yet despite naming names and detailing wrongdoing, nothing came of it. Even if Lloyd's insurers had shown a desire to break up this alleged fraud ring, what could they have done? Fighting crime in Greece was the job of the Greek police, who had a patchy record when it came to prosecuting members of their country's most successful industry.

In any case, the modern structure of Lloyd's makes tackling fraud an even lower priority than it was in earlier years. For most of its history, the money behind the market came from "Names," the moniker given at Lloyd's to private individuals who pooled their wealth into underwriting syndicates. In theory, Names bore unlimited liability for losses: if claims were large enough, they could be forced to give up everything they owned. But in practice, premiums usually exceeded claims by a comfortable margin, and Names received excellent returns. The group included British dukes, baronets, members of the landed gentry, banking scions such as the Rothschilds, and commercial dynasties including the Guinness family. The Lloyd's market was, in effect, an invitation-only investment club for preserving wealth and privilege.

From the 1960s, a series of scandals and expensive natural disasters led to a liquidity crisis among the syndicates. To raise more funds, Lloyd's eased its membership requirements, welcoming the not-so-blue-blooded as Names, including sports stars, musicians—notably, the members of Pink Floyd—and thousands of dentists, doctors, and small-town stockbrokers. But it still wasn't enough to feed the world's growing appetite for insurance, not just for ships, but for planes, nuclear power stations, and spacecraft.

So in 1994, the leadership of Lloyd's allowed companies to serve as Names for the first time. The arrival of American and Swiss conglomerates vastly increased the capital available for syndicates to write insurance policies. It also changed the fundamental nature of the place. Underwriters used to answer to a list of wealthy individuals, often from the same social circles, who'd bought into what were supposed to be safe investments. Now they dealt with giant corporate entities, which took out their own insurance policies from reinsurers. Losses were passed on, again and again, in a cycle of transactions so complex that it could be impossible to know who was left holding the bill.

Court defeats and risk-averse corporate legal departments made managers in the new Lloyd's so queasy about alleging fraud, and so terrified of the potential consequences, that they essentially stopped using the word. Instead, the market adopted lawyerly euphemisms: "material non-disclosure" or "misrepresentation." Scuttling became "willful casting away." Claims departments, responsible for investigating fraud, were underfunded and understaffed, because big corporations have a habit of neglecting teams that don't bring in any money.

Today, no one knows how many ships are scuttled. Vessels get in trouble all the time. Very few accidents are fully investigated. Even when a sinking looks deliberate, Lloyd's syndicates have understandable reasons not to challenge a claim, since the odds are stacked against them in court. It's also bad for business to sue your biggest customers. Shipowners could just as easily get their insurance someplace else, where they might find less combative partners. So rather than fighting fraud, the underwriters normally settle, offering 50 percent of a ship's value or less, citing "difficulties" in assessing the claim.

By some estimates, maritime crime costs the global economy several billion dollars a year, although the real figure is likely much higher, since so many cases are never reported. Once you know what scuttling looks like, and that it pays well with little chance of consequences, you start seeing it everywhere. Every tanker that runs aground; every freighter that goes down in a storm. Was it really an accident? Who can ever know for sure?

CHAPTER 14

WAR RISKS

Richard Veale decided to call his investigation into the hijacking of the *Brillante Virtuoso* "Project Tundra," a code name chosen at random to obscure any connection to shipping or insurance. After getting the initial assignment from Paul Cunningham, the claims manager at Talbot Underwriting, in September 2011, Veale put together a plan to help the hull insurers at Lloyd's get a clearer sense of what they were looking at.

It was, in some ways, like any other marine case that Veale might take on. There was a corporate paper trail to follow and an evidentiary picture full of holes and inconsistencies. Veale couldn't talk to the crew, nor could he examine the ship. There was nothing especially unusual about any of that, and so, for now, he would have to do the best he could from his office in London. Incredibly, the underwriters weren't sure who was on the other side of the multimillion-dollar insurance contract protecting the *Brillante*. Veale's first goal was to untangle the web of offshore structures around the ship and find out who actually owned it. This sort of task was precisely why Veale had created EBIS, his private detective agency. EBIS was building a reputation within the Lloyd's market as one of the top investigative firms for thorny insurance disputes, and Veale knew that the more he demonstrated his expertise, the more challenging—and lucrative—mandates would come his way.

Still, Veale had a sense, almost from the start, that this job would be different from most. The inescapable fact of David Mockett's death cast a grim shadow over the case, putting everybody involved on edge. No one at Lloyd's wanted to believe that one of its representatives had been killed because of work they'd hired him to do. It was too awful to contemplate.

Veale got to work at EBIS's small office in Canary Wharf, the cluster of polished skyscrapers that had sprung up not far from his East London birthplace. It was the right postcode, at least, for someone as impatiently ambitious as he was. Admittedly, Veale's desk was only a few feet off the ground, and didn't share the view enjoyed by the investment bankers in the neighboring towers, who could gaze out their windows at the glittering Thames snaking off to the horizon. Still, EBIS's base was discreet, had a secure private entrance, and was an easy commute from Veale's home.

Talbot executives had told Veale that they believed the *Brillante Virtuoso* belonged ultimately to Top Ships Inc., a Greek-run shipping company with twelve tankers and shares trading on NASDAQ. He quickly discovered that was wrong. An entity listed on the insurance documents called Central Mare, part of the Top Ships group, was only the ship's manager, an external service provider hired to keep the *Brillante* fueled and crewed. Veale pulled several hundred pages of documents from Liberia, where the tanker was flagged, as well as the Marshall Islands, where the shell company that officially owned it, Suez Fortune, was registered. Both countries' corporate registries had offices in the US, and it was, in theory, a simple matter of requesting the right files and paying a fee. In practice, you had to know exactly what type of document to ask for—whether you needed the RLM-101A, for example, or the RLM-101BCR. Veale often found it helpful to reach an official on the phone and lay on some Cockney charm.

As he reviewed the files at his desk, Veale noticed that some of them had been signed by an individual whose name he hadn't seen before: a man called Marios Iliopoulos. Iliopoulos had also offered personal loan guarantees. Based on that fact, Veale told Cunningham, he had a "high level of confidence" that Iliopoulos was the *Brillante*'s ultimate owner. When Cunningham heard the name, the Talbot executive nearly fell off his chair. "That's the bloke from the *Elli*!" he exclaimed.

The *Elli* was a tanker that had run aground off the coast of Yemen in 2009, after a fire broke out in its radio room. Talbot was part of the syndicate insuring its hull. A salvage team eventually towed the *Elli* away for repairs, but while they were in the process of pumping water into its ballast tanks for stability, the tanker suffered what lawyers called a "catastrophic hogging" near the Suez Canal. In layman's terms, the ship's bow and stern halves had sheared apart midway down the hull, splitting in two like a watermelon. It was such a strange accident that, although Cunningham wasn't personally involved in the case, he knew all about the vessel's demise.

In a seemingly improbable coincidence, the same two salvage firms that attended to the *Brillante Virtuoso* had also tried to save the *Elli*. Poseidon Salvage, run by the gnarled diver Vassilios Vergos, was first on the scene from nearby Aden after its grounding. Poseidon later was replaced by another Greek outfit, Five Oceans Salvage, just as it had been when the *Brillante* was hauled out of Yemeni waters. There were two other parallels. The *Elli*'s chief engineer was Nestor Tabares, the same Filipino sailor who'd bravely stayed aboard the *Brillante* after the other crewmen fled. And its owner was none other than Marios Iliopoulos.

Veale hardly needed decades of investigative experience to know a good lead when he saw one. He started compiling what he could from public records, news outlets, and other sources within the universe of data that feeds the Lloyd's market. A couple months later he presented his initial findings in person, at Talbot's offices in the City of London. Veale had discovered that Iliopoulos, who was best known in Greece as the owner of Seajets, a popular ferry service connecting Athens with the beaches of the Cyclades, was also behind several other high-value insurance claims, including one for a damaged catamaran that carried tourists between the islands.

But other than his position at Seajets, there wasn't much other information about Iliopoulos to be found. According to Veale's research, whenever there was a dispute over insurance, Iliopoulos kept a low profile, presenting himself as a manager, rather than the owner of a fleet. Financial records showed that the companies he was involved with were interlinked with loans and cross-guarantees, making them "highly interdependent," Veale explained. Some of them were showing signs of stress: large debts and missed loan repayments. Iliopoulos had borrowed heavily to acquire his fleet and, in 2011, he appeared to be struggling under the burden.

Although it was still preliminary, Veale felt his report contained enough evidence for the *Brillante*'s insurers to depart from the normal Lloyd's practice of paying claims promptly and in full. The underwriters already knew that its hijacking didn't fit the typical profile of a Somali pirate attack. Veale's research indicated that the ship's owner had a history of dubious casualties and an apparent financial motive to get rid of his asset. Much more investigation would be needed, but it seemed that something questionable could be going on. Veale would need to act quickly, though, to stop the process that was in motion. Suez Fortune had just presented the hull insurers with a "notice of abandonment," officially informing them that the *Brillante* was damaged beyond repair—a key step toward making a claim. In January 2012, the same month Veale gave his presentation at Talbot's office, Suez Fortune formally claimed on the tanker's "war risks" insurance policy, which covered against acts of piracy.

The underwriters now had two options: write a substantial check, or prepare to invalidate the claim in court. Veale hoped it would be the latter, and not just because of the fees that EBIS might earn. He still felt like a cop at heart, and was more than a little intrigued by the possibility of unraveling such an unusual case. But Veale knew that it wasn't up to him to decide whether it went ahead. Answerable to corporate boards and compliance departments, the claims managers at Lloyd's wouldn't so much as write a letter without consulting attorneys from one of the august law firms serving the London market. Paul Cunningham, who would later testify in court that he was "reliant on legal experts" to guide him, soon introduced Veale to the man who would be leading the *Brillante* matter for the hull insurers. "This guy has a brain the size of a planet," Cunningham said approvingly.

The lawyer's name was Chris Zavos. He had a fastidious demeanor, thick-rimmed glasses, and the immaculate hair and refined diction of a BBC anchor—in sharp contrast to Veale's expletive-dense East London slang. Zavos's firm, Norton Rose, boasted a prestigious list of City clients and offices opposite the Tower of London, where partners racked up average salaries of nearly half a million pounds a year. In their first encounter, Zavos's commanding manner left Veale with little doubt about who would be calling the shots. At one point, he tossed a folder across a table in Veale's direction as though dispensing a royal decree.

In the first months of 2012, there was every chance the hull insurers would ignore the warning signs and pay the *Brillante* claim, just as the Lloyd's market had done with countless other suspicious casualties over the years. In that scenario, Iliopoulos would have taken the money, satisfied his creditors, and carried on squeezing profit out of his aging fleet. Veale would have gone back to tracing pirates' bank accounts, or whatever else came across his desk at EBIS. Talbot would have split the cost with the other nine insurers named on the war risks policy and barely noticed the loss. The real story of what happened to the *Brillante Virtuoso* might never have emerged.

But the hull syndicate, led by Talbot, decided not to pay, at least not yet. Veale wasn't part of the discussion and couldn't be sure of exactly what swayed their deliberations. Perhaps it was the sheer size of the potential loss: more than $70 million, and set to grow larger with additional costs and lost income. Perhaps it was the existence of the *Elli* dispute, which was still being litigated and might yield proof that a fraud had been committed. Or perhaps, as Veale later came to believe, David Mockett's death had shocked the Lloyd's market into a rare moment of conscience.

In response to the underwriters' decision, Suez Fortune filed a lawsuit in London, claiming they were legally obligated to pay out. Veale was in business; a messy legal battle seemed likely. We're off, he thought. As a first step, he asked to see the statements taken from the *Brillante*'s crew in the aftermath of the attack. As he read through the transcripts, they struck him as strangely formulaic, with multiple Filipino sailors using the same English words and phrases. To Veale, they seemed scripted. The crew might have been under duress. "They've got to be redone," Veale told Cunningham. But he was informed that reinterviewing the crew was impossible. The sailors were back in the Philippines or spread on ships around the globe, and the other side's lawyers might object.

Veale knew there was at least one other ongoing investigation into the *Brillante* hijacking. In parallel to the hull insurers, the syndicate insuring the cargo had begun its own, separate probe. It had recouped some of its money by siphoning off and selling the *Brillante*'s oil. But the syndicate was still obliged to compensate the salvors, Poseidon and Five Oceans, for their work recovering it—a sum likely to be in the tens of millions of dollars. Veale tried, without much success, to get the two inquiries working together. Yet he wasn't permitted formal access to the two private-detective firms the cargo syndicate had hired.

The same went for the Lloyd's arbitration, already under way, to determine the size of the salvage award. In that process, an independent expert would weigh the nature of the job, and the value of the salvaged cargo, before arriving at a figure. Veale had plenty of questions about the salvage, not least about how Poseidon's crew had arrived so quickly in the middle of the night. But he wasn't allowed to see any material from the arbitration. Nor would the legal team working on the *Elli* case provide any substantive information. The tanker's insurers had, in fact, rejected Iliopoulos's claim for the ship on the seemingly reasonable grounds that tankers don't just break in half in calm seas. The shipowner had responded by suing in London to force the issue. Whatever its underwriters knew about the *Elli* was hidden behind legal privilege.

As Veale saw it, the problem was that the different components of the Lloyd's market were terrified of opening themselves to accusations that they were colluding against customers, which might lead to an antitrust complaint. For a Lloyd's outsider like him, the atmosphere of secrecy was maddening. At the same time, the police investigation into the murder of David Mockett seemed to be reaching a dead end. Prior to the inquest into his death, an officer from Plymouth, representing the local coroner, informed Chris Zavos that he thought it was unlikely anyone would ever establish who was behind the bomb that killed Mockett, or whether it was related to the burning of the *Brillante*.

To Veale, the situation was crying out for real investigation—finding witnesses, persuading them to talk, and cross-checking the information they provided. Zavos made clear he saw it differently. To defeat Suez Fortune's lawsuit, he and Paul Cunningham settled on a more technical, legalistic strategy. They filed their defense against the *Brillante* claim at London's Admiralty and Commercial Court late in 2012. The document made no mention of scuttling or fraud. Instead, it was a narrowly targeted argument that Ilio-poulos's company had breached the terms of its insurance policy and therefore had no right to be compensated. Specifically, the insurers argued that the *Brillante* had not been fully destroyed and could have been repaired, and that the tanker had failed to observe basic maritime security practices by lingering in a high-risk area without a naval escort, thus invalidating its coverage. The insurers reserved the right to make more specific allegations after the two sides exchanged evidence, prior to trial.

To Veale, the approach was nonsensical. The Lloyd's market was fully aware of what had happened at Mockett's inquest. Everyone had seen news reports describing how Jonathan Tottman, the Metropolitan Police detective dispatched to Yemen, had claimed that the surveyor might have been killed because of an insurance scam. Veale couldn't understand why the underwriters were still treating the *Brillante* like any other contract dispute. From the lawyers' point of view, however, alleging fraud was a major escalation, not something to be done lightly—and certainly not if a case could be won by less aggressive means. Despite all the suspicion and rumor, they had no hard evidence, at that point, that contradicted the reported version of events. And even if they discovered that evidence, the history of scuttling cases in London made clear just how difficult it was to pin criminal activity on a shipowner.

But as the legal team moved ahead with its contractual arguments, Veale received just enough encouragement from Cunningham and the other insurance executives to keep Project Tundra going. If the destruction of the *Brillante* was a fraud, and all of Veale's instincts were screaming that it was, it would be the largest in maritime history, bigger even than the notorious case of the *Salem*, which was worth about $50 million. A lifetime of experience told Veale that he could be heading toward a confrontation with serious criminals, and he was going to need help, from someone he knew he could depend on. Which was why he decided to call an old friend.

CHAPTER 15

METAL MICKEY

Veale had known Michael Conner for thirty years, since they'd begun working together in London's Metropolitan Police. When Veale called him in late 2012, Conner was at the end of a distinguished career, serving most recently as a detective chief inspector in the small agency responsible for law enforcement in the British military. Veale asked his friend how he was. "I'm retired now, Dick," Conner said, in a tone that suggested he was reluctant to get pulled into whatever Veale might be getting in touch about. He was sixty and recovering from an eight-hour heart operation, no doubt related to the toll of four decades pursuing gangsters, fraudsters, drug traffickers, and pedophiles. His first marriage had also fallen apart, but Conner wasn't bitter. He considered himself fortunate to have been given the opportunity to pit himself against "arseholes," as he described the criminals he faced. It was his life's work, and he was exceptionally good at it.

Though he stood just over five feet tall and had the deeply lined face of a man nearing pension age, Conner could still end an argument with little more than a hard stare from his glacier-blue eyes. At the Met, his colleagues called him Metal Mickey—both for the toughness of his leathery, muscular frame and his unyielding personality—and his misshapen knuckles suggested that he wasn't someone you wanted to offend. But Conner had a soft side, too. He loved gags, which made his craggy features soften and melt into laughter. And he liked to say that police work offered the chance to see the best, as well as the worst, of human nature.

"What do you fancy doing now?" Veale asked him.

"Getting on my bike and going around the world," Conner joked. Veale, who employed a handful of former police officers as consultants at EBIS, told him not to do that. "I've got this job I'd like you to take a look at," he said. He'd pay Conner for his time, of course.

Conner was interested enough to read the file Veale had prepared on the *Brillante Virtuoso*. It took him a few days to come back with an initial assessment. "This is major organized crime," he said. Of all the cops Veale had worked with over the years, Conner was the best qualified to make that claim.

Like Veale, Conner had grown up in London—in his case, in a spacious Victorian house in a middle-class neighborhood, with a view of Big Ben in the distance from his bedroom window. His father died when he was fifteen, leaving Conner in the care of his Irish mother. He didn't encounter much crime as a youngster in the city's southern suburbs, but between Conner's willingness to confront those who crossed him and his total lack of deference to authority, it's not so hard to imagine that he might have ended up on the wrong side of the law. After his father's death, the headteacher at his school, who was also a priest, refused to let Conner's friends come to the funeral. They weren't well dressed enough, the clergyman said, and despite Conner's pleas, he wouldn't discuss it any further. So Conner punched him. He was promptly expelled; his only regret about the incident was that it upset his mother.

After leaving school, Conner got a job at an ad agency close to the Old Bailey, Britain's most important criminal court. From his office one day, he saw a heavily guarded convoy flash past, escorting the Kray twins, the infamous East End gangsters, to trial. The Krays were lowlifes, he thought, but he liked the look of the detectives escorting them. Conner signed up with the Met in 1971, as a nineteen-year-old. He was assigned to Islington in North London, largely because he was a capable boxer and the local precinct had a good club. Despite his small stature, Conner quickly earned a reputation for making arrests. The natural next step was the Criminal Investigation Department, to train as a detective, where he did stints in the drug hotspot of King's Cross and in Brixton, on the robbery squad.

In the early 1980s, a smartly uniformed young constable walked up to Conner's desk at Canon Row police station, in Westminster. He introduced himself as Richard Veale, and asked for help processing an arrest. Conner, by then a credentialed detective, sent him away with a long list of instructions, thinking he wouldn't see him again for days. Veale was back within a couple of hours, the job done. Conner was impressed enough to take the younger officer under his wing. They came to know each other as Mick and Dick. Together they targeted pickpocket gangs, which they were convinced were linked to more serious crime. One of the suspects they pursued turned out to also be an armed robber. When they broke down his door to arrest him, he blurted out: "What am I nicked for? We haven't done it yet!" Veale and Conner found duct tape and a mask nearby. They laughed long and hard as they dragged the man away.

While Veale, with his studious manner, was sometimes mistaken for an accountant, Conner had a gift for speaking to criminals in terms they could understand. His specialty was recruiting and handling informants. He'd pull up alongside a suspect in a van with blacked-out windows and say, "Jump in. I need to talk to you." Mostly, they did. He worked out that crooked lawyers and bookkeepers were the easiest to flip. "There are two chairs in the courtroom," he would tell them. "Witness, or defendant. Which one would you like to sit in?" He went on to work in an antiracketeering unit in Northern Ireland during the Troubles, investigating drug smuggling and contract killings by militants, and then spent a few years going after Turkish heroin traffickers in London.

Conner's refusal to bow to pressure made him an effective investigator, a respected "thief-taker" in the language of the Met. One former colleague described him as "one of the hardest blokes you will ever meet." But the same qualities that made him Metal Mickey also made Conner difficult to manage. He saw many of his superiors as overconfident careerists, eager for Conner's help with difficult investigations but quick to blame him if anything went wrong. He regularly ignored senior officers who disagreed with him, a habit that prevented him from rising to the level that others felt he deserved. As often as he made a breakthrough in an important case, Conner would find himself butting heads with someone of higher rank, and then being shunted sideways to another unit.

After Veale departed the force to build a career as a private investigator, Conner stayed in touch. Sometimes he'd quietly ask for help on a case; Veale was often better at getting information than Conner's contacts in Britain's intelligence services, and working with him left no electronic footprints for well-sourced criminals to pick up on. Once, Conner was trying to break up a ring of suspected pedophiles who met at a pub they called the Elephant's Graveyard. He couldn't find any reference to a venue with that name in London, nor could any of his fellow detectives. After Conner asked him to see what he could find out, Veale started trawling the internet and concluded that the Elephant's Graveyard was a nickname for a real pub by Marble Arch. It had taken him less than five minutes.

When Conner was fifty-one, he left Scotland Yard to join the CID of the Ministry of Defence Police, which was charged with keeping members of the military in line and protecting Britain's nuclear arsenal, among other tasks. By the time he retired in 2012, his work had included hunting pedophiles across the armed services and leading an inquiry into a mysterious explosion on a nuclear submarine, HMS *Tireless*, that killed two sailors.

While Conner had seen more varieties of criminality over the course of his career than anyone Veale knew, he was amazed by the *Brillante Virtuoso*. The more he learned about the case, the more he wanted to help crack it. He was in. Yet Conner was surprised, in his first few weeks working with Veale, that some of the Lloyd's executives and lawyers he met seemed more interested in avoiding conflict and finding a commercial solution than in determining conclusively whether a fraud had taken place. Incredibly, they were contemplating writing a check to the man Veale and Conner believed had orchestrated the plot, so long as the number on the end didn't have too many zeroes. "What's wrong with these guys?" Conner asked his old colleague. Veale didn't have a good answer.

Even more frustrating was the fact that, as far as the pair could tell, no meaningful criminal investigation was going on—an oversight they hoped to correct. Early in their work, Veale introduced himself to a former Met detective at a boozy social event for ex-cops. The man was a specialist in financial fraud and was working at the time for the National Crime Agency, the nominal British equivalent of the FBI. Sensing an opportunity, Veale steered the conversation to the *Brillante* and David Mockett, sketching out the basics of the story. "What are the cops doing about it?" his new acquaintance asked.

"Nothing," Veale answered.

The official was astonished. "You are fucking joking," he said. He promised to do what he could to get someone interested.

As they looked for evidence, Veale and Conner decided to visit Cynthia Mockett in Plymouth to see what they could learn about her husband's murder and his connection to the ship. Veale went first, on his own, in early 2013. It was more than five hours' drive from London, much of it through idyllic English countryside, along narrow roads fringed with hedgerows.

Cynthia was surprised by Veale's engagement in the case, which was then nearly two years old. He was the first person to come to talk about David's work since the inquest into his death, more than six months earlier. She'd heard nothing more from the police, the coroner's office, or Noble Denton, the firm that hired Mockett for his last job. Veale explained that he was investigating on behalf of the *Brillante*'s insurers at Lloyd's. He'd seen Mockett's reports, he said, and something didn't look right. He left promising to return soon.

A few weeks later, Conner joined Veale for the trip back to England's southwest. After Cynthia invited them inside, Conner got straight to business, opening with a question that had been bothering him ever since he learned about Mockett's work in Yemen. "Was David working for the CIA?" Conner asked. Cynthia shrugged and held up her hands. If he was, she didn't know anything about it. The notion wasn't as far-fetched as it sounded. Mockett had a range of allies among the small network of European and American officials and businesspeople in the country. It was possible that some of them might have been connected to intelligence agencies. While Cynthia knew he'd helped the British Embassy from time to time, there were still things about her husband's life that she didn't fully understand.

Still, Conner figured it was unlikely that Mockett was killed because he'd been discovered to be an intelligence operative. Even if he was working with the Americans, or for some other nation, government agents aren't routinely assassinated, even in turbulent corners of the Middle East. Such actions bring unwelcome consequences. Then there was the timing of his murder, only a week after his survey of the *Brillante*, and at a crucial moment in the operation to salvage the tanker.

Cynthia invited her visitors to Mockett's office upstairs to look through his correspondence. There, Veale picked up a letter from Roger Stokes, the lawyer who was one of Mockett's regular dining partners in Aden. "Roger's a friend of mine," Cynthia told them. Indeed, Stokes had attended Mockett's funeral in August 2011 and returned to Yemen after promising to help Cynthia collect his final paycheck. But she'd heard nothing since. "I haven't been able to reach him for a while," she said. Veale and Conner glanced at each other. Then Conner told her something they'd learned in their investigation. "I'm so sorry," Conner said. "He's dead." Cynthia's legs gave way in shock. She stumbled to the floor murmuring, "Poor Roger, poor Roger."

Conner and Veale told Cynthia what little they knew. In October 2012, some fifteen months after the attack on the *Brillante*, Stokes's regular driver had apparently arrived at his apartment overlooking Aden harbor to find him bleeding from a head wound. Stokes was still conscious when the driver discovered him, but died on the way to the hospital. News reports at the time cast the death as "mysterious." At first, Stokes's family worried that he'd been attacked, until they learned that the apartment was securely locked from the inside. "It was just a silly, awful accident," his sister told a newspaper in his native Tyneside, in northeast England. She believed Stokes had fallen and hit his head. But his body wasn't returned to the UK for an autopsy, and there was never an official explanation for his death. According to an aunt, "His employer said there was no indication of foul play, but it is still unclear. It is so horrible to think of." British police considered the possibility that it wasn't an accident. At one point, National Crime Agency officers investigating the *Brillante* attack contacted the US Navy to ask for any available information on Mockett and Stokes. Both, the NCA said, had died "under suspicious circumstances."

Veale had been curious enough to contact the Stokes family to get permission to review the lawyer's records. From those files, he learned that Stokes was also connected to the *Brillante*, tracking the vessel's movements off Yemen on behalf of one of its owner's many creditors. Meanwhile, his employer was involved in the salvage operation. Shortly after the hijacking, port officials in Aden had inexplicably seized one of the tugboats sent to help. Stokes's firm was hired to help get it released, just before Mockett was killed. Veale wasn't sure why the tug had been held. There seemed to have been a dispute over money owed to some branch of the Yemeni government, perhaps port charges or the payment for a license to run a salvage operation. Given the rampant corruption at the Aden port, it might have been a ruse known as a "squeeze and release," in which officials "arrest" a vessel on a pretense and extort bogus fees for themselves.

Whatever the cause, the tug's seizure had caused a serious problem for anyone with a financial stake in the *Brillante*. Without its pulling power, the tanker couldn't leave Yemeni waters, which meant the $100 million of oil below its deck couldn't be recovered. There would also be no chance to properly assess or repair damage, which meant it couldn't be sold, nor declared a loss so that a claim could be made on its insurance. In short, there was a fortune riding on the *Brillante* being towed away from Aden. With no other options, after several days the salvors made the required payments, and the tug was permitted to take the *Brillante* up to the United Arab Emirates.

After the shock of learning about Stokes, Cynthia promised to help Veale and Conner as best she could. Conner, in particular, took to her immediately. She was tougher than he'd expected. She stubbornly refused to accept the idea that because it was hard to discover the truth, they should stop trying. Cynthia felt a strong connection to Conner, too. Here was someone, she thought, who appeared to have the resolve to truly take the *Brillante* investigation forward—perhaps even far enough to get some answers about her husband's murder.

Around the time that Conner first met Cynthia, Veale made a minor break-through against the resistance he was encountering at Lloyd's. After asking for months, he received permission to team up with the private detective working on the same casualty from another corner of the market. Malcolm Jull, a veteran investigator who'd been hired by the firms that insured the *Brillante*'s cargo, had narrow, wary eyes half hidden under an unruly gray brow. He'd worked for the insurance industry since the 1960s, discovering early in his career that he had a knack for sniffing out scams. He'd investi-gated everything from stolen copper barges to phantom beef shipments, and in the process developed a finely tuned bullshit detector. The *Brillante* story set it off, he told Veale.

The two investigators began sharing files and contacts. Jull proved to have sources all over the world, including some in Greek law enforcement. He took Veale with him to Cyprus to visit Solal, the chartering firm that had hired the *Brillante* to transport oil from Ukraine to China. There, a helpful Russian manager turned over all of Solal's communications about the pas-sage. Jull and Veale walked out with cardboard boxes containing hundreds of pages of email printouts.

But Jull had his own problems. The firms employing him had recovered most of the oil protected by their policy. The $100 million they originally stood to lose was off the table. The cargo insurers' remaining liability—paying the Greek salvage crews for their work saving the payload—was considerably smaller: an arbitrator had decided that the salvors were due about $30 mil-lion. That was still one of the most generous salvage awards anyone at Lloyd's had ever seen, but a lengthy legal dispute might not cost much less. As a result, the insurers were considering paying the salvors' fee, despite their suspicions about the *Brillante*, which would make the problem disappear immediately.

Jull, who had little patience for niceties, made clear what he thought about the possibility of millions of dollars ending up in the hands of people he considered criminals. But he'd been around Lloyd's long enough to know how things worked. As the market debated how to proceed, he wasn't actively prevented from doing his job; instead, there was a lack of engagement. Any mention of the case would result in silence and awkward glances, he found. Requests for materials were delayed. Meetings were put off. When one insurance executive announced that he was bored with hearing about the *Brillante*, Jull struggled to keep his temper in check.

Matters came to a head in the spring of 2013. Jull was visiting sources in Jordan when he learned about a "market meeting" to be held at Lloyd's the next day. The purpose of the gathering was to decide what to do about the *Brillante*. Both the tanker's cargo and hull insurers would be represented, but the most pressing matter was whether to honor the salvage claim, which fell on Jull's clients. He flew back to London and went straight from the airport to Lloyd's headquarters in the City. There he took the elevator to the eleventh floor, where the most important business of the market was conducted, high above the bustle of the Underwriting Room. About thirty attendees were seated around a long conference table. Behind them, a window displayed a sweeping view of the London skyline, its historic spires competing for attention with modern monuments to international finance.

The most important members of the cargo syndicate were RSA Insurance Group (formerly Royal and Sun Alliance), Zurich Insurance Group, and Allianz, three industry behemoths with combined assets of more than $1 trillion. All had sent senior executives. Also present were Talbot's Paul Cunningham and other members of the hull syndicate, alongside a supporting cast of attorneys, accountants, and investigators. Veale and Conner hadn't been invited, but a few detectives from the City of London Police, who'd finally taken a tentative interest in the *Brillante* affair, were seated at the head of the table. Separate from the much larger Metropolitan Police, and responsible only for the crowded financial district, the City force had jurisdiction over the vast majority of the capital's insurance headquarters, and would therefore play a lead role in any investigation.

It quickly became clear that the room was divided over how to proceed. Several of the underwriters wanted to do something about what looked like a brazen fraud against the entire Lloyd's market. Someone suggested that if the police opened a formal investigation, it would give the insurers a legal basis to delay any payments. That wasn't how things worked, a detective explained. For the police to investigate properly, they would need a letter officially requesting help from all the members of the syndicate. The cops weren't going to intervene to halt a suspected fraud without firm support from its ostensible victims. But not all the insurers agreed. An executive from RSA was particularly hesitant, according to others who were in the room. "Our main concern is the reputation of the Royal Insurance companies and its clients," she said. Many of those clients happened to be members of the Greek shipping community. Getting in the habit of rejecting claims might lead to embarrassing lawsuits that were impossible to win.

In the end, the meeting broke up without a definitive resolution. Afterward, Jull spoke to the police detectives, who were surprised at the insurers' reluctance to make a criminal complaint. To them, it seemed crazy to even think about rewarding illegal conduct. "I'm here as an investigator," Jull told them. "I can't do anything about it."

Talbot and the hull syndicate decided not to change course. They would continue to pursue a defensive legal strategy against Marios Iliopoulos, the *Brillante*'s owner, while searching for concrete evidence of fraud. But a few weeks after the market meeting, RSA, Zurich, and Allianz quietly settled with the salvors, writing out a check for $34 million. Some in the cargo syndicate were disgusted at how easily their colleagues had given up. According to a person who was present, one argument over the decision, between an insurance executive and a lawyer in a City pub, got so heated that they nearly came to blows.

But as far as the cargo insurers were concerned, the *Brillante* case was closed. A few months later, the dispute over the *Elli*, the Iliopoulos-owned tanker that had run aground near Aden in 2009, was also settled out of court. The *Elli*'s insurers agreed to pay an undisclosed sum and committed themselves to keeping the matter confidential. Iliopoulos now had extra money in the bank to fund his *Brillante* litigation. And Veale and Conner were on their own.

CHAPTER 16

CIRCUMSTANTIAL EVIDENCE

On a gray afternoon in October 2013, Veale and Conner pulled into Whitehall, the broad avenue that hosts the great institutions of the British state. A few weeks earlier, Conner had reached out to an official at the Foreign & Commonwealth Office, explaining that they were working on a civil case they believed had substantial ramifications for Britain's maritime sector. They needed assistance getting information out of Yemen, he said, and finding out what evidence the government might hold on a tanker called the *Brillante Virtuoso*. A significant pirate attack, and the subsequent murder of a UK citizen, would surely have drawn the attention of the authorities in London, and presumably produced considerable amounts of documentation. But Veale and Conner had access to virtually none of it.

The official was sympathetic, and agreed to set up a meeting between the investigators and other key personnel to discuss what assistance they might be able to provide. Veale and Conner hoped that a trove of government-sourced evidence would be enough to convince their clients to take a firmer position on the case—a harder line that might then push the police to investigate more seriously. As they took their seats, Veale noted with satisfaction that some fairly serious people had turned up, including specialists in maritime security and counterpiracy operations from the FCO and Ministry of Defence. A representative of the National Crime Agency was also present.

Although the NCA had a mixed reputation—frustrated over the years by its bureaucratic inertia, Conner sometimes called it "Never Caught Anybody"—its attendance was still a good sign.

Veale had prepared a pitch that he figured would have the broadest possible resonance. A fraud against Lloyd's amounted to "an attack on part of the critical national infrastructure," he told the group—a threat to a core element of the UK's position as a nexus of global trade. In order to respond, he said, "We need to unlock the evidence jam." The people in that room had access to many different types of information that might be relevant: military records from the aftermath of the *Brillante* hijacking, diplomatic cables, and intelligence reports, among other documents. Veale explained that, according to various British laws, official files could be released to the private sector for the purposes of "preventing or detecting a crime," or for safeguarding the "economic well-being of the UK." He and Conner were trying to do both of those things, he said. "What we want is to establish a legal conduit for sharing information."

Some of the officials were hesitant. One wondered aloud why the government should play any role in what he referred to as a "civil matter." But by the end of the meeting, it appeared that Veale's arguments about the centrality of Lloyd's to Britain's larger interests had sunk in. He left the room hopeful that they'd made a breakthrough, and for the next several weeks he checked his inbox expectantly, looking for an update from the various agencies they'd met with. But none arrived, despite repeated nudges. The evidence jam hadn't cleared.

Veale and Conner continued on their own, slowly and methodically collecting evidence, bit by tiny bit. Through a source, they got their hands on a transmission sent by the USS *Philippine Sea*, the American vessel that had come to the *Brillante*'s aid after it was attacked. Time-stamped at 5:12 a.m. "Zulu" the next morning—8:12 a.m. in the Gulf of Aden—the message had been written by an officer on the warship, and contained a summary of what naval personnel had learned from the tanker's crew. It appeared to be drawn from CENTRIXS, an encrypted system that functioned as a sort of high-seas WhatsApp, used for coordinating operations and identifying pirate activity by the dozens of navies working to protect the sea-lanes.

As Veale read through it, he noticed something surprising. In statements given in Aden shortly after their rescue, *Brillante* crewmen had said the intruders who hijacked and burned their ship had been able to board by claiming to be from "the authorities." When he first saw the statements, Veale had thought the term was odd, especially because it was used so consistently by different sailors. They didn't mention a specific agency; it was just "the authorities." Had the attackers described themselves as being from the Coast Guard? Customs? Police? It wasn't even clear what country these "authorities" purported to represent. But at the time, the repeated phrase was just one of several things the crew members said that Veale found curious, and he hadn't dwelled on it.

Now, though, he saw that the US Navy received a quite different description of the ruse employed by the hijackers. "THE ATTACKERS WERE DRESSED LIKE MILITARY MEMBERS AND CLAIMED TO BE FROM THE VESSEL'S 'AGENT' AND WERE TASKED WITH PROVIDING THEM SECURITY FOR THEIR TRANSIT," the *Philippine Sea* officer wrote. "THAT WAS HOW THEY WERE ABLE TO GET ALONGSIDE WITHOUT MUCH ALARM."

For Veale and Conner, the message raised a series of pivotal questions. The first was about the attackers themselves. A roving band of pirates had no obvious way to know that *Brillante* was expecting a security team—the ostensible reason it was drifting off the Yemeni coast. So how had these gunmen come into that critical knowledge? The second question was related to the crew's behavior. Why would they give one account to the US Navy, in the immediate aftermath of the hijacking, and a different one to a lawyer in Aden, just days later? Why had they changed their stories?

Veale and Conner's clients, however, appeared strangely unmoved by the new evidence they were turning up. The person who seemed least impressed was Chris Zavos, the punctilious attorney leading the legal team for Talbot and the other hull insurers. A graduate of St. Paul's, an ultraprestigious private school on the banks of the Thames, he was the detectives' temperamental opposite in almost every way, and the differences seemed to become more pronounced the longer they worked together. In meetings, Zavos spoke with the precise cadence of a man ever attentive to how his words might be interpreted, and was often accompanied by another lawyer who would take copious notes, as though anticipating that any conversation might have to be cited in court. To Veale and Conner, he came across as so stiff that smiling might cause him physical pain. But Zavos's awkward manner hadn't stopped him from becoming a bona fide insider at Lloyd's, where Paul Cunningham, who'd first introduced him to Veale, seemed to regard him with awe.

Zavos and the insurers' other lawyers had asked the judge handling the *Brillante* case to split it into two trials. The first would deal mainly with "quantum," or the amount at stake. Under the strategy Zavos had helped formulate, their primary defense against Iliopoulos's lawsuit would be to try to shrink it. First, Talbot would apply pressure by arguing that the *Brillante* breached the terms of its policy by lingering in the Gulf of Aden. Failing that, the insurers would claim the ship could have been repaired despite its extensive damage, and that Iliopoulos botched its sale for scrap, off-loading it too cheaply. Their goal was to reduce the amount of money the shipowner could claim he was due to a few million dollars, small enough that a settlement to put an end to the dispute would begin to look attractive to both sides. In insurance cases, that was often how things were done. From Zavos and his colleagues' point of view, the plan made sense: their job was to get the best deal for their clients.

Since only the second trial would deal with the cause of the fire on board, this approach didn't require the underwriters to accuse Iliopoulos of wrongdoing, yet. Under the gentlemanly code of Lloyd's, with its basic assumption that everyone associated with the market was acting honorably (or that any dishonorable acts could be resolved in low-profile ways), insurers simply didn't suggest that major clients had committed fraud unless they absolutely had to. When Veale tried to press the matter, Zavos or one of the other lawyers would bring up the *Alexandros T*, an ugly dispute that was still rumbling through courts in London and Greece. The vessel at the center of the case was a Greek-owned bulk carrier, loaded with iron ore bound for China, that had sunk in the waters off South Africa. After the ship's insurers rejected the resulting claim, alleging that the *Alexandros T* was sailing with safety flaws that should have been disclosed, its owners retaliated ferociously. They filed nine countersuits in Greece, accusing the underwriters of defamation and fabricating evidence. The litigation would ultimately drag on for more than seven years, rising all the way to the UK Supreme Court, and was interpreted at Lloyd's as a warning about the risks of taking on a well-connected shipowner.

Veale was still surprised that the underwriters weren't ready to fight Iliopoulos. He kept returning to the same principle: if his and Conner's suspicions were correct, a substantial fraud, one of the biggest in maritime history, had been committed against the Lloyd's market, and paying out would only incentivize more of the same. It would also put legitimate funds into the hands of the people responsible—settlement proceeds that could be deposited at virtually any bank in the world, hassle free. In Veale's former line of work there were words for that kind of behavior, and he was certain that respectable Lloyd's members would never want them used to describe how they did business. He couldn't claim to be entirely high-minded about it. As the man hired to find out whether Iliopoulos had perpetrated a fraud, Veale could make a considerable amount of money by taking that effort as far as possible. But there was still a moral dimension that he believed couldn't, or shouldn't, be ignored.

Late in 2013, Veale arrived for a meeting at Talbot's offices across from the neoclassical Royal Exchange, where Lloyd's was housed through the nineteenth century. About fifteen people took their places around a large conference room table: representatives of the *Brillante*'s insurers as well as their lawyers, there to discuss the latest developments in the case. After the lawyers spoke, explaining the finer points of litigation procedure, it was Veale's turn to present, and he pulled up a PowerPoint presentation on a wall-mounted screen. He was supposed to be giving a synopsis of his investigation's progress so far, as well as a rundown of next steps. But in the middle of the deck, he'd inserted a slide that wasn't strictly part of the work he was being paid to do. It contained just one image: David Mockett's burned-out car, photographed just after the bombing that killed him. "It's important to remember," Veale said to the group. "A really decent man was murdered."

The quantum trial, which was held in November and December 2014, ended with a decisive defeat for the underwriters. In a decision handed down the following January, the judge, Julian Flaux, ruled that even though it hadn't sunk as a result of the attack, the *Brillante* had been rendered a "constructive total loss." As far as the legal system was concerned, it would be treated as though it were on the bottom of the ocean, irretrievable. Flaux said he was unimpressed by the allegations made by the insurers up to that point, including that Iliopoulos and his agents had exaggerated the *Brillante*'s damage and what it would cost to repair, and racked up unnecessary expenses along the way. Those were small-fry arguments, given the scale of what had occurred, and Flaux seemed to sense that the insurers were holding back. Once, during the court proceedings, he'd observed that they were "willing to wound, yet afraid to strike."

The ruling meant that if Iliopoulos prevailed in the second trial, which would decide what caused the fire on the *Brillante* and who was to blame, the firms that insured the tanker stood to lose as much as $85 million. That would be a very large bill, even at Lloyd's—and Veale and Conner believed it gave them an opening. The detectives argued that it was time for the insurers to finally get aggressive, by filing a civil fraud case and doing everything they could to help the police pursue Iliopoulos criminally. They still met resistance. During a postmortem meeting they attended after Flaux's decision, the group got into a discussion about evidence—specifically, what the underwriters would be able to prove about the *Brillante* if they decided to fight. Everything they'd learned so far was "circumstantial," one of the attendees said. Incensed, Veale interrupted him.

"Throughout this I've heard you all talk about circumstantial evidence," Veale said. "Do you actually know what that means?"

"That there's no smoking gun," the man replied.

"A smoking gun is *the best* example of circumstantial evidence," Veale said, his voice rising with frustration. It could only be otherwise if someone had witnessed the weapon being fired. "Circumstantial evidence isn't weaker evidence," he continued. "DNA and fingerprints are circumstantial evidence." None were proof, on their own, that a crime had been committed or by whom. They were building blocks, to be combined into the foundation of a persuasive case, one that Veale was confident would succeed if the insurers were willing to make it.

He and Conner kept lobbying for a more forceful approach, bombarding Talbot's Paul Cunningham and another of the main underwriters, Dean Allen of the Bermuda-based insurer Hiscox, with arguments for why a fraud case was winnable. They weren't sure if they were getting through. Veale had succeeded in convincing the insurers to formally report the *Brillante* case to the City of London Police as a suspected fraud, and both Cunningham and Allen had spoken of their distress about what happened to Mockett. But the customs of Lloyd's still seemed to be more powerful than any logic the detectives could muster. There was another factor, just as problematic. Although the insurers were the ones paying the bills, to Veale and Conner it was clear that the lawyers were in control. Zavos, in particular, exuded a confidence that appeared to have convinced his clients it was best to let him take the lead. He periodically told them about some of the many comparable cases he said he'd worked on, with the implication that he knew exactly how to handle this one.

Veale wasn't persuaded. The only kind of knowledge Zavos really valued, he thought, was legal expertise. But the more he and Conner learned, the more they became convinced that the *Brillante* case was nothing like an average insurance lawsuit. Veale took to regularly challenging Zavos's statements, asking him to justify his advice. The lawyer didn't always appreciate it. "I think I'm being questioned here," he declared during one exchange. "We're all under scrutiny," Veale responded.

Conner's relationship with Zavos was even worse. Fairly or not, he saw a set of traits in Zavos that he'd encountered again and again in his dealings with corporate lawyers: absolute certainty, imperviousness to criticism, and a deep aversion to unpleasant conversations. What bothered Conner most was the way Zavos waved away his references to Mockett's death, dismissing it as irrelevant to the litigation. In the legal sense, that was an entirely accurate statement. But to Conner, it couldn't have been more mistaken in the moral one. He found he could barely spend time with Zavos without getting fed up.

In his irritation, he began staring intensely at the lawyer during meetings, a habit so unnerving to Zavos that he asked Veale to make Conner stop.

The two investigators weren't the only ones frustrated with the underwriters' approach to the *Brillante*. Encouraged by the formal police report, British law enforcement agencies were trying to gauge whether a prosecution was feasible. But they still weren't sure they had the full support of the insurance market. In a meeting at Lloyd's to discuss the case, representatives of the NCA, the City of London Police, and Financial Conduct Authority—the UK's main financial-market watchdog—stressed that insurers had a legal obligation to prevent fraud and money laundering, one they needed to ensure that they were honoring. Some of the government officials had been surprised to learn that Lloyd's didn't appear to have a central database of its customers, let alone reliable information about who stood behind the shell companies that typically owned ships. "You need to do more," one of them urged.

In 2015, Veale and Conner began to sense the mood changing in their favor, although, since they weren't involved in many of the discussions between the insurers and their lawyers, they couldn't be sure exactly why. Veale had always had the impression that the underwriters viewed cost as the most important factor in their strategy, and the quantum ruling meant that a settlement to make the *Brillante* affair go away was likely to be expensive. There was also the growing pile of evidence that he and Conner were collecting, even if, to them, the signs of wrongdoing had been clear from the start.

In the spring of that year, the insurers filed new documents at London's High Court, revealing a dramatic change in strategy. To Veale and Conner's delight, the members of the *Brillante* syndicate had agreed to accuse Iliopoulos of fraud, and sought permission to make that argument at the second trial—the one that would determine if they had to pay up. "There was no attack by Somali pirates," they said in their new pleadings. In fact, they went on, "Any such attack on the vessel was staged with the involvement and connivance of the owner," and members of the crew: Captain Gonzaga, who'd ordered the ship to drift and given permission for the supposed pirates to come aboard, and Chief Engineer Tabares, who'd been alone with the intruders in the engine room. Drawing on the reports they commissioned from explosives experts, the underwriters claimed the fire that gutted the *Brillante* "was initiated by an explosive incendiary device," planted by people "acting on the instructions of the owner." Iliopoulos had been deeply in debt, they argued, giving him a strong incentive to destroy a vessel that carried insurance far in excess of its economic value.

The reasons for the reversal were essentially financial, as Veale had suspected. In a statement to the judge, Zavos provided a detailed map of the logic that the detectives found so strange. "Underwriters have from an early stage been extremely suspicious of the cause of the casualty," Zavos wrote. But despite those misgivings, they "would have wished to avoid making this allegation, if it was not necessary to do so, e.g. if the quantum of the claim was such that 'the game was not worth the candle'"—an obscure expression, coined before the advent of electricity, about avoiding card games with stakes lower than the expense of illuminating them. There it was, Veale remarked to himself: a clear statement of the priorities at Lloyd's. Losing the quantum trial, and being faced with a larger bill, "led to a serious and careful review of all the available evidence," Zavos explained, "and to the present decision."

For Veale and Conner's purposes, the insurers' motivation wasn't particularly important. The detectives were eager to get going on a more intense, structured investigation. Without their clients tapping the brakes, they were optimistic about getting to the truth of what happened to the *Brillante*. They arranged a meeting with Zavos, Cunningham, and Allen for a Monday in mid-May. Veale and Conner intended to brief the group on their strategy, which encompassed dozens of "investigative actions": tracking down potential witnesses in Yemen, reinterviewing the *Brillante*'s crew, and digging into the salvage companies that had responded to the attack, among other inquiries. All of that work might take a year or more, but at the end of the process they were confident they could deliver a decisive body of evidence.

They arrived early, taking seats in the brightly lit lobby of Talbot's offices. Cunningham emerged a short time later to collect them. His ashen expression struck Veale immediately. He brought them to a meeting room where Zavos was waiting. After Veale and Conner entered, he began to speak about the investigation. "I need to run it," Zavos said firmly. "I can't have you going off doing things I don't know about." Cunningham was more apologetic, but he reiterated the lawyer's statement. Everything would have to go through Zavos from now on. Veale wanted to contradict them, to argue that he and Conner had been transparent about their work from the start. But something about Zavos's tone told him there was no point arguing. The message was clear. They were being sidelined.

CHAPTER 17

MARKED

D ressed in funereal black, the woman standing at Cynthia Mockett's door announced solemnly that she was a police family liaison officer. She seemed very young, Cynthia thought as she invited the visitor inside. FLOs are employed to act as conduits between law enforcement and members of the public affected by crime. They are supposed to offer support, guide families through the complexities of the justice system, and, importantly, update them on the progress of investigations.

It was early 2016, almost half a decade after David Mockett's death; nearly four years since Detective Jonathan Tottman had suggested, in the public setting of a coroner's inquest, that Mockett was murdered to cover up an insurance scam; and three years since Veale and Conner had come to Cynthia's home to tell her they wouldn't let the case go cold. As far as she knew, however, the police were no closer to identifying her husband's murderers. A visit from an officer was a surprise, and Cynthia briefly hoped that it indicated some new developments.

In Cynthia's living room, the young woman sat down on a sofa and placed a briefcase on her lap. She opened it, reached inside, and pulled out some papers: a brochure on how to deal with bereavement. Cynthia sat with her jaw clenched and arms folded as the officer leafed through the pages, showing her pointers about coping with grief. Anger management would have been more appropriate, Cynthia thought bitterly. But she decided to bite her tongue rather than say what she was really thinking: that a pamphlet on bereavement was worse than useless, except as a reminder of what the police had failed to do. The Mocketts' older daughter Sarah, who happened to be visiting, watched what was unfolding and couldn't stay silent. She tore into the FLO about the inadequacy of the police response and how little information the family had received. Years of pain and rage came pouring out in the direction of the unfortunate officer, who hurried away from the house, clutching her briefcase.

Mockett's death had been hard on the whole family, but especially on his two daughters. With so many questions still unanswered, their grief was formless. It couldn't fit into any shape they recognized as a meaningful response to loss. While they had rich, busy lives and children of their own, neither had been able to fully move on. Their distress compounded Cynthia's own sadness.

She also had more tangible frustrations to deal with. Mockett's partner in the Middle East had dropped out of contact, and she'd been unable to claim on his professional life insurance. The only compensation Cynthia had received was 100,000 pounds from a policy bought through an advertisement in *Reader's Digest*. And she'd had to complain to a consumer-rights agency to get even that. It wasn't enough to keep up the mortgage on the Vicarage, the beloved home where she and Mockett had raised their family. Cynthia knew she'd have to sell the house and leave behind the lush garden and flowerbeds that she'd carefully tended over the years.

Still, Cynthia tried to find solace in her grandchildren, her plants, and her deepening alliance with Michael Conner. The retired detective had begun to visit her regularly in Devon, and they met in London when Cynthia traveled up for the Chelsea Flower Show. No one was paying Conner to help her; assisting Mockett's widow wasn't part of the work he and Veale had been hired to do. But he felt a certain responsibility to Cynthia, who he thought had been treated appallingly. Conner kept her informed about the progress of the insurance investigation, including the setback of the quantum trial defeat, as well as his and Veale's sidelining by Chris Zavos, the lawyer now running the inquiry. Conscious of his decades of experience in law enforcement,

Cynthia had come to rely on Conner to represent her family's interests to the authorities. She knew that he and Veale had been furiously lobbying the police to make a priority of the *Brillante Virtuoso*, and of Mockett's murder.

Veale and Conner did receive occasional hints that British cops were still engaged with the case. A few months after Cynthia's encounter with the family liaison, two officers arrived at her home: a detective sergeant from the City of London Police and a member of the Metropolitan Police antiterrorism unit, which had taken over the Mockett file. Their presence was encouraging. But the policemen, who insisted they were there to help Cynthia, looked uncomfortable. They weren't willing to share any information about Mockett's death or the status of their investigation. If anything, they appeared to be trying to find out what *she* knew.

In the middle of the discussion, Cynthia's phone rang. Her daughter Sarah came in to announce that Conner was on the line. The antiterror officer was visibly irritated. "That man no longer works for the police," he said sternly. Cynthia was furious. "Don't you dare," she hissed. Conner had done more to help her than anyone, and certainly more than the two men sitting in her living room.

While Cynthia fumed at police inaction, Veale and Conner found themselves on the outside of the insurance syndicate's legal fight. Since Zavos made clear he was taking charge, the lawyer had hired his own detectives and consultants to gather evidence in Greece. The two friends had a reasonable idea of what was happening, but they weren't involved. Months passed, and they began spending more time on other projects.

Then one afternoon in March 2016, Veale's phone lit up with a call from Zavos. He was talking into a speaker, with several other attorneys in the room, and sounded shaken. The *Brillante*'s owner, Marios Iliopoulos, had somehow gotten hold of forty-five confidential emails sent between Zavos's team and the Greek lawyers they were working with. Apparently, printouts of the messages, sealed in a large white envelope, had been left for one of Iliopoulos's associates at the entrance to his apartment building. Zavos had no idea who'd put them there, or how that person had obtained them. The documents were then passed to Iliopoulos's legal team in London, who'd been obliged to inform their opponents.

Whether the emails had been hacked or taken in some kind of burglary, their loss represented a major security breach. For one thing, they contained detailed information on the strategy the insurers planned to deploy against Iliopoulos in court. Worse, the Iliopoulos associate claimed the emails showed that the investigators Zavos hired had violated Greek privacy protections as they gathered information. In response, he'd filed a criminal complaint with the Athens public prosecutor, making wild allegations against the Lloyd's market and its agents. Among other things, the complaint alleged that Zavos was somehow an accessory to money laundering, and that the Greek gumshoes working for him were part of a criminal gang.

Those claims were bizarre and scarcely credible. Yet the insurers knew from the infamous *Alexandros T* case that legal proceedings in Greece couldn't simply be ignored. The complaint particularly rattled Zavos and his colleagues at Norton Rose. They'd spent decades climbing to the pinnacle of the British legal profession, a genteel environment where trial lawyers refer to each other as "my learned friend" and, even in the most adversarial cases, the combatants down arms during court breaks to chat about their summer homes in France or crack jokes in Latin. They had never experienced anything like this.

The stakes were even higher for their colleagues in Greece. There, Norton Rose had teamed up with the Piraeus firm of Lallis Voutsinos Anagnostopoulos, led by an attorney named Gerry Lallis, a former merchant captain who'd studied in the UK before building a practice representing insurers in shipping disputes. Captain Lallis was a heavyset man in his sixties, with a mole the size of a quarter on one cheek and thick fingers better suited to a deckhand's duties than to filing depositions. He was known as one of Greece's leading experts on scuttling fraud, which made him an unpopular figure among some of his compatriots. Through bitter experience, he'd learned how dangerous it could be to go up against Greek shipowners in a Greek shipping town. During his long career he'd been screamed at, threatened, sued, and offered numerous bribes, all while safeguarding a reputation for integrity with his clients in London.

Sometimes the consequences were physical. On a spring morning in 2013, Lallis had been walking from the Piraeus railway station toward his office, as he did every day. Suddenly he felt a sharp impact to his head—and then more blows, which he would describe in a report to prosecutors as a "storm of punches," delivered with speedy precision. His attacker, a tall man whose face was concealed by a motorcycle helmet, kept beating Lallis after he crumpled to the pavement, continuing until he was barely conscious. Then he calmly turned and walked away. During the entire encounter the assailant hadn't said a word.

Lallis never found out which of his many enemies was behind the assault, though he had his suspicions. In the Greek maritime world, he told his British friends, you had to pick one side or the other. He'd chosen his long ago. It was a stressful line of work, but lucrative. Lallis opted to live a good distance from Piraeus, in a secluded village with his wife and dog.

When Zavos approached him about the *Brillante* case he'd agreed to help, as long as his assistance remained confidential. But the theft of the emails left him exposed. Soon after the leak, Lallis came home to find a single kite, fluttering in the wind, at the entrance to his garden. Someone had tied the string around the branch of an old olive tree. It could have been local kids, Lallis told the insurers' legal team. Or it could have been a warning, identifying him as a target. Days later, Zavos received word of a chillingly specific threat. One of the Greek investigators working for Norton Rose reported that he'd heard Lallis was, as he put it to Zavos, "marked for extermination." The investigator didn't know the details, but Zavos took the information seriously. He called Lallis immediately, instructing him not to leave his office. Then he called Veale to ask him and Conner for help. Keeping Lallis alive was well beyond the expertise of a City law firm.

The news made Veale deeply suspicious of who had been hired in Athens. "How the hell does the investigator working for us know about a hit on Lallis?" he thought. But an examination of the man's loyalties would have to wait. Veale's contacts in British law enforcement had no jurisdiction in Greece, so he arranged for a team of private bodyguards, paid for by the insurers, to pick Lallis up at his office and escort him home. They placed him in the center of a convoy, with cars full of armed guards in front and behind, plus a motorbike on his flank. Gunning through the streets of Piraeus, Veale hoped they would convince anyone observing that hurting Lallis wasn't worth the trouble. The security team would keep watch over him for weeks.

Conner took the first flight to Athens he could find, to manage the protection effort. After he arrived, he and Lallis went to meet a senior commander in the economic crime division of the Greek police. At first, the officer seemed concerned that Conner might be a British spy. After Conner set him straight with some lawman-to-lawman small talk, he agreed to sit outside while the officer and Lallis discussed what to do. Greek law enforcement seemed to be taking the matter seriously. Conner was soon invited to a "summit meeting" at a police headquarters, with a dozen or so local officials as well as a representative from the British Embassy. There, the authorities agreed to step up patrols in Lallis's neighborhood and to assign a detective to check on him. Just as important, the economic crime officer agreed to cooperate with the UK investigation into the *Brillante*.

At the end of the discussion, the officer decided to seal the arrangement in traditional Greek fashion. He produced an unmarked bottle of clear liquid while a captain distributed shot glasses. The spirit was his own personal distillation, he explained through a translator. Oh, shit, thought Conner, who'd given up drinking twenty years earlier. But it seemed unwise to spoil the collaborative mood. Conner raised his glass to join in the usual toast of "*ya mas*"—to our health. The moonshine burned all the way down.

In the London lawsuit, Iliopoulos was stonewalling. Every request by the insurers' lawyers for supporting documentation was refused for one reason or another. The shipowner's attorneys said they had tried their best to acquire records from the *Brillante*'s shipping agent, the crewing firm that supplied its Filipino sailors, and the security outfit that was supposed to provide the tanker's escort, among others. In each case, the files had been destroyed, or lost, or the company had ceased operations, or it had stopped responding to letters from London.

Iliopoulos claimed that his capacity to deal with the insurers' requests was reduced because of stress-induced labyrinthitis, an ear ailment made worse by the burdens of the court case. When pressed to explain what happened to a missing electronic archive from one of his companies, the shipowner said he'd given it to a business partner who refused to return it, for reasons so convoluted they defied coherent explanation.

There would be no way to hold a fair trial without more information. The open exchange of documents between defendants and plaintiffs, a process known in English law as "disclosure," is critical to the administration of justice. If it didn't occur, decisive evidence might be hidden, and any court decision could be tainted by unfairness. After months of obfuscation, in early 2016 the judge assigned to the case lost patience with Iliopoulos and his legal team, and ordered the shipowner to come to London to testify in person about the missing archive. If he refused, he risked having his claim thrown out.

Veale and Conner were thrilled. Finally, they would have a chance to come face-to-face with the man at the center of the storm around the *Brillante Virtuoso*.

CHAPTER 18

SUPER MARIO

liopoulos received his summons at his office in Piraeus, opposite the ferry terminal where he'd built much of his fortune. Centered on a hook-shaped peninsula extending southwest from central Athens, the city of 160,000 is the undisputed center of Greece's shipping industry. Along its densely packed commercial blocks are the offices of virtually every one of the country's maritime tycoons. That, in turn, makes Piraeus the ship-owning capital of the world. Roughly 18 percent of the worldwide merchant fleet is Greek owned, a volume wildly out of proportion to the country's overall economy, which is barely among the twenty largest in Europe. The marine assets controlled from Piraeus dwarf those held by Japan, with 11 percent of the total, and the US, with just 3 percent.

Collectively, Greek shipowners have done better out of the seventy-five-year explosion in international trade than almost anyone else. No geopolitical or macroeconomic event—not the fall of the Soviet Union, the rise of China, or the emergence of COVID-19—has thrown them off course for long. Not even their country's recent financial collapse, which drove unemployment to nearly 28 percent and threatened to split the Eurozone, diminished their power. At the nadir of the crisis, with Greece's government desperate to raise revenue to fend off creditors, the shipowners of Piraeus fought successfully to retain an astonishingly favorable set of fiscal advantages, some of them written into the Greek constitution. To this day they are largely exempt from corporate taxes.

There's no single explanation for how a small group of businesspeople from a country of 11 million citizens, with no other globally competitive industries, came to exert such outsize power over seaborne commerce. Geography plays a role, of course. Spread across some two hundred inhabited islands, in an archipelago stretching five hundred miles from Corfu to Rhodes, Greeks have depended since antiquity on marine transport. Some of the longer-lived Hellenic shipping dynasties got their start with short runs in the Aegean and Mediterranean, shifting gradually into longer, transoceanic journeys. A history of emigration is also a factor. Ethnically Greek communities have existed since the nineteenth century or earlier in countries like Egypt and Ukraine, predating the more recent waves of arrivals in New York, London, and other world cities. Those widely dispersed populations provided a ready commercial network in key ports, linked by blood, language, and culture to the business community at home.

But the most important element of the story is nimble twentieth-century entrepreneurship. The Second World War devastated Greek shipping, destroying more than 70 percent of the country's commercial fleet by the end of hostilities. But enterprising Greeks soon found a way to replace that lost tonnage: by acquiring surplus Liberty Ships produced for the Allied war effort, which were being sold off in large numbers. Despite the demands of fighting a well-organized Communist insurgency, and the severe poverty of large parts of the population, the Greek government managed to find the resources to guarantee the 1947 purchase of one hundred Liberties by a group of local businessmen— an early example of the influence of shipping concerns over the country's politics. The vessels were awkwardly designed and sometimes of dubious quality, but they had the crucial attribute of being cheap, and therefore easy to pay off. With so many ships available, Greeks soon carved out strong positions in what's known as tramp shipping—running vessels with no fixed schedules, willing to transport whatever cargo they can find—just in time to be enriched by the booming postwar economy.

Much of the trade they exploited was in oil. As cars became mass-market conveniences in Europe and North America, crude went from the periphery of the shipping business to its very center. In an earlier era, ships collected their cargoes in industrial cities—Liverpool, Philadelphia, Montreal. In the new automobile age, the most important loading ports would include places like Mina Al Ahmadi, in Kuwait, and Ras Tanura, on the edge of Saudi Arabia's seemingly limitless oil fields. Sixty percent of the growth in maritime trade between 1948 and 1973 was in "liquid cargo," overwhelmingly petroleum and products related to it.

Moving larger quantities of oil over longer distances required a huge increase in tanker capacity, which a pair of Greek operators were particularly eager to provide. Stavros Niarchos and Aristotle Onassis, the most prominent shipping tycoons of the postwar era, arguably deserve more credit than anyone for the development of the supertanker, which transformed the energy business after its introduction in the 1950s. Contemporaries and bitter rivals, Niarchos and Onassis competed to build the fanciest yachts and to wed the most beautiful women (one of whom, the maritime heiress Tina Livanos, they both ultimately married). They vied to dominate the tanker trade, commissioning larger and larger ships that would dramatically cut the cost of carrying each barrel between continents.

The two men also played a significant role in creating the legal framework that supports and dictates the rules of modern shipping. Their ideas weren't entirely new. Greek maritime families had long known that obscuring responsibility for what happened in their business could be convenient. In a rare memoir of life inside the industry, the shipping heir Elias Kulukundis described how his family firm, R&K, "had an office in Bermuda which was nominally the head office of the company. Decisions were supposedly taken there and transmitted to R&K in London." The London office was meant to act only as an "agent," though in reality the decisions were made there and "telephoned to the Bermuda office, which created a paper trail by sending back a telex" with the same instruction it had just received. Such small-bore juggling was useful enough in shedding legal and financial burdens. But Niarchos and Onassis had much grander ideas than working up a bit of misleading paperwork. They were among the earliest to grasp the potential of putting their ships and their money entirely beyond the reach of the countries where they lived and did business.

The very first vessel to be registered under Liberia's flag was the *World Peace*, a Niarchos-owned tanker that entered the nominal jurisdiction of that West African state in 1949. He and Onassis quickly became some of the most enthusiastic users of so-called flags of convenience, which allowed them to escape the rules on maintenance, inspections, and sailors' wages that prevailed in the Western world. As with their other innovations, this one was quickly adopted by the rest of the Piraeus shipping fraternity. By 1959, over half the "Liberian" merchant fleet was owned by Greeks, who also piled into the Panamanian registry. Other financial sleights of hand pioneered by Onassis in particular, like dividing the ownership and management of ships into separate companies domiciled in tax havens, became similarly commonplace. Once he had proved the concept, the basic appeal of such regulatory dodges was too attractive to resist: all of the profits, little of the accountability.

Veale and Conner hadn't found it easy to compile a substantive dossier on how Marios Iliopoulos came to be among Piraeus's shipping tycoons. The problem wasn't that he was obscure. Though he didn't emerge from one of the great Greek maritime families, Iliopoulos had been a major purchaser of tankers, with his activities tracked diligently by the shipping press. He was well-known for his other main business, a huge ferry operation linking Piraeus to islands like Mykonos and Santorini, and had clearly accumulated considerable wealth and influence in his home country. But he'd done so with very little of the financial and legal exhaust that businesspeople in less secretive industries generate. None of his companies were listed on a public stock exchange, and when he borrowed money, it was from Greek banks, not international bond markets. Countries like the Marshall Islands, where some of his assets officially resided, were hardly known for their transparency.

It would also be challenging to get anywhere through quiet inquiries in Greece. Piraeus was a shipowners' town, not the kind of place where a couple of detectives working for the London insurance market could expect a warm reception. The threats to Gerry Lallis, the Greek lawyer assisting the *Brillante* underwriters with their case, were proof enough of that.

But gradually, through interviews with the few people who knew his history and were willing to speak with them, Veale and Conner pieced together a biography of Iliopoulos. His father, Panagiotis, had entered the shipping business in the late 1960s. Niarchos and Onassis were then at the peak of their fame—the best known of the latter's marriages, to the woman formerly known as Jacqueline Bouvier, began in 1968—and ambitious Greeks were entering the industry in large numbers, seeking their own fortunes. The elder Iliopoulos was a goldsmith by training and had no maritime background to speak of. Yet he found that he was a natural. "I have a restless spirit," he would later tell a Greek court, a personality ideally suited to the wide range of financial and technical challenges a shipowner might encounter. Panagiotis reveled in being the ultimate decider on every question about the vessels he operated: "the machinery, the crews, the repairs, about everything," he recounted. He traveled frequently, visiting distant yards to personally supervise repair and maintenance work.

Greek shipping firms are generally family operations, with sons and sons-in-law (it's rarely daughters) expected to join the business and then relocate to wherever its operations demand. But the youngest of Panagiotis's three boys had little interest in joining his father. Marios Iliopoulos's passion was on land: driving powerful vehicles at extreme speed. As a high school student in the 1980s, according to a Greek news outlet, he was known around Psychiko, an upmarket Athens suburb, for roaring down the quiet, villa-lined streets on a powerful motorbike. Almost as soon as he learned to drive Iliopoulos began competing in rally races, competitions that bear little resemblance to the controlled environments of Formula One or NASCAR. Instead of doing laps on a track, rally drivers hurl their cars along rugged mountain roads, navigating steep climbs and sharp bends. Winning takes considerable technical ability, as well as a degree of courage that can be hard to distinguish from recklessness. While powering down a steep hillside, one mistake can mean the difference between victory and sliding over a cliff.

After finishing high school, Iliopoulos studied economics in the UK and performed his mandatory military service in the Hellenic Navy. He found that nothing about those commitments, let alone joining the family shipping operation, could compare to the high of rallies. "Everything else I did was a pointless chore," he said later. "I was born to race." By all accounts Iliopoulos was a talented driver, winning multiple championships in Greece. But Pan-agiotis didn't approve of his son putting the rest of his life on hold to keep competing, especially given the constant risk of being hurt or worse. By 1997 Iliopoulos had undergone at least five surgeries to treat injuries from rallying. And he was spurning a secure career, including the prospect of equity in the family business. Yet Iliopoulos insisted on making racing his priority, strain-ing his relationship with his father.

Even if he wasn't engaged in it firsthand, Iliopoulos learned early on about the harsher realities of the shipping industry. In August 1994 the *Iron Antonis*, an aging freighter owned by the family (and bearing the name of Iliopoulos's eldest brother), departed the port of Tubarão, Brazil, with a load of iron ore. To operate commercially, merchant vessels require certificates from "classification societies," private companies that inspect a ship's condi-tion and verify that its hull and machinery are in working order. The *Iron Antonis*'s certification, issued by the French provider Bureau Veritas, had been withdrawn earlier in the year. A Greek classification society, the Hellenic Register of Shipping, had stepped in to provide clearance, allowing it to sail from Brazil to Shekou, in southern China.

Not long after it left Tubarão, the *Iron Antonis* encountered ferocious seas in the South Atlantic. The crew would have followed their training, seal-ing hatches and tying down gear, while their captain did all he could to keep the bow pointed into the waves—the best way to prevent them from capsizing the vessel. But the heavy seas kept coming, slamming with terrifying force onto the *Iron Antonis*'s deck. On September 3, the captain reported that its hull had cracked amid the swells. The vessel was listing badly, he said, and the twenty-four men on board might need to abandon ship. Later that day, the *Iron Antonis* stopped responding to hails. It sank in some of the loneliest waters on earth, about 1,700 nautical miles west of Cape Town. A small, empty lifeboat was all rescuers were able to find.

Despite his resistance to joining his father's firm, Iliopoulos's name was on the *Iron Antonis*'s paperwork, along with those of his two brothers. Greek prosecutors charged all three with the "negligent homicide" of the men on board, claiming they sent the freighter to sea knowing it was in dangerously poor condition. The brothers denied wrongdoing at their trial, which was held in 2000 and 2001 at a utilitarian courthouse near Panagiotis's office in Piraeus. On the stand, Iliopoulos said that he had no role in his father's operations beyond providing his signature when told. When asked to endorse documents, he testified, "I didn't even know what I signed." Panagiotis, who wasn't charged, appeared as a witness for the defense, testifying about his maritime career and denying that he would ever have tolerated an unseaworthy ship in his fleet. "I would never dare to throw a twenty-five-year-old vessel to the wolves," he said.

Iliopoulos and his middle brother, Ioannis, were acquitted. But Antonis, who worked full-time for the patriarch, was found guilty and received a five-year suspended prison sentence. During his appeal, the judges heard testimony from a woman named Varvara Kiourani, the sister of the man who was second mate on the *Iron Antonis*. "The ship wasn't sunk because of the weather conditions as we were initially told, but by those who held the fate of the crew in their hands," she said. Kiourani recalled that in their last phone call, her brother "told me that the ship was a mess," headed for the scrapyard after one more voyage. "We want justice to be served. These maritime crimes need to stop."

In a fortunate stroke of defendant's luck, Antonis had moved to a new house while he was under indictment, informing the court of the change in address. But the authorities sent some official documents about the case to his old home by mistake—an error his lawyers claimed violated Greek law. The appellate court accepted their argument and overturned Antonis's conviction. He never spent a day in jail.

As best as Veale and Conner could tell, by the early 2000s Iliopoulos had changed his view of working in shipping. He founded his ferry company, Seajets, in 2002, gradually expanding it into a significant presence on the Piraeus docks, a barren patch of concrete that might be transited by more tourists than any other site in Greece. As it grew, he learned to eke out an advantage by playing hardball.

In 2012, for instance, Iliopoulos agreed to buy the *Snaefell*, a seventy-four-meter catamaran operated by a ferry line based on the Isle of Man. After it arrived in Piraeus, he claimed that it was riddled with defects, faults he said would necessitate a significant drop in price. Executives at the company that sold him the catamaran believed Iliopoulos's allegations were, at the very least, heavily exaggerated, since he'd had every opportunity to inspect it during earlier negotiations. With the purchase apparently up in the air, they wanted to bring the *Snaefell* out of Greece so it would be in neutral waters during any renegotiation. But they found they couldn't. Required permits were mysteriously held up, and local oil companies refused to provide any fuel. In the end, the ferry line had to go to court to get the ship released. It and Iliopoulos eventually reached a deal that he found acceptable; despite its alleged deficiencies, the *Snaefell* went on to become a workhorse of the Seajets fleet.

By the late 2000s, Iliopoulos had augmented his passenger operations with a major presence in the oil trade. In 2008, a marine publication reported that he'd gone on a "buying spree," picking up eight older tankers. One of them was the *Elli*, which would later come to grief off the Yemeni coast; another was the *Brillante*, which Iliopoulos acquired for $46 million, far more than his other purchases. He paid for it with a mortgage from Piraeus Bank, one of Greece's largest lenders, which seemed to have provided Iliopoulos with much of his financing since he came into the industry. Iliopoulos's assets weren't assembled under a single corporate umbrella, making it difficult for Veale and Conner to determine their full extent. Like other Greek shipowners, he held his vessels inside a wide array of shell companies with generic names: Sea Ventures Shipping, Aegean Jet Company, Karite Shipmanagement, to cite a few. But he was undoubtedly a significant player.

Not that Iliopoulos bore any resemblance to the polished, polyglot operators who dominate the top ranks of shipping. Overweight, with long, stringy hair and an unruly beard, he was certainly no Aristotle Onassis. One negotiating partner recalled being shocked by his manners at a business dinner, where Iliopoulos barked over subordinates and carried on conversations with his mouth full of food. Another businessman arrived for a meeting at his office to find Iliopoulos in a tracksuit, sprawled on a sofa. And while many Greek shipowners serve as prominent patrons of the arts or other worthy causes, his main interest outside of work remained rally racing. Seajets sponsored a major race, the Acropolis Rally, and Iliopoulos frequently competed himself, taking the wheel of a souped-up Ford with "MARIO" printed in huge white letters across the windshield. He posted videos of his performances to Facebook, depicting him skidding around sharp bends at hairraising speed, trailing clouds of dust. He remained a strong driver even in middle age. The racing press often referred to him by a nickname: "Super Mario."

The summons requiring Iliopoulos to testify in the *Brillante* case marked him out in a different way from the rest of the Greek shipping world. For decades, Piraeus's maritime elite had engaged in a vigorous effort to insert layers of intermediation between themselves and what actually occurs at sea. Shell ownership, management companies, crewing agencies—all had the benefit of diffusing responsibility, whether for something as quotidian as paying taxes or as grave as losing a ship and its crew. Being called to appear in a foreign court, where the shipowners of Piraeus had no influence, was extremely rare. Being directly accused of fraud was even more so.

In a statement prepared ahead of his testimony, Iliopoulos made clear that he viewed the allegations against him as an affront. "The suggestion that I arranged for a party of foreign intruders to board a ship and detonate an explosive device is as desperate as it is extraordinary," Iliopoulos wrote. "I am a respectable businessman, welcomed by such individuals as the Archbishop of Athens and the Vice-President of Greece. Yet I am being vilified," he continued, "as though I were a criminal."

CHAPTER 19

AN UNRELIABLE WITNESS

arios Iliopoulos marched up to the witness box with the swagger of a professional wrestler approaching the ring, his unshaven features twisted into a scowl, arms swinging by his sides, untucked shirt stretched over an ample stomach. He sat down in front of a microphone in the corner of the stall, a translator at his side. Outside the room, an electronic sign listed the participants in the pretrial hearing—*Suez Fortune Investments Ltd v. Talbot Underwriting Ltd & Ors*—and the day's date: April 11, 2016.

The space was among the larger venues in the Rolls Building, one of the busiest dedicated commercial courthouses in the world. On any given day, the modern complex on the fringes of London's legal district might host an indebted shopkeeper declaring bankruptcy, hedge funds fighting over the scraps of long-dead banks, and, in the biggest rooms on the top floors, Russian billionaires suing each other for possession of mining rights in Central Africa. Despite London's status as an international legal hub, a place where judges are deemed reliable enough to settle the biggest of big-money disputes, some of the capital's courthouses are a century old and infested with rats. The vast Royal Courts of Justice, for example, is sometimes used in movies for its Hogwarts-worthy spires, winding stone staircases, and halls lined with busts of ancient grandees. By comparison, the Rolls Building can seem as sterile and bright as an operating theater. Behind Iliopoulos, a contemporary take on the Royal Coat of Arms—a lion and unicorn prancing alongside a decorative shield—gleamed on the rear wall. In place of dusty bookshelves full of legal tomes, there were computer screens and audio equipment. The walls were painted beige, the floors covered with wall-to-wall carpet in a corporate gray.

From his seat, Iliopoulos looked out at a phalanx of attorneys, maybe two dozen in total, divided down the middle by an invisible line separating the opposing legal teams. Unlike in the US, British lawyers fall into two distinct camps: barristers and solicitors, with different skills and training. In the front row were the barristers, trial specialists whose job it would be to address the judge and question the witness. Behind them sat the solicitors, who deal directly with clients and do most of the preparation for a case. The most senior solicitors sat immediately behind the barristers. On Talbot's side they included Chris Zavos, who was absorbed in one of the dozens of ringed binders of documents arrayed on the lawyers' tables, which were so heavy they had to be hauled in on trolleys. Behind were the ranks of junior solicitors, associates, and clerks, whispering and passing notes. All the attorneys wore suits: the commercial courts had long since dispensed with the white horsehair wigs and starched collars still used elsewhere in London. Finally, at the back, there was a single row for spectators, largely empty apart from Veale, Conner, and a gray-haired older woman. Cynthia Mockett had traveled to London to see Iliopoulos in the flesh for the first time.

The judge, a stern, owlish figure wearing a simple dark robe, was last to appear in the room. Outside it, his name was Julian Flaux. Inside, he was the Honorable Mr. Justice Flaux. The barristers greeted him as "my Lord," in keeping with English tradition. Flaux had a fierce reputation. Lawyers who came before him ill prepared could expect a dressing-down, and he presided over his court with the authority of the most feared teacher at school, the one no student would dare mess with.

Iliopoulos confirmed his identity and swore an oath to tell the truth, leaning in to listen as the man seated to his left translated the court clerk's words into Greek. Despite studying in the UK in his youth, Iliopoulos had said his English wasn't strong enough to withstand the rigors of cross-examination. The formalities dealt with, Talbot's barrister, Jonathan Gaisman, rose to his feet and began to press the shipowner on the subject of the day's hearing: the missing company archive containing information about the *Brillante Virtuoso*'s final voyage. Why had Iliopoulos given up possession of the hard drive that contained it, knowing its contents were likely to be vital to his insurance claim? Why hadn't he made copies?

Iliopoulos argued that his efforts to retrieve the records were hampered by a mistrust of computers. "I'm the kind of person that never touches technology," he explained through his translator. He wasn't even comfortable using a credit card, he said, let alone dealing with electronic archives. Then he pleaded ignorance of the very words Gaisman was using: "I still don't understand the question. If you can just simplify it for me?"

The barrister paced up and down as Iliopoulos spoke, occasionally pushing a thick pair of glasses up the bridge of his nose. As a Queen's Counsel, an honor awarded to only the top barristers, Gaisman was a courtroom veteran, with a deep voice and a bald dome of a head. He made no effort to hide his skepticism of Iliopoulos's answers. The shipowner, in response, radiated contempt for his inquisitor as the day wore on. "Your question is irrelevant, and I disagree," Iliopoulos snapped at Gaisman at one point.

The missing records were from a company called Worldwide Green Tankers (WWGT), one of the myriad off-the-shelf corporate entities Iliopoulos used to manage his fleet. They were said to contain a cache of email communications about the *Brillante* and Iliopoulos's other businesses, though the insurers had never seen it. While Iliopoulos admitted controlling WWGT, he said it was now defunct and the businessman in possession of the archive was refusing to hand it over. He recounted a series of face-to-face meetings in which he claimed to have pleaded for its return. The story seemed to get more complicated with each telling. First, the businessman had agreed to release it, then changed his mind, then expressed concerns that handing it over would leave him open to lawsuits, then refused to discuss the matter any further.

The day ended in a bad-tempered stalemate. The shipowner and the barrister resumed their duel the next morning, with Iliopoulos earning a reprimand from Judge Flaux for failing to give satisfactory answers to Gaisman's questions. "No, no, no," Flaux exclaimed in frustration. "I really am going to draw a line under this. You are not answering the question you have been asked."

Gradually Iliopoulos grew more animated, thumping his fist on the desk in front of him as he squinted in Gaisman's direction. "I'm used to these unreasonable expressions of yours," he said in response to one provocation. He accused Gaisman of misleading the court, and the underwriters of running "secret investigations" in Greece, trying to access private flight records and medical details. "You committed crimes," he said, referring to the Greek criminal complaint against the insurers. Soon Flaux's patience frayed further. He asked Iliopoulos again to focus on what he was being asked. "I'm not the slightest bit interested in hearing you repeating insults to Mr. Gaisman or insults to the underwriters," Flaux declared. "You have come to give evidence."

This sort of open hostility was rarely seen in London's commercial courtrooms, and Gaisman was clearly enjoying himself, relishing the opportunity for verbal combat. At one point, he turned around and leaned over to where Zavos and the other insurance lawyers were sitting. "He's good, isn't he?" Gaisman whispered.

Gaisman steered the cross-examination to the theft of the insurers' emails that had exposed Gerry Lallis. The hacked files had mysteriously ended up in Iliopoulos's hands. In fact, the lawyer who'd found the envelope containing printouts of the messages represented the same businessman who Iliopoulos claimed was refusing to return the WWGT archive. Wasn't it true, Gaisman suggested, that the main beneficiary of the stolen emails, and the subsequent criminal complaint in Greece, was Iliopoulos himself?

At first Iliopoulos was reluctant to engage with the question. "I will not play Mr. Gaisman's game," he protested.

The barrister tried a more direct approach. "I'm putting it to you," Gaisman said, staring at the witness, that it was "you who sponsored the illegal acquisition of these emails, Mr. Iliopoulos. Would you like to comment or not?"

Iliopoulos answered in a steady voice: "If there is any responsibility for any of the assumptions in the allegations against me, you will be held responsible for those."

At this, Flaux erupted. "You will not use this court to threaten counsel or English lawyers. You will behave yourself!" he thundered. Iliopoulos tried to explain that he was talking about legal consequences, and that he was merely protecting his reputation, but the damage was done. "You have just, Mr. Iliopoulos, exposed your motive very clearly," the judge said.

At the end of his second day on the stand, Iliopoulos asked if he could make a statement to Flaux, through his translator. "I'm a very emotional man," he said. "I would like to apologize for anything that's not right." Then he walked down the aisle muttering to himself. Though it was hard to make out, it sounded like he was saying: "Wikipedia . . . Wikipedia." It had been one of the most extraordinary court sessions anyone present could remember. Conner and Veale were buzzing, chuckling to themselves in the corridor outside. Iliopoulos's performance was plainly disastrous for his case.

It took fifteen minutes for everyone to file out of the courtroom and into the elevators, headed for the lobby of the Rolls Building. The courthouse had a central entrance hall decorated with a large drawing of old and new London, overlaid together in a panorama. Iliopoulos, with his legal team in tow, passed a line of counters where clerks milled around, either fetching or delivering bundles of paperwork. The space was narrow enough that the two sides of a lawsuit couldn't help but rub shoulders with each other on the way out. As Iliopoulos made for the exit, he spotted Zavos and approached the lawyer for a brief, animated conversation. Later, Veale and Conner would learn that he'd asked Zavos, with his conspicuously Hellenic name, if he spoke Greek. Zavos said he didn't.

It was only as Iliopoulos passed the metal detectors that he noticed four police officers wearing stab vests waiting at the edge of the lobby. They were from the City of London Police. "Mr. Iliopoulos?" the tallest of them said. "I'm arresting you for conspiracy to commit fraud." The shipowner looked surprised, but offered no resistance as they led him outside, toward an unmarked blue sedan. Veale and Conner, who suspected the arrest was coming, had been waiting on a street corner to get an unobstructed view. They watched in silence as Iliopoulos was guided into the backseat and driven away.

The police had planned the arrest carefully. As soon as Iliopoulos was in custody, a team swept his hotel room, looking for documents or electronic devices that might contain evidence about the *Brillante*. Detectives were waiting for him at a bunker-like police station in the City, where they asked him to empty his pockets. True to his courtroom testimony about avoiding technology, Iliopoulos wasn't even carrying a phone. Officers also found nothing of substance at his hotel. It was as though he'd been expecting the room to be searched.

In an interrogation room, the detectives tried for hours to get Iliopoulos to talk. Yet to each of their questions, his response was the same: "No comment." He'd clearly decided to give them nothing, perhaps betting the police didn't have enough evidence to hold him. That turned out to be a shrewd decision. He was released that night without charge, and was soon on a plane back to Athens. The British police had taken their shot at Iliopoulos, and missed.

But the drama of his appearance at the Rolls Building had other consequences. A few days later, Flaux oversaw another hearing in the Talbot case, in which the judge made his feelings about Iliopoulos clear. "He demonstrated himself an aggressive and arrogant man," Flaux told the shipowner's lawyers. "He was rude to everyone here, including me."

Iliopoulos's barrister made a final plea for understanding. "Yes, he gets upset," she said. "Yes, he takes the case very personally." Iliopoulos felt the London insurance market was mounting a campaign against him, she went on. "He takes exception to the allegation that he had the ship deliberately set on fire." Flaux was unpersuaded. In his written judgment, issued several weeks later, he delivered a scathing assessment of Iliopoulos's testimony, describing him as "evasive and non-responsive and, on occasions, aggressive and threatening." Overall, Flaux had formed a clear view that "he was not telling the truth." He dismissed the convoluted explanation offered for the missing archive as a "fabricated story" and "a complete invention."

As for Iliopoulos's promise to make sure the insurers and their agents were "held responsible" for any allegations against him, the judge was unequivocal: "With this intemperate and menacing evidence, Mr. Iliopoulos lost any remaining shred of credibility." It was clear, Flaux wrote, that his real intention was to build up a case against the insurers in Greece, the same diversionary tactic that had been employed in the *Alexandros T* affair.

Since Iliopoulos had deliberately breached a court order requiring him to deliver the archive, Flaux ruled that his claim against Talbot and the other insurers in the hull syndicate would be "struck out." His participation in the *Brillante* lawsuit was over. The litigation, however, was far from dead. In the confusing netherworld of insurance law, the owner of a wrecked ship wasn't the only one who could pursue compensation from Lloyd's. Instead, an owner's claim could be "assigned" to another entity that had suffered a loss when the vessel was destroyed.

That's precisely what happened in the case of *Suez Fortune v. Talbot Underwriting*. Iliopoulos's company had financed the $46 million deal to buy the *Brillante* with a loan from the Greek lender Piraeus Bank. It was later refinanced, leaving him owing more than $60 million. At some point after 2011, the bank had decided it was not going to be repaid and wrote off the entire debt. As a result, it was suing the Talbot syndicate for about $80 million on the basis that it was "co-assured"—entitled, in other words, to continue the claim on the *Brillante*'s hull policy without Iliopoulos. In a twist so confusing that only Lloyd's insiders could contemplate it without inducing a migraine, Piraeus Bank *also* had separate insurance covering losses on its loan book. That meant that even if the bank lost the *Brillante* case, it could reclaim most of the money from a different policy. The upshot: *Suez Fortune v. Talbot Underwriting* had become an argument about which group of insurers would be left holding the bill.

Zavos and his colleagues were pleased with Flaux's ruling. Veale and Conner, however, were more circumspect. Between the destruction of the money-losing *Brillante*, Piraeus Bank giving up on collecting his loan, and no longer facing the burden of participating in a costly lawsuit, Iliopoulos was, at least, tens of millions of dollars better off. That was before whatever he might have received out of the more than $30 million paid to the *Brillante*'s salvors. "Not a penny lost in Greece" was how Conner summed it up. Iliopoulos's position had improved so much that he and Veale suspected his disastrous performance in London might have been intentional, to execute an elegant exit from the legal proceedings. "It's genius," Conner told anyone who would listen.

But the insurers' legal team had other priorities. They still had a trump card to play against Piraeus Bank. If they could prove that the *Brillante* had been destroyed through the "willful misconduct" of its owner, the hull insurance policy would be declared void. But for that to happen, they needed positive evidence of fraud. Five years after the attack, they still had almost none.

Iliopoulos's arrest in London was big news in Greece. In the days that followed, an Athens-based lawyer at Zavos's firm, Norton Rose, was contacted by a man called Christos. (His name was not disclosed in legal documents describing these interactions and has been changed here.) Christos said he was representing another individual who'd seen media reports of Iliopoulos's legal troubles and claimed to have important information about the *Brillante*. But, Christos made clear to the lawyer, that person would need financial compensation before he agreed to help the insurers.

Paul Cunningham called a meeting in London to discuss the offer. After the email hack and the threat to Gerry Lallis, everyone working on the case was wary. Veale fretted that this new source could be a plant, sent by Iliopoulos to trick them into handing over cash so he could accuse the insurers of bribery. Still, Veale was keen to meet Christos and his client to sound them out, and didn't think it was the type of encounter that was best handled by a lawyer. Zavos, however, was adamant that he should be in charge.

Apparently, Christos and the other man were seeking as much as $10 million. There was no way the insurers could consent to such a demand, but Conner urged them to ignore the numbers. "Don't even talk about the figures," he told Cunningham. The most important thing was to sit down with the guy to find out whether he was for real. If anyone knew how to handle complicated witnesses, it was Metal Mickey. After some debate, Cunningham agreed to a compromise. Veale and Conner would fly to Athens to meet the source, accompanied by John Liberopoulos, the local Norton Rose lawyer who'd received the first approach. The two detectives decided to give the man a code name to protect his anonymity in case of another security breach, as they would have during their years at the Met. He would be known as X-Ray.

CHAPTER 20

BEARING GIFTS

V eale and Conner arrived in Greece a few days before their meeting with X-Ray. They needed time to assess what they were walking into. It was early September 2016, and despite the country's economic troubles, Athens was lively, its cafés crowded with prosperous residents returned from summer retreats on the islands. The venue the detectives had chosen for their rendezvous was familiar to every well-heeled Athenian. Located right on Syntagma Square, the city's central plaza, the Hotel Grande Bretagne was a five-star palace favored by statesmen and film stars, with a reputation for discreet luxury—even if, in recent years, its managers had been periodically forced to pull down metal shutters to protect guests from chaotic antigovernment protests taking place outside.

Veale and Conner hadn't selected the Grande Bretagne for its amenities. They were more interested in its security profile. They liked that it was busy and public, with several popular restaurants and a stream of people coming and going throughout the day. It was also across the street from the Greek parliament and a stone's throw from several embassies, which guaranteed a heavy police presence nearby. Even the most determined criminal, Veale and Conner figured, would hesitate to plan an ambush there. If X-Ray really had crucial new information on the *Brillante* case, it wasn't inconceivable that someone would try to stop him from sharing it, perhaps violently. Nor could they be sure that he wasn't secretly working for Iliopoulos, sent to lure them into a trap.

The same level of scrutiny applied to picking a meeting place within the hotel. Ideally it would be somewhere relatively inaccessible, forcing attackers to navigate a substantial chunk of the building to reach it—and, just as important, to get back out. After studying the Grande Bretagne's floor plans, Veale and Conner settled on a small conference suite on a mezzanine level above the lobby. The room had thick wooden doors, and the detectives noted with satisfaction that they opened slowly even when pulled very hard. If assailants tried to burst in, that momentary delay could buy them just enough time to get themselves and X-Ray onto the floor.

As a further precaution, they were staying at a different hotel in town, in case the location of their appointment leaked. Neither spoke much as they arrived at the Grande Bretagne on the morning of the meeting, stepping from the square into a lobby decorated with gilt-edge paintings of nautical scenes. Both Veale and Conner tended to get quiet before an important engagement. In their preparatory conversations, they had gamed out the likely scenarios, formulating a clear plan for dealing with X-Ray, assuming they got to the point of actually speaking. They would be friendly but firm, making clear that they, not he, would decide exactly how the meeting would proceed. What Veale called "silly games"—providing inconsistent information, waffling about the veracity of an account, threatening to walk out—would not be tolerated. The only objectives that mattered were those of the investigation, and if X-Ray wanted money he would have to meet them. "We are going to drain him for everything he knows," Veale told his clients. Conner used a different shorthand for how he hoped the relationship would work. "He should live to regret the day he ever met us," he said.

In the meeting room, the pair went over their plan a final time with John Liberopoulos, the Norton Rose lawyer. Although Veale and Conner would have preferred to be on their own, with full control of what happened on their side of the table, Zavos had insisted Liberopoulos sit in. They hoped he wouldn't say much. As the clock neared 10:00 a.m., Liberopoulos went to the lobby to wait. Soon he came back, accompanied by X-Ray and his adviser Christos. Everyone introduced themselves. A marine engineer by training, X-Ray's name was Vassilios Theodorou. Over six feet tall, with huge arms, long hair, and a rough beard, Theodorou hadn't been hard to pick out in the lobby. He looked almost like a real-life version of Bluto, the hirsute villain in the *Popeye* cartoons. This was a guy who could look after himself, Veale thought as he sized Theodorou up.

The five men sat down around a rectangular table. Theodorou and Christos told the detectives that they didn't want any notes taken; they were willing to have only an informal conversation to gauge whether they wanted to go further. Veale politely refused, explaining that he needed to have at least a limited record of what was said. He was willing to accept their demand, however, that nothing discussed in the meeting would be used as evidence in court. His and Conner's priority was to determine what Theodorou knew—and to verify that he hadn't been sent by Iliopoulos to intimidate or entrap them, or otherwise interfere with their investigation. If his knowledge was as significant as he claimed, and he really was willing to help the insurers, they could conduct more structured interviews later.

Speaking in a mixture of English and Greek, with Liberopoulos translating, Theodorou began by explaining how he came to be involved with the *Brillante*. He said that in 2011 he'd been working in Cuba when he got a call from Vassilios Vergos, the limping Greek salvor whose company, Poseidon Salvage, had set up a branch in Yemen. There was lucrative employment for him in Aden, Theodorou recalled Vergos saying—a salvage job that "hadn't happened yet." Theodorou flew back to Athens, where he said he'd attended a meeting with Iliopoulos to plan what would happen to the tanker. He'd then gone to Yemen to work with Vergos, where he claimed to have been privy to the most intimate details of the operation. As a member of Poseidon's salvage crew, Theodorou said he'd been one of the first people on board the *Brillante* after the crew fled the burning ship, its deck so hot that it singed the soles of his boots. Yet despite providing Vergos with what he described as crucial assistance, Theodorou said he'd never been paid.

Veale and Conner had been in the investigative game long enough to know that it was critical to keep a poker face when interviewing an informant. Showing obvious surprise or enthusiasm could influence what a source said next, or give him unhelpful ideas about the value of his information.

They kept their expressions fixed as Theodorou continued his story. But privately, they were both thinking the same thing. If he was telling the truth, they were on the verge of a breakthrough.

Theodorou knew he needed to prove his bona fides, and had brought some evidence. After taking a laptop from his bag, he pulled up a series of photographs depicting the salvage of the *Brillante*. Though they didn't say it, all of them were new to the detectives. Theodorou told them he had more than 750 in total. Before he would consider parting with the archive, or providing a comprehensive statement, he wanted some assurances. In the years since the attack, he said, Iliopoulos had threatened him repeatedly to keep quiet. He added that Vergos had warned him that if he ever revealed what he knew, "we'll end up in jail, but you'll end up in the ground." If the insurers wanted his help, Theodorou would need immunity from prosecution and assistance securing a new identity. Of course, there would also need to be a great deal of money involved—"millions," as Christos put it.

Veale and Conner couldn't make any guarantees on behalf of law enforcement. But money was something they might be able to provide, given time to verify the accuracy of what Theodorou had told them. Soon afterward they drew the meeting to a close. They'd gone some way toward establishing his credibility, and that he was willing in principle to cooperate. For a first interview, that was more than enough. The detectives escorted Theodorou and Christos into the lobby and out to the street, to make sure the two men weren't seen hanging around the hotel.

Back in the meeting room they waited for Liberopoulos to leave. After he walked out, Veale and Conner looked at each other for a moment in silence, then burst out laughing. The weight of the last several days had lifted. Finally, they had found a real source. In London, Zavos and the other lawyers had endlessly debated experts' reports, arguing over whether this explosives specialist or that marine engineer made a more persuasive case. As well credentialed as they were, none of those experts had even a speck of firsthand knowledge. None of them was there. Theodorou was, and he could substantiate what the detectives had so far only surmised.

Conner opened up his notebook to record all he could remember while it was still fresh. After being asked not to take notes at all, he hadn't wanted to spook Theodorou by writing too much during the meeting. "Motivation: revenge and money," he wrote.

Veale needed to get his hands on some cash. It was March 2017, some six months after their first meeting, and he was preparing for another conversation with Theodorou. This one would occur on neutral ground: a hotel in Zurich, where he and Conner could be more confident they weren't being watched. Switzerland had other advantages. As they explained to Theodorou, who feared being detained if he left Greece, its status as a non-EU country meant it was beyond the scope of a European Arrest Warrant. British police had no power there.

In the intervening months they had learned a great deal from the Greek. Theodorou claimed to have actually bought some of the guns carried by the supposed pirates who boarded the *Brillante*, paying 1,500 euros for three Kalashnikov-style rifles in Aden before the attack. Much of the damage that had rendered the vessel useless, he told them, had been inflicted by Vergos's salvage team—himself included. Rather than trying to save the ship, he said they'd gone around the vessel smashing open tanks and pipes, providing plenty of fuel for the fire that the gunmen had started. The salvors' firefighting efforts had been entirely for show, he said; their job was to ensure that the *Brillante* was consumed by the blaze.

Despite all he'd told them, Veale and Conner still didn't have Theodorou's full cooperation, nor did they have access to the photographs that could corroborate his account. They had suggested he go to the police; if he gave a formal statement to British law enforcement, the insurers might be able to obtain it via a court order. But Theodorou said he had no interest in doing so unless Veale and Conner could guarantee he wouldn't be prosecuted. They couldn't, obviously, which left money as their only lever. During their second meeting, Christos had suggested a reward of 10 percent of the insured value of the *Brillante*, in exchange for the photos and full download of what his client knew. That amounted to the better part of $10 million, a figure Veale and Conner viewed as preposterously high. Theodorou's adviser then made a series of other proposals, all in the millions. To each one Veale responded with a mock-outraged "fuck off," though in their notes, which might have to be entered into evidence one day, they employed a gentler euphemism: "immediately rejected." At times the discussions had grown tense. "The only reason we're here is because my client is willing to help you," Christos remarked at one point, exasperated. Conner corrected him. "The only reason we're here is because you blew up our ship."

Though they were still far from an agreement, the detectives had succeeded in talking Christos and Theodorou into a much more realistic range of numbers, and Veale thought they might be able to close a deal during their upcoming meeting. To show they were serious he wanted to arrive with a pile of banknotes, big enough to look impressive. That was how Veale found himself early one morning at London City Airport's foreign exchange counter, asking for all the US dollars they had.

The clerk wasn't sure he'd heard correctly. Veale repeated the request: He wanted as much cash as they could give him. The staff on duty began cleaning out their drawers. The total amount of American currency they had on-site turned out to be about $5,000, in bills as large as $100 and as small as $5. The clerks formed the bills into a brick secured with plastic cling film, and Veale zipped it into his backpack. After it went through the bag scanner at security, one of the guards pulled him aside. Even before a flight to Switzerland, departing from a terminal favored by the bankers of Canary Wharf, an Escobar-style stack of bills was something airport staff didn't see often. Though it was perfectly legal to carry any amount under 10,000 euros onto a plane without making a declaration, Veale had a white lie ready anyway. His wife's birthday was coming up, he told the guard, and he planned to buy her a watch in Zurich as a gift. He didn't want to spoil the surprise by having the transaction show up on their joint credit card. To help sell his cover story, he'd even put a Rolex catalog in his bag before leaving home. After consulting with a colleague, the guard waved Veale through to his gate.

Conner was flying separately, traveling with Paul Cunningham, the underwriter from Talbot. Conner had argued with Veale about the wisdom of bringing Cunningham on the trip. Theodorou had good reason to be nervous about helping the insurers, and discussions with him needed to be conducted with extreme delicacy. Any mistake might scare him off, perhaps permanently. Cunningham would have no idea how to carry himself, Conner worried; he handled insurance claims, not confidential sources. He'd never dealt with an informant in his life. But Veale thought it was important to have a representative of the insurers hand over the money, and directly receive the information it purchased. Cunningham was coming, he told Conner.

The three men met up at a hotel in Zurich, where the detectives unwrapped the cash and began restacking it on the bed. To make more of an impression, they informed Cunningham, they wanted to put the hundreds on the outside, hiding the tens and fives in the middle. Cunningham was clearly nervous, filling the air with jittery small talk as they worked. To keep the mood light Veale and Conner joked around, talking about how Ray Charles, the blind soul legend, insisted on being paid for gigs in $1 bills so he couldn't be cheated.

To give Cunningham time to settle in, and Veale and Conner a chance to assess the risks to themselves and Theodorou, they'd again arrived a couple of days before their meeting. Among other tasks, they wanted to visit an old friend of Conner's, a prolific gun collector, to quiz him on Swiss firearms laws. If someone flew in from Greece looking to do harm, how easy would it be for him to get a gun? But they also took the opportunity to rib Cunningham a bit—partly to pierce his anxiety, and partly because they couldn't resist making him the straight man in their ex-copper Laurel and Hardy routine. "I'll take the Sig," Veale said, theatrically, as Conner's friend showed off his cache of weapons. "Mick will have the Glock. Paul, what do you want?" It took Cunningham a long moment to realize Veale was joking.

For their discussion with Theodorou, they'd booked a meeting room at a blandly contemporary Radisson overlooking Zurich Airport, Switzerland's primary international air hub. There were plenty of police in the vicinity, and Veale appreciated that the hotel's elevators, situated in a central atrium, had glass doors, so he could see who was coming up. He'd mentally mapped the route to the fire escape in case they needed to get out in a hurry. Conner and Cunningham waited in the reception area for Theodorou to arrive. Accompanied again by Christos, he strolled in at the appointed hour, looking tough and confident. The last thing Conner wanted was for his client to feel intimidated. "Imagine him in prison," he joked to Cunningham as Theodorou approached. "He's just another bare bum in the shower." The underwriter broke into a grin.

After some pleasantries in the meeting room, Cunningham put the money on the table. "This is just to cover your expenses," he said. Christos moved to take the stack of bills, but Theodorou stopped him, pushing it back toward Cunningham. Accepting the cash, everyone knew, would create at least some obligation, which made Theodorou pause. It was a scenario that Veale and Conner had planned for. Following instructions they had given him beforehand, Cunningham pushed the money forward again. This time Theodorou didn't stop Christos.

Once the money changed hands, Veale knew he had an opening. He asked Theodorou to open his Fujitsu laptop, with access to his database of photos. Before discussing further payment, Veale explained, the insurers needed to take copies of some of them to verify their authenticity. From his backpack he pulled out a USB key, still in its stiff plastic packaging, as well as a penknife to open it up. Christos flinched in his seat at the sight of the knife, prompting Theodorou to burst into a laugh that eased some of the tension in the room. Taking control of the laptop, Veale plugged in the USB. He would be allowed to download only a small part of the directory, a sample set of twenty-three photos and videos from the *Brillante* salvage. For the rest, Christos said, the insurers would need to hand over a lot more money. As Christos emphasized the point again and again, Veale shot Conner a glance: they weren't going to get any further that day.

After wrapping up the discussion, Veale, Conner, and Cunningham returned to their hotel. Cunningham was pale with fatigue and nerves, and the detectives bought him a beer to calm him down. As they drank, Cunningham asked Veale what he would have done with his knife if Theodorou had gotten violent. "I'd have stabbed him," he deadpanned.

At his desk in London, Veale had time for a detailed examination of the photos he'd downloaded. He ran them through a forensic program called Proof

Finder, to confirm they were taken when Theodorou said they were: the day after the attack on the *Brillante*. Viewed sequentially, they showed something remarkable. Early on July 6, the inferno that began several hours before appeared to have died out, with only faint wisps of smoke visible from the salvage tugs attending to the tanker. Yet in images taken later that day, thick black plumes billowed from its hull. In between, it appeared, the salvage crews had reignited the fire, just as Theodorou said.

While the photos were tantalizing, Veale and Conner would need more from Theodorou. They thought he wanted to make a deal. Theodorou was a heavy smoker, and during their meetings Conner always accompanied him for cigarette breaks outside, chatting with him about his girlfriend, his tax problems, and anything else that was on his mind. Theodorou seemed impressed by Conner's police background, and his familiarity with the seamier sides of business. During one of their exchanges, he told Conner that he'd be a valuable asset in the Athens underworld. Conner was pleased by the comment. It was a sign that he'd succeeded in building a rapport, a skill he'd honed over decades handling sources. Theodorou reminded Conner of many of the informants he'd dealt with as a cop. He was a chancer, a percentage man, instinctively weighing the prospects for financial gain in any situation. He wasn't someone who would give up tens of thousands by insisting on millions. "Tell me, Michael," he'd once asked. "Will I get anything?" Conner gave him the only truthful answer: "I don't know." Theodorou replied that he wouldn't have believed Conner if he said anything different.

But in two further meetings, they still couldn't get to an agreement. At one point, in May 2017, Theodorou suggested he'd accept $65,000 for the full image database. That was a sum Veale and Conner could work with. But afterward Christos corrected him. In fact, he said, the price was $3 million. They held a final discussion that July, back in Athens. In a meeting room at the Grande Bretagne, Christos kept insisting on seven-digit figures. He also added a new twist. "We're not stupid," he said. He and Theodorou knew the insurers would try to use the photos they already had in court, whether they came to a final accord or not. To make that more difficult, he claimed the images Theodorou had allowed Veale to download had been selected carefully: "Some good, some not so good, some to confuse." The same was true,

Christos said, of what his client had told them, although Theodorou himself insisted that he'd been truthful. The only way to get a clear account would be to pay up.

There was nothing else to say, and Veale and Conner were soon on a flight back to London. They were deeply frustrated. Theodorou had helped fill in some gaps in the story they were trying to piece together, and provided a taste of evidence that could make a real difference. But they were still a long way from knowing the full truth about the *Brillante* or the murder of David Mockett—let alone being able to prove it.

CHAPTER 21

I'M NOT AFRAID

The town of Donges sits near the very end of the Loire, where the silty flows of France's longest river enter the Atlantic. It has none of the medieval charm that can be found farther upstream: no handsome stone buildings or gracious boulevards, elegant bistros or fairy-tale fortresses. Instead, the primary feature of Donges is its oil refinery, one of the largest in the country. Allan Marquez, the former *Brillante Virtuoso* crewman, had gotten a good view as his vessel approached in July 2017, not that there was much to see. A vast collection of pipework and exhaust towers, the facility sprawled heedlessly across the river's right bank, ringed with a perimeter of razor wire that gleamed in the summer sun. Marquez's arrival, on one of the hundreds of vessels that moored there every year, was routine. France's domestic oil reserves are minimal, and to produce the gasoline demanded by its consumers the Donges refinery relied on a steady flow of tankers making their way up the estuary—all of them crewed by men like Marquez.

After months on the oceans, it would be Marquez's last port for a while. He was booked on a flight to Taipei, connecting onward to Manila for a well-deserved break. Trips home are momentous events for Filipino seafarers, not only because they're a rare chance to spend time with the families for whom they work so hard. The visits also serve as occasions to distribute the relative prosperity afforded by their wages, and, in performing that ritual, to show off a bit. Gifts would be all but obligatory, for children and parents of course, but also aunts, uncles, cousins, friends—concentric circles of obligation for every returning sailor. The women might be hoping for perfume; the men, cigarettes and watches, the kids, T-shirts bearing the names of foreign brands or places. While Marquez was home, few of the relatives he spent time with would be likely to reach into their pockets. Whether for a meal in a restaurant or tickets to the cinema, it was understood that the visiting seafarer picked up the bill. It could get expensive, but the opportunity to help his family was what drew Marquez to the sea in the first place. The isolation, the long hours, the imperious captains—there was no other reason to endure it all. He would remain in the Philippines for a little over a month before beginning his next assignment.

Shortly before his flight, Marquez saw that he had a Facebook message from someone he didn't know—a reporter at Bloomberg, based in London. "I'm working on a story," the note began, "about a ship called the *Brillante Virtuoso*." The name got Marquez's attention. For over half a decade he'd tried not to think about his time on the vessel. Assigned to the evening watch on the night the *Brillante* drifted off the Yemeni coast, awaiting the arrival of its security team, Marquez had been the first crew member to spot an unidentified boat approaching. He was the one who'd been told to extend a ladder and let the men inside come aboard, initiating the chain of events that would force Marquez and his crewmates to flee for their lives. It had been the most harrowing experience of his maritime career.

The journalist and a colleague—the authors of this book—had been trying to reach Marquez for weeks. They'd read the statements he gave to investigators, revealing his small but critical part in the events of July 2011, and wanted to speak to him before publishing their article. He could easily have ignored the message. In addition to the psychological impact of reliving what happened to him, Marquez had his livelihood to consider. Shipping is not an industry that looks kindly on employees having unauthorized conversations with the media, and his wife wouldn't want him doing anything that could jeopardize the work their family depended upon. Manila's manning agencies employed thousands of seafarers, any of whom would be happy to replace Marquez at a moment's notice.

The *Brillante Virtuoso* at sea

The main deck
of the tanker

Fleeing the
Brillante after
the attack

US Navy sailors rescuing the crew

Crew members aboard the USS *Philippine Sea*

The *Brillante* after the fire

Wreckage on the bridge

David Mockett in Yemen

The Mocketts on their wedding day

David and Cynthia

Roy Facey (left), hiking on a Yemeni island

Mockett's car after the bombing

A Poseidon salvage tug alongside the *Brillante*

Ringing the Lutine
Bell at Lloyd's

Private investigators Richard Veale (left) and Michael Conner

Poseidon's owner, Vassilios Vergos

Marios Iliopoulos, the owner of the *Brillante*

Mockett in
the garden

Mockett's grave
in Devon

DAVID JOHN MOCKETT
27 MARCH 1946 – 20 JULY 2011
DEVOTED HUSBAND
DAD AND GRANDAD
ALWAYS MISSED
LOVED FOREVER

But something inside Marquez made him want to respond—a feeling more powerful than his fear. Later that day, he picked up the phone to call the reporter who'd contacted him. The journalist had barely spoken when Marquez's words began pouring out. He'd been keeping his story to himself for a long time.

"I'm afraid of the owner of the vessel," Marquez said, "that they would kill me if I told the truth." He spoke rapidly, in uneven but comprehensible English. "They said they would kill my family."

The reporter tried to get Marquez to slow down, asking who, exactly, he was referring to. "Do you mean Marios? Marios Iliopoulos?"

"The Greek owner," Marquez replied. "When I made a true statement, they said make it new."

The reporter again asked Marquez to clarify. "The man who threatened you, the owner, are you certain it was Marios Iliopoulos?"

"One hundred percent sure it was Mario," Marquez replied, using the shortened version of the shipowner's name. "He came, he looked for me, and he said, 'Change your story.' Or he will kill me." Terrified, Marquez said he'd lied in his statements to investigators, altering the details as he was instructed. It had taken him months to shake the trauma. "For a long time, I couldn't sleep," he said. "I was afraid for my family."

The reporter sent Marquez a photo of Iliopoulos, standing on the sidelines of a rally race, asking if he was sure the image matched the man who had told him to change his account. Marquez said it did—and that now he wanted to go on the record with the full truth. Several times, the reporter asked Marquez if he was sure he was comfortable being quoted by name in a story that would be read widely, including, certainly, by Iliopoulos. Marquez insisted, in that and subsequent conversations, that he was. In messages over Facebook he explained why. "im afraid to God," he wrote. "how long i can hide the truth in my conscience." He said he was ready to accept the consequences for speaking out. "As of now," he said, "im not afraid to die."

Early on a Saturday morning, in late August 2017, Marquez left his house in a modest subdivision on Manila's northern outskirts and boarded a train toward the center of the city. The article quoting him had been published in *Bloomberg Businessweek* the month before, prompting a flurry of calls to Marquez from London. A couple weeks earlier, a detective from the City of London Police had flown in to interview him at the British Embassy. Now he had an appointment with a group of men representing the *Brillante*'s insurers, who were waiting for him at the Dusit Thani hotel in Makati, Manila's financial district. They wanted Marquez to provide formal testimony, explaining exactly what happened to him on board the ship and afterward—and to identify where his previous statements were false.

Marquez knew what he was doing was dangerous. The oceans are perilous. Hundreds of seafarers are killed or go missing every year—crushed by heavy loads, scalded by faulty boilers, swept away by rogue waves. No police force in the world, let alone insurers from Lloyd's of London, could guarantee his protection at sea—where the loss of one more sailor, who happened to have crossed the interests of a powerful shipowner, might hardly be noticed. But his determination to tell the truth hadn't flagged. Like many Filipinos, Marquez was a devout Christian, and had come to think of his choice in religious terms. After committing the sin of lying, he now had a chance at redemption.

In the lobby of the Dusit Thani, Chris Zavos was getting anxious. It hadn't been easy to book time with Marquez; he had to finish a training course before returning to duty, and was free only on a weekend. Their session was supposed to begin first thing in the morning, but at 10:30 a.m. the sailor still hadn't arrived. The underwriters had hired an interpreter—Marquez's English, while serviceable for most occasions, wasn't quite up to a British legal proceeding—and she called him on his mobile to check where he was. "Will he be here?" Zavos asked.

Richard Veale and Michael Conner were trying to stay relaxed. Compared to much of what they'd dealt with in their investigation of the *Brillante*, a tardy witness was hardly a crisis. They were more perturbed at being stuck with Zavos, who needed to be present to collect a formal statement. Their relationship with him had been steadily worsening, to the point that Conner, who'd never been good at hiding his opinions of authority figures, spoke with Zavos only when absolutely necessary. It didn't help that some months earlier, Conner had written an angry email to Veale describing the lawyer as a "scorpion" determined to undermine them—and then sent it to Zavos by accident.

But as the morning ebbed away, the detectives began to get impatient too—and to worry that their witness might be having last-minute doubts. "I'm going to walk out," Conner announced, to see if he could spot Marquez in the metro station. He returned not long afterward, accompanied by Marquez and a man the sailor introduced as his cousin. Marquez wanted him to sit in as he gave his statement. No one had a problem with that, but still, Marquez seemed wary, anxious enough that Veale felt they needed to treat the next few minutes with extreme care. Marquez was an ordinary seafarer whose involvement in the *Brillante* case was the result of simple bad luck. It was important to make him feel comfortable, and not as though he were being treated with suspicion.

Once they got to the suite Veale had reserved for the meeting, he called room service to send up cake and coffee while Conner chatted with the Filipinos about their families, the weather, the traffic—anything but international maritime conspiracy. After a little while, it felt to Veale like Marquez was ready to begin the interview. He admitted that much of what he'd told investigators previously was fabricated. "I am still scared," he said through the translator, "but I believe I am less at risk if many people know about my story." With Veale, Conner, and Zavos taking notes and occasionally interjecting to ask for clarifications, he told them what really happened.

From the start, Marquez said, he'd been suspicious of the men he was instructed to let on board the *Brillante*, and initially refused a superior officer's order to lower a ladder to them. When he argued with the officer, he was told that "if I did not lower the pilot ladder, I would be written in the book for insubordination." He found the insistence odd at the time; why would anyone be so determined to let armed men onto the ship? But he followed the order, and his immediate questions were quickly consumed by the events that followed.

It was only later, onshore, that Marquez realized something deeply unsettling was afoot. After a few days on the USS *Philippine Sea*, the *Brillante* sailors were taken to Aden to await flights home. Marios Iliopoulos had flown in, installing the men in a hotel by the airport. Iliopoulos knew his insurers would require testimony from the crew, and shortly after arriving at the hotel they were instructed to write out their recollections. Marquez did as he was told, and prepared a longhand statement describing his experience.

Not long after he handed over the document, Marquez said, Iliopoulos and Nestor Tabares, the *Brillante*'s chief engineer, appeared at the door of his room. (Unaccustomed to shoreside accommodation, he referred to it as a "cabin.") Tabares had Marquez's statement in his hands. As Marquez looked on, unsure what he'd done to attract the attention of the shipowner and a senior officer, Tabares began tearing up the paper. He "told me to write another statement," Marquez recalled. He wasn't to refer to his doubts about letting the gunmen on board, or to mention that he'd been ordered by the captain to lower a ladder. And he needed to change his recollection of a particular detail: who the crew believed the apparent pirates to be when they were allowed onto the ship. Marquez said Tabares ordered him "to say the intruders said they were the authorities"—and not, as the crew told US Navy personnel immediately after their rescue, the security team with whom they planned to rendezvous. From that point onward, Marquez and the other sailors used "authorities"—though it was unclear exactly which authorities they were referring to—when describing how the men who boarded the tanker had identified themselves. (Tabares would say in later court testimony that he had no recollection of threatening Marquez.)

As Marquez spoke, Veale and Conner felt that an important piece of the puzzle was clicking into place. There was no reasonable way for true pirates to have known the *Brillante* was expecting a security detail. Claiming that the attackers posed as the "authorities," by contrast, dealt with that logical problem. Since getting their hands on US Navy records that exposed the inconsistency, the detectives had been trying to account for this crucial change in the crew's stories. Now Marquez was providing an explanation for how it happened—and, even more important, implicating Iliopoulos in the fabrication of evidence. Before he wrote his new statement, Marquez said, the shipowner "told me not to tell anything" to investigators. Iliopoulos's words, he said, were: "I will kill you and your family if you tell them what you know about what happened on the ship."

The same menace followed Marquez home. While they recuperated in the Philippines after the attack, the *Brillante* crew were summoned to a hotel on Manila's waterfront promenade to provide another, more extensive round of statements. Before he could enter the building, Marquez said, Iliopoulos and Tabares intercepted him. That the Greek had even been in Manila at the time was news to Veale and Conner; as far as they knew, the only people handling those interviews were lawyers. Iliopoulos and Tabares again told him "not to say anything about what happened," Marquez said, or even reveal to anyone that Iliopoulos was in town. He recalled that Tabares was carrying a pistol on his belt—the Philippines has a vibrant gun culture—and touched it suggestively as he spoke. (Tabares denies that this occurred.)

Veale was trying to watch Marquez's expression closely. The insurers had no power to compel his testimony, and he was free to leave at any time. Aside from providing an honorarium that amounted to a few hundred dollars, they weren't even paying him to be there. Push too hard, Veale worried, and he might walk out, taking with him their chances of using his evidence in court.

Around the middle of the day, Veale spotted an opportunity to lift some of the pressure on his subject. "Why don't we go down to lunch?" he asked. Grateful for the break, the group trooped into the Dusit Thani's buffet. With stations for Italian, Indian, and pan-Asian dishes, it was a typical five-star affair of luxurious abundance—or abundant waste, depending on one's perspective. Having access to that kind of spread was a new experience for Marquez and his cousin, and Veale couldn't help but laugh as they piled their plates with more shrimp and grilled meat than he'd ever seen anyone consume. It was another reminder of a reality he hoped Zavos would keep in mind: Marquez was from a very different world. They needed to tread lightly.

There was much more to get through, and Veale, Conner, and Zavos's discussions with Marquez continued over the rest of the weekend. One of Marquez's most important tasks was to go over the audio from the Voyage Data Recorder, the black box that recorded conversations on the *Brillante* bridge, to corroborate his account of events there. It was laborious, time-consuming work, and Zavos sat with Marquez well into Sunday night listening to the tapes. Veale had stepped out when, around 9:00 p.m., Conner came and found him. Zavos was getting impatient with Marquez, he said, demanding the sailor give more precise answers when he was clearly exhausted. If it didn't stop, Conner warned, "We're going to lose Allan." Veale walked briskly back into the room. "Allan, thanks so much," he said, making clear they were done for the day. "We'll get you a cab home."

Marquez returned at 7:30 the next morning, a national holiday in the Philippines, to complete his testimony. Later that day, Zavos took him through the formalities that would render his words into a document fit for presentation to a London judge. Marquez signed all ten pages of his official statement in a looping script, placing his final signature below the standard boilerplate of a witness before an English court: "I understand its contents to be true to the best of my knowledge and belief."

Marquez noted in the document that he would have liked to provide more extensive assistance, identifying all the instances where his previous accounts were inaccurate. But there wasn't enough time. He'd signed a new, nine-month contract, and he was about to go back to sea.

CHAPTER 22

ZULU 2

Marios Iliopoulos thrashed his Audi R8 LMS up a winding route that started at the bottom of a hill in Ritsona, near Athens, and ended at its rocky summit. Painted candy-apple red, with a "MARIO" decal across the top of the windshield, the Audi screamed in protest as Iliopoulos pushed its engine to its limit. As he approached a hairpin bend, its rear wheels started to skid out toward spectators gathered behind a reinforced barrier, but Iliopoulos kept the vehicle glued to the road. The crowd applauded as he roared by.

Ritsona is the site of one of the oldest and most prestigious rally races in Greece, where competitors test their skills against an unforgiving course: barren rocks on one side and a steep drop on the other, the Aegean shimmering in the distance. Inevitably, not all of the participants get to the finish line. Each year, a handful make a mistake that sends them spinning into a ditch if they're lucky or careening off a cliff edge if they're not. For the 2017 event, organizers had placed large sandbags on the most dangerous corners to reduce the risk of calamity. Bombing up the hill at ninety kilometers per hour, most drivers take around five minutes to finish. Iliopoulos completed the course in an impressive four minutes and seventeen seconds, placing third out of ninety-nine competitors. In a public letter to fans afterward, he compared his car to a purebred racehorse, speedy on the flat but ill suited to the slopes. His preferred vehicle, a four-wheel-drive Ford, had been out of action because of a broken suspension, he explained. The backup Audi was "stroppy and wild," but nonetheless "breathtaking."

After the unpleasantness of the London court case and his arrest, Iliopoulos had returned enthusiastically to what brought him the most joy: cars, the kind with engines so powerful they sound like a jet taking off. There was no sign of the stress-induced illness he'd complained of a year earlier. Instead he gave the impression of a man enjoying the life of wealth and privilege to which, as a successful shipowner, he'd long been accustomed. Iliopoulos's marriage began breaking down in about 2012, he'd said in one of his witness statements for the insurance lawsuit. Now he seemed free of romantic troubles, photographed at parties in the company of a blond marketing director from Seajets, his ferry business. In June 2017, a little over a year after he'd testified in London, Iliopoulos's company sponsored the Acropolis Rally, the biggest racing event in Greece. Next to the Seajets stand and a tent emblazoned with his name, Iliopoulos performed the Zeibekiko, a traditional dance that's supposed to convey an embattled man struggling through suffering, overcoming it with a display of masculine defiance. A huddle of young models wearing short PVC skirts and sunglasses crouched in a circle to clap as Iliopoulos staggered back and forth, awkwardly slapping his thighs to the Greek folk music blaring from speakers nearby.

The only public sign of the trouble in London was a message posted on his racing team's Facebook page. Iliopoulos thanked his supporters and paid tribute to his brother Ioannis, who'd recently died. Then, referring to himself as "the warrior Mario," he said cryptically that he'd been fighting "the establishment" not just in sport but in his personal and professional life. "I am used to dealing with evil and mud on all levels," he said. "Jealousy and envy is a subconscious process. All of you are my strength, energy, passion and driving force in my soul to keep on fighting for our ideals."

Veale and Conner watched the exploits of Super Mario, as he was called in the racing press, from afar, occasionally with amusement, mostly in disbelief. Given that Judge Flaux had just called him an aggressive and arrogant liar, and the real possibility that he could be facing criminal charges in the UK, they had half expected the shipowner to lay low. "He doesn't care," Veale remarked to Conner as they watched the YouTube footage of him dancing. They tried not to let his antics distract them. There was a lawsuit to win.

Flaux's decision to throw out Iliopoulos's claim against his insurers left them in an odd position: having to prove fraud against someone who was no longer involved in the litigation. Technically, it was now a dispute between the Talbot syndicate and Piraeus Bank, which had loaned Iliopoulos the money to buy the *Brillante*, and claimed the Lloyd's insurers were responsible for covering what it lost with the vessel's destruction. Iliopoulos no longer had any obligation to answer questions or share evidence, nor provide explanations that could be picked apart in court. And the bank could justifiably claim to have no direct knowledge of what happened on board. Proving that an owner destroyed his own ship was hard enough; Zavos and his colleagues could count on one hand the number of times anyone had recently managed that in a London courtroom. Now they needed to do it against an opponent who didn't even have to play the game.

With Veale and Conner's help, the insurers had assembled a huge volume of evidence, including a formal statement from Allan Marquez claiming that Iliopoulos had forced him to lie about what happened on the *Brillante*. But they knew their arguments would have to be airtight, strong enough to overwhelm the legal and procedural obstacles that had sunk so many previous fraud cases. Marquez's testimony, while damning, wouldn't be enough.

Nor would what Veale and Conner had learned from Vassilios Theodorou, the shaggy-haired salvor who'd tried to sell them his photo archive. His arrival, far from corroborating the insurers' allegations, had in fact exposed a damaging rift within their team, just when it most needed to pull together. Everyone knew that Theodorou could never be called as a witness at trial. His piratical appearance alone was likely to unsettle a judge, quite apart from his demands for cash, his dubious motivations, and the fact that his own adviser had discredited his evidence by claiming some of it was "not so good," in order to confuse things until Theodorou got his money.

As far as Veale was concerned, that was fine. They could treat Theodorou like any other underworld informant, as a source of information that needed to be verified independently, not as a witness of fact. But the other members of the team, specifically those with law degrees, didn't see it that way. They were more interested in what they could learn from professional experts, hired to review documentary evidence that already existed. Some of them had never so much as set eyes on the *Brillante*. "The experts weren't there!" Veale told Zavos, exasperated. Even the surveyors who'd boarded the ship off the United Arab Emirates had been inspecting a badly damaged crime scene, caked with soot and so hot that spending more than a short time belowdecks risked exhaustion. Theodorou had been present while the *Brillante* burned, Veale kept saying. Yet Talbot's attorneys seemed quick to dismiss him.

One telling example of the difference between Theodorou's evidence and the experts' analysis was the question of whether a bomb had exploded on board. All the expert witnesses agreed that a conspicuous dent, discovered just outside the *Brillante*'s engine room, was the result of an explosive device. But Theodorou had been insistent: there was no bomb. The men who attacked the tanker, he said, had just filled a couple of jerry cans with gasoline and set them alight. In the combustible environment of an engine room, that had been enough, he claimed. It seemed like a pointless thing to lie about, since Theodorou had already admitted to helping the blaze spread by smashing open fuel tanks. But Talbot's lawyers couldn't believe their hired specialists would get it so wrong. "Petrol isn't explosive," one of them objected. "How do you think a car engine works?" Conner shot back.

Whenever the two detectives tried to argue the point, someone would remind them that they weren't experts, at least not of the kind that corporate lawyers were used to consulting. That irked Conner in particular, who'd served in Northern Ireland, investigating attacks by militants, and worked on a government inquiry into a gruesome explosion on a nuclear submarine. If there was a bomb, he pointedly asked, why was there no evidence of fragments from the device? They shouldn't have been too difficult to find: when a Pan Am 747 was blown up over the Scottish town of Lockerbie in 1988, investigators had been able to pick pieces of the mechanism out of gardens more than thirty thousand feet below.

As that and other conflicts simmered, at least one member of the legal team felt that Veale and Conner had developed an inflated sense of their importance to the case—and that they were increasingly behaving like "bullshitters," determined to put themselves at the center of every decision. The lawyers were confident that they knew how to win a lawsuit. In their eyes, running around after criminals was at best a distraction, and at worst a significant waste of resources. Veale's firm, EBIS, was being generously compensated for its work. Combined with legal fees, the *Brillante* dispute was burning through money. An executive from one of the insurance companies joked privately that he didn't want to be responsible for getting Veale and Conner rich.

For their part, the detectives felt that when it came to criminal conspiracies, they were the experts. They had decades of law enforcement experience between them. Zavos and Paul Cunningham, the Talbot claims manager, had never even contested a scuttling case before. Veale tried to convince them that normal litigation procedure—an exchange of letters and evidence, followed by the measured testimony of professors and forensic scientists and skilled legal analysis by barristers—wouldn't work against people willing to torch an oil tanker.

At one point, Veale requested approval for a trip to the Gadani shipbreaking yard in Pakistan, where the *Brillante* had been torn apart for scrap. Theodorou claimed to have stashed the tanker's sprinklers there, part of a vital firefighting system that he said had been filled with concrete to stop it from working. If Theodorou was telling the truth, the sprinklers, with identifying serial numbers, could offer evidence that the fire was planned in advance. When Zavos refused to give Veale and Conner permission to go, the rift between the lawyers and investigators widened into a chasm.

In the summer of 2017, while Iliopoulos was roaring around the mountains in superpowered cars, Veale and Conner returned to Greece to meet some of their sources. By then the two were spending almost all their time either working on the *Brillante* or talking about it, sometimes bickering like an old couple. They spoke so often on the phone that their wives started to joke about them having an affair. Sometimes it felt like they were going in circles. Every new lead either fizzled into a dead end or yielded so many avenues of investigation that it would take weeks to chase them down. There were too many potential witnesses, scattered to the four winds, and too few reliable ones.

On their trip to Greece, Veale and Conner learned about another man who, like Theodorou, had boarded the *Brillante* in the immediate aftermath of the hijacking. He was "close to home," their source said.

"What does that mean?" Veale asked.

"He's in London."

The man's name was Dimitrios Plakakis. He was a former computer technician and financial controller who'd somehow ended up in business with Vassilios Vergos, the ex-diver whose ramshackle salvage outfit had, according to Theodorou, helped destroy the *Brillante*. Veale and Conner traced Plakakis to the flat where he was staying and sent some old colleagues from the Met to do surveillance. They came back with photographs of a slender, bookish man in glasses, talking into a mobile phone—Plakakis. To conceal his identity, Veale decided to refer to him by a code name, Zulu 2. He didn't look like much of a criminal, and so the detectives figured the best approach would be to show up on his doorstep and put him on the spot.

It was the sort of thing they'd done countless times together as police officers. Still, Veale was cautious. For all they knew, Plakakis might have been a captive, watched over by a team of Greek enforcers. He and Conner drove past the flat a few times to get a sense of the street scene, then went to the local library to scan the electoral register, which could tell them who else was living there. Veale also pulled the building plans from the land registry to work out where the entrances and exits were located.

Conner knew they had to inform the City of London Police that a potential witness to the *Brillante* attack was on their doorstep. He called a detective he'd met to tell him they had located Plakakis and planned to visit him. Better to be transparent, Conner thought. But instead of expressing gratitude or curiosity, the detective insisted they couldn't contact the Greek. "We can," Conner said angrily. "This is a courtesy call. We don't need your permission." He hung up. At no point in his career had Conner let orders from his supposed betters overrule his instincts. He wasn't about to start now.

Plakakis's flat was on the second floor of a grand Victorian house in a wealthy part of town. The detectives approached it on a July morning, walking casually down the tree-lined street. They split up, Conner going to the front door while Veale stayed on the sidewalk, checking to see if anyone appeared in a window. There was no answer when Conner knocked. "Dimitrios!" he called out. Still no response. Veale crept around the back as Conner kept knocking. There he noticed that the doors to the patio were wide open, letting in the summer breeze.

After a silent nod to each other, the pair tried an old cop trick. "There's no one here," Conner hollered, loud enough to make sure he could be heard. Then he walked down the road a few paces before suddenly turning around. Plakakis was peering out from behind a curtain. Their eyes met, and Conner curled his index finger to beckon the man down. Standing at his front door, Plakakis was shaking. Conner reached out and took both his hands. "You don't need to be afraid," he said. "We are gentlemen. We are from the insurers."

They had a brief conversation on the doorstep, as much as the two detectives thought Plakakis could handle. Once he realized they weren't there to harm him, he began to relax. But he also made clear he couldn't talk further without first checking with the police. "I need to talk to my handlers," Plakakis said. Veale and Conner exchanged a brief glance that, in the telepathic understanding shared between old friends and longtime partners, they both knew to mean, basically, *holy shit*. As they walked away from the house, Conner turned to Veale in amazement. "Fucking hell," he said. "Handlers!" Neither man had any inkling that Plakakis had already spoken to the cops. The City of London Police didn't seem to know anything about it, even though they were supposed to be investigating the *Brillante*. Veale and Conner soon learned that Plakakis's handlers were from the National Crime Agency. Whatever the nature of their relationship, it was sensitive enough for the NCA to have kept it from their colleagues in London's Square Mile.

The next day, Plakakis called Conner on his mobile. He'd talked to the NCA and was apologetic. "I've been told I mustn't speak to you," he said. While he was keen to tell his story, Plakakis said, he was only prepared to do "what is legal."

Veale and Conner's efforts to find out why the NCA was interested in Plakakis got nowhere. The agency didn't want to cooperate with private investigators. But eventually their contacts at the City of London Police revealed that Plakakis had agreed to come in to give a detailed statement for their fraud probe. The interview had lasted for several hours. Concerned about his safety, Plakakis asked the police to keep his identity a secret and signed the statement using a pseudonym, Theo Blake, apparently picked at random.

After the leak of the insurers' emails in Greece, Veale and Conner were reluctant to tell the Talbot legal team too much about Plakakis, in case the information found its way to Piraeus. They kept to themselves, for example, exactly how they found him, attributing the tip to a loose network of informants they called RITA, a catchall acronym for "Regional Investigative and Tasking Activities." RITA was one source and RITA was twenty sources, was how Conner later described it: "That's how you protect people."

But when Zavos heard that Plakakis had provided a statement to the police, he spotted an opportunity. He knew that private-sector lawyers could apply for court orders requiring law enforcement to disclose evidence relevant to a lawsuit. There were technical hurdles to clear, and the insurers would have to book a day in court, but it might offer a way to get Plakakis's testimony and use it at trial. It would be several months before the strategy paid off. But eventually, the judge ordered the police to submit the statement as evidence in the *Brillante* trial. When it finally arrived, the document was a revelation. Not only did it provide minute detail about an audacious fraud that was planned in Greece and executed in Yemen. It contained alarming new information about the death of David Mockett.

CHAPTER 23

TWO GREEK GUYS

According to the account that Plakakis gave to the police,* he'd stumbled into a position near the center of what happened to the *Brillante*. Conner was instinctively skeptical of stories like it; over the years, he'd met plenty of people who claimed they'd never wanted to get involved in whatever situation he was investigating. But something about Plakakis's manner suggested that he was being truthful. In his fear and bewilderment, the Greek didn't seem like someone who'd known exactly what he was getting into.

Plakakis had grown up in the 1980s in Piraeus, where he proved himself to be an excellent student, particularly in math. He relocated to the UK in 1991, moving in with an aunt and later studying for a master's degree in financial mathematics at City University, a brief walk from the trading floors and sleek offices of London's ancient banking district. The City was in the middle of the long boom that began with Margaret Thatcher's deregulation campaign, and that was where Plakakis wanted ultimately to make his career. But when he returned to Britain in 2001 after completing his mandatory Greek military service, he found he couldn't get hired. Sharp as he was, Plakakis hardly stood out among the thousands of young Europeans then flooding

---

*The account of Plakakis's role in the *Brillante* case in this and the following chapter is based on official law enforcement records, court testimony and documents, and interviews with people who spoke to him about his involvement.

into the British capital. It took him almost a year of fruitless searching to find a job, though it was a long way from the City, both physically and spiritually. Hellas Helvetia, where Plakakis worked as a financial controller, had its office in a scruffy district on the north side of Hyde Park, and its business was property management—finding tenants for apartments and dealing with formalities like boiler inspections.

Plakakis struck up a friendship with one of the firm's clients, George Costoulas, a Greek diplomat in his sixties, who owned a London flat that Hellas Helvetia managed for him. Despite an age difference of decades, the two men became close, talking regularly on the phone and meeting during Plakakis's visits to Greece. In one of their conversations, Plakakis mentioned that he was thinking about a career change. He was working sixty or seventy hours a week and had begun to wonder if it was time to leave London and try his luck somewhere else, or perhaps return home permanently.

As it happened, his older friend had a proposal for him. Though he was nearing retirement, Costoulas was still popular at the foreign ministry in Athens and had been offered a job as Greece's ambassador to the United Arab Emirates. In Abu Dhabi he would need a private secretary, someone he could rely on to manage his professional commitments and help him with day-to-day organization. Would Plakakis be willing to do it? After giving it some thought, he decided that he was. It wasn't a huge risk, he reasoned. The post would probably be Costoulas's last before he retired, and a couple of years living on the Persian Gulf would be an exciting change while Plakakis figured out what to do next.

He soon moved to the UAE, living in the Greek Embassy and accompanying Costoulas to all of his engagements. While the economic relationship between Greece and the Emirates was hardly critical to either country, there was still investment to chase and flesh to press, and Costoulas spent much of his time making connections with businessmen. In September 2006, Plakakis accompanied his boss to a meeting with an entrepreneur named Sharif Ba'alawi. Plakakis liked him immediately. Thin, with a gentle face and a neat beard, Ba'alawi struck Plakakis as polished and educated, but also street smart, like a man who clearly knew how to operate in difficult environments. Though he had lived for decades in Dubai, Ba'alawi was of Yemeni and Somali extraction, and seemed to be invested in a wide range of businesses in both countries: logistics, sugar trading, real estate. He apparently even had a stake in a Coca-Cola bottling plant in Mogadishu.

In conversation with the Greeks, Ba'alawi mentioned a new venture he was considering. Ships passing the Yemeni coast often needed to refuel. Coming into port for "bunkering," as the process of refueling a merchant vessel is called, cost time and therefore money. That created an opening, Ba'alawi explained. Vessel managers would pay a premium to avoid the delay, and with a license from the local authorities and a small tanker, it was possible to buy oil from the refinery in Aden, then resell it at a markup five or ten miles offshore. But Ba'alawi needed an employee with experience bunkering ships to help run his new operation. Plakakis happened to know another man with the right background. Spying an opportunity, he was soon working with the bunkering expert to help set up the new company, which would be called Adoil.

By 2009 Plakakis had relocated to Aden, where he would be paid $5,000 a month to manage Adoil's daily operations. He'd never lived anywhere like it. Harsh and only lightly governed, it was nothing like Abu Dhabi, let alone London. In the city center, Victorian buildings left by the British had been neglected to the point of rot. Even the newer structures, exposed to the dusty wind, looked battered, as if decades of wear had been concentrated into a few years. Plakakis spoke little Arabic and had only a faint understanding of Yemeni customs; in his dealings with locals, he relied heavily on one of Ba'alawi's brothers, who was based in Aden.

He was nonetheless happy to be there. Despite appearances, the city was a promising place to operate, with a location critical to maritime commerce and considerable margin for profit, as long as you had some connections and an eye for opportunity in the liminal spaces of its economy. Aden's drastic unfamiliarity was also part of its appeal. Plakakis had wanted a change from managing flats in West London, and he'd certainly got it.

He'd only been in his new job a couple of days when he was introduced to Ahmed Nashwan, a tall, well-fed Yemeni with a distinctive gap between his front teeth. Nashwan was one of Adoil's local shareholders, and from what Plakakis gathered he was a powerful man. Rumored to be a veteran of the Republican Guard, the branch of the Yemeni military closest to President Ali

Abdullah Saleh, Nashwan, Plakakis was told, came from the politically dominant north and had extensive connections in Sana'a. Bureaucratic tangles were a constant concern for Adoil, and Nashwan seemed to have a unique ability to untie them. Whether a problem involved the police, port authorities, or politicians, he was almost always able to resolve it. Plakakis didn't quite know how Nashwan managed to jolt usually uncooperative officials so effectively, but he was pretty sure it wasn't with polite requests. The Yemeni could be more than a little menacing. He was always carrying a gun when Plakakis saw him, and was a prodigious chewer of qat. When he was high on the leafy stimulant, Plakakis thought, he seemed at once vacant and volatile. "He was a feared person," Plakakis would tell police years later.

Plakakis was in a restaurant, about a month after he arrived, when another Greek, a thickset man who walked with a noticeable limp, came over to say hello. He introduced himself as Vassilios Vergos, and, to Plakakis's surprise, he was also in business with Ba'alawi and Nashwan, who were investors in the local branch of his salvage company, Poseidon. Plakakis was pleased by the coincidence. What were the odds, as he later put it, that there would be a pair of "Greek guys in the middle of nowhere"?

Vergos lived on one of Poseidon's boats, and Plakakis began visiting him frequently. Often, the salvor hosted him for Greek meals that he prepared in the tiny galley, simple affairs of grilled fish or stew that, for a man so far from home, felt like the height of luxury. Vergos was hopeless with technology, and in return for his hospitality, Plakakis began teaching him to send emails and make Skype calls, the two men sitting shoulder to shoulder as Vergos fumbled with the mouse. They also tried to push business each other's way. When he spoke to ships' captains and port agents about bunkering, Plakakis might mention that Poseidon was available for services like underwater cleaning. The company could also furnish security details, putting groups of armed Yemenis sourced by Nashwan onto a Poseidon tug called the *Voukefalas*—named, rather grandiosely, for the horse that Alexander the Great rode into battle—to escort passing ships.

Plakakis soon learned that Vergos had an extreme emotional range. With people he deemed friends he was garrulous and genial, greeting them with kisses on both cheeks and warm exclamations of "Brother!" Anyone who crossed him, though, was a *malakas*—a hard-to-translate Greek insult, roughly equivalent to "wanker"—and subject to furious tirades. Vergos had led an eventful life, and when they ate together he liked to recount boastful tales of his diving exploits, sexual conquests, and, most of all, his long career in the salvage business. The salvor's limp, Plakakis learned, was the result of a case of the bends after a dive went wrong, so severe that he was lucky to live through it. Though he'd rarely worked anywhere outside Greece before coming to Aden, Vergos had handled a broad range of maritime mishaps: grounded ferries, sunken yachts, stranded tankers. Once, Poseidon had helped retrieve the wreckage of a helicopter from more than 250 meters beneath the surface, which the company said was the deepest recovery ever performed in Greek waters.

One of the stories Vergos shared with Plakakis, according to what the younger man told police, was that of the *Elli*, the Iliopoulos-owned tanker that ran aground near Aden in 2009, then split in half catastrophically, resulting in a substantial claim against its London insurers. Poseidon had set up its Yemeni subsidiary only weeks before the grounding, and its tugs had been able to race to the scene. As he recounted his involvement, Vergos made a frank admission. The timing, he said, had been no coincidence. He'd known before leaving Greece that the *Elli* would soon require his services. "In the salvage business I don't wait for things to happen," he told his friend. "I make them happen." Plakakis, who knew next to nothing about the workings of Lloyd's or the salvage industry, was confused. How could a salvor know in advance about an accident? It wouldn't be long before he understood what Vergos meant.

Despite Plakakis's efforts, Adoil was a failure, crippled by disagreements between its Greek and Yemeni investors. Yet moving oil around the Gulf of Aden was still an attractive business, and Vergos wanted to start an operation of his own, which he suggested Plakakis could run. In 2010 the two men were back in Greece, holding meetings at Poseidon's headquarters, near the Piraeus docks, as they looked for a bunkering vessel.

Since getting to know each other in Aden, their relationship had evolved from a friendship to a loose commercial partnership, and Plakakis accompanied Vergos to many of his meetings, looking for opportunities. While Plakakis enjoyed their time together, he'd concluded that Vergos's swaggering manner—in Athens he drove a red Hummer, hardly a practical vehicle for the city's narrow streets—masked a deep insecurity. Many of the men at the top of the Greek shipping world came from storied maritime families, tracing their roots to idyllic Aegean islands. Vergos, by contrast, grew up in Levaia, a village of just nine hundred people in Greece's agricultural north, which many residents still called by its former name: Lakkia, or "pit," possibly in reference to a nearby coal mine. The place was so removed from the sea that Vergos hadn't even been taught to swim as a child. He wanted badly to be counted among the salvage industry's elite, entrepreneurs whose gleaming fleets were stationed all over the world, ready to respond at a moment's notice to the most difficult accidents. Plakakis got the sense that Vergos intended to prove himself their equal.

The two men were at Poseidon's offices one day when Vergos received a call from Iliopoulos. There was something the shipowner wanted to discuss, and Vergos brought Plakakis along with him to Iliopoulos's nearby office. At first the talk was about selling the wreck of the *Elli*, but at a couple of points, Plakakis remained in his chair while Vergos and Iliopoulos stepped away to discuss something in private. Afterward Vergos handed Plakakis a sheet of paper. Printed on the page, Plakakis realized, were the names of several vessels. "This is the list Iliopoulos gave me," Vergos said. "One of them will be the next *Elli*."

Plakakis would later claim that he hadn't paid much attention to the remark; Vergos was a big talker, and Plakakis was much more focused on their new bunkering business. He returned to Aden in early 2011 to get it running. Vergos had found a small tanker, the *Sweet Lady*, that they planned to use after making some repairs. As he stepped on board for the first time, Plakakis's heart sank. Poseidon had salvaged the vessel after an accident in the Red Sea, and in the photos Vergos showed him it seemed to be in reasonable shape. But close up it was a mess, heavily waterlogged and totally unready for use. Getting it into working condition, even with the help of some of Poseidon's Bangladeshi crewmen, would be a huge job. The only good news was that

Plakakis would have a skilled partner. Vergos had brought an engineer into the project, with far deeper marine expertise: Vassilios Theodorou, whom Veale and Conner would later get to know in Athens.

The two men slept in one of the *Sweet Lady*'s filthy cabins and rose at dawn each day, downing a cup of sludgy coffee before getting to work. The labor was exhausting, but Plakakis needed to get the vessel seaworthy as quickly as possible. He wasn't being paid a salary—instead, Vergos had promised him a 20 percent stake in the bunkering business in exchange for rendering the ship operational—so every day the *Sweet Lady* remained in its berth was a day of lost money. Plakakis was covering costs out of his own pocket, expenses that were climbing steadily into the tens of thousands of dollars, and had grown frustrated, particularly because Vergos seemed distracted by other concerns. He wasn't even in Yemen. After one of Poseidon's Greek personnel, a grandfatherly sailor named Spyros Protogerakis, hurt his leg in a crane accident, Vergos had flown back to Athens to make arrangements for his treatment, leaving Plakakis to run the salvage business in his absence.

After a little over a month away, Vergos reappeared in Aden in the spring of 2011. On one of his first days back, he summoned Plakakis and Theodorou to a meeting. Plakakis could see the delight on his face; the salvor clearly had news that he couldn't wait to share. Vergos explained that he'd been given a "job" by Iliopoulos. It was a grand plan; if it succeeded, he said, they'd all be rich. This time, however, a grounding like that of the *Elli* wouldn't work. No one would believe that particular lightning could strike twice.

CHAPTER 24

THE JOB

Plakakis spent his time in Aden largely offshore. When not working on a salvage, Poseidon's vessels sat at anchor, lashed together in the middle of the harbor a couple of miles from land. In one direction, he could see the dun-colored buildings of the city center, rising on rocky slopes away from the water's edge. On the opposite side, he could make out the gantries of the city's container terminal, on a pancake-flat island that had been reshaped to orthogonal dimensions to accommodate ocean freighters. The unofficial flagship of Poseidon's flotilla was the *Vergina I*, a blue-and-yellow barge that carried a thirty-five-ton crane for use in salvage missions. It was controlled from a large open-plan cabin, where Plakakis sometimes worked during the day. Vergos was usually there, too, and Plakakis noticed that, since returning to Aden in April 2011, he had added a new element to his routine. Just before six o'clock each evening, he would grab a cheap cellphone from one of Poseidon's Bangladeshi crewmen, loaded with a prepaid local SIM card. A moment later it would ring, with Iliopoulos or one of his associates calling from Athens. Portions of the discussions that followed appeared to be in a crude code; sometimes Vergos referred to the arrival of something he called "the wolf." But beyond that precaution, he made little effort to hide what he was talking about, speaking at full volume with little regard to who might be listening. Plakakis was in no doubt: Vergos and Iliopoulos were making preparations to destroy a ship, somewhere off the Yemeni coast.

Plakakis would later say to police that he wanted no involvement with the plan, and told Vergos not to expect him to be an active participant. He'd come to Aden to start an oil business, and while that might bring him into some ethical gray areas, what Vergos was contemplating was in another category. Nor, Plakakis recalled thinking, would he have ever wanted Iliopoulos as a coconspirator. The shipowner struck him as mercurial and untrustworthy. And it wasn't as though Vergos had any power over Plakakis. They were partners in the fuel venture, not boss and employee.

Yet despite his refusal to help, Plakakis told detectives that Vergos seemed unconcerned about how much he learned about the operation. Getting into the city from Poseidon's vessels required a trip in a small motorboat, but Vergos's old diving injury made it difficult for him to climb in and out of the craft. In May and June 2011, he asked Plakakis to ferry him to a series of onshore appointments. The younger man used the time to pick up groceries or spare parts, trying to keep clear of the violence that was becoming a regular concern in Aden, before bringing Vergos back to the floating crane at day's end. Vergos was happy to tell him what he'd been up to: meeting with Sharif Ba'alawi, the Yemeni-Somali businessman; Ahmed Nashwan, the qat-chewing fixer Poseidon employed to iron out bureaucratic problems; as well as various government officials, who were all involved in what he called "the job." From overhearing Vergos's calls, Plakakis had learned that Iliopoulos wanted it organized quickly, complaining that he was losing $20,000 per day operating the ship in question. He'd also surmised that Nashwan expected a payment of $2 million to cover his role, and to secure the cooperation of Aden's power brokers. If the Greeks wanted to operate on Yemeni turf, then the Yemenis would need to be cut in.

Vergos soon dropped any pretense of secrecy among the men he worked with. Early in the summer of 2011, he gathered Plakakis, Theodorou, and the older sailor Protogerakis, who'd returned from Greece after getting his leg patched up, around a table on the *Vergina*. Vergos was in an upbeat mood, eager to impress his colleagues with the scale of the plan he'd helped devise. It was evening, and Aden's lights were blinking on across the water as he began to speak. The vessel they were waiting for was a supertanker, Vergos boasted, not some little ship. It would be attacked by supposed pirates, who would round up everyone on board apart from the captain and chief engineer. The chief engineer would then show the intruders where to detonate a grenade in the engine room, ensuring that the ship was badly damaged, if not effectively destroyed. For weeks, Vergos had been reminding Protogerakis to make sure he had a Lloyd's Open Form, the standard contract for salvaging a vessel, close at hand. Poseidon would handle the recovery, positioning it for a generous award from the Lloyd's market.

Organizing the attack had required complex preparation, Vergos explained, not least to deal with the most fundamental problem: finding a group of pirates willing to do it. For one thing, there weren't any in Yemen. The country had plenty of terrestrial bandits, but piracy in the Gulf of Aden was an overwhelmingly Somali phenomenon. And even if some bona fide pirates could be found, they would be too difficult to control. What was to stop the gang from simply taking the ship for themselves? Vergos told Plakakis and the others that he'd found a solution. The "pirates," he said, would be men from the Yemeni Coast Guard, sourced by Nashwan.

Plakakis had learned enough about Yemen not to be shocked by the idea of employing agents of the state for a bit of unconventional freelance work. Set up in the aftermath of 9/11, as President Saleh attempted to ingratiate himself with the US, the YCG was supposed to be a government showpiece, a capable counterterrorism force that would secure a nearly two-thousand-kilometer coastline. Eager to build the service's capacity, the US government had provided it with more than a dozen patrol boats, and American naval experts trained its sailors. It received about $30 million of Pentagon funding in 2009 alone.

Yet no amount of financial assistance could protect the YCG from the spiraling disorder Plakakis had witnessed in Aden—or the avarice of officials looking to take advantage of the chaos. In the final phase of the Saleh regime, the YCG was so short of money that it sometimes couldn't afford fuel for its vessels. Early in 2011, *The Wall Street Journal* reported that it had begun renting out boats and crews for antipiracy escorts in the Gulf of Aden, putting assets paid for by US taxpayers into the service of private shipowners—and, almost certainly, YCG commanders. (A Yemeni government official interviewed by the *Journal* claimed, laughably, that revenue generated by such commercial missions went only to the state, and "didn't enrich anyone personally.") In those circumstances, taking an assignment posing as pirates, rather than stopping them, was not so great a leap.

As the date of the operation approached, Plakakis became increasingly determined to get out of Yemen. The bunkering business that had brought him to Aden was going nowhere. Even after he'd sunk most of his savings into the project, the *Sweet Lady* remained a wreck, and he felt betrayed by Vergos, who still hadn't paid him a cent. He booked a flight to Athens for mid-June. But Vergos said he wanted him to stay—probably, Plakakis would later conclude, to keep an eye on him until the *Brillante* job was complete.

To convince him, Vergos tried appealing to Plakakis's compassion for a member of the Poseidon team. Despite his treatment in Greece, Protogerakis's leg still hadn't healed. Every day, Plakakis had been gently lifting his bandages to clean the gash below his knee, pulling away the gauze with all the delicacy he could muster. The wound suppurated with thin, yellowish fluid, and an aureole of angry reddish skin had developed around its perimeter. Plakakis had come to like Protogerakis, and was worried that he could be in the early stages of a severe infection. His anxiety was something Vergos could exploit. "If you don't stay for me, stay for Protogerakis," the salvor said.

Plakakis realized he was trapped. If he didn't take care of his colleague, he wasn't confident that anyone else would, and in the grubby conditions offshore that neglect could be catastrophic. Reluctantly, he canceled his plans to depart. With little to do other than look after Protogerakis, he settled into an irritable funk. He started sleeping late, trying to kill time until he could leave. Yemen had brought Plakakis only disappointment, and he just wanted to go home.

In the close quarters of Poseidon's rusty vessels, however, he couldn't ignore what was about to happen to the *Brillante*. The salvage crew was working long hours to get ready, and Plakakis had a front-row seat. On the afternoon of July 5, he and Vergos were on the deck of the *Vergina*. A small ship was heading out to sea, pushing away from the ash-dark peaks that framed Aden's harbor. Plakakis recognized the gray hull: it was a YCG patrol cutter. Vergos motioned toward the vessel as it slipped past. "That's the boat that's going to do the job," he said.

That night, Vergos instructed the Poseidon crew to get to bed early, to be ready to leave in the early hours of the morning. The firm's salvage tug, the *Voukefalas*, had already been stocked with food and water for an extended deployment. At around 3:00 a.m., Plakakis heard an urgent message burst from the radio. "Help, help, help," he would recall the voice saying. Somewhere in the littoral darkness, the *Brillante* was on fire.

Plakakis refused to go with Vergos and the rest. He stayed on the *Vergina* after the *Brillante* attack, alone apart from a Bangladeshi crewman who'd been too sick to join the salvage. Scanning the headlines with an erratic internet connection, he saw that the cover story appeared to have sold: the shipping press was reporting that the vessel's near destruction was the work of pirates, almost certainly Somalis. Plakakis had spent several tedious days on board when one of Poseidon's boats appeared on the horizon, moving steadily toward the barge. The salvors needed to use the *Vergina*'s crane, and the boat would be pulling it out to the *Brillante*.

Plakakis had nowhere else to go, and he remained on board after the Poseidon sailors connected their towline, beginning the ponderous journey out to the tanker. Vergos and Theodorou were there when he arrived, weary from long days working on the skillet-hot deck. Vergos was on edge. In the hours immediately following the raid, Iliopoulos had demoted him from what he assumed would be his position as the *Brillante*'s primary salvor, relegating him to a subcontractor's role. He'd be reporting to a larger, better-funded Greek firm called Five Oceans Salvage, which had been appointed to lead the operation. Vergos had protested furiously, bellowing that he wouldn't allow another company to have access to the vessel; an incapacitated tanker full of oil was a rich prize, one that Vergos didn't want to share. But Iliopoulos's decision was final, and Vergos had no choice but to accept his diminished status—subordinate, once again, to the salvage industry's big men. He'd been in a foul temper ever since.

Shortly after Plakakis arrived, a fishing trawler pulled up alongside the *Brillante*, mooring next to one of Poseidon's boats. Dusk was approaching as one of its passengers, a broad-shouldered British man with a bald, sun-worn head, clambered off. Thanks to his years in London, Plakakis spoke better English than the other Greeks, and he helped David Mockett get oriented. Mockett's survey wouldn't begin until morning, and Plakakis showed him to the bed on the *Vergina* where he would spend the night. Though he was still new to the world of salvage, Plakakis understood Mockett's role: to evaluate the condition of the ship and send a report back to Lloyd's, where its insurers would decide whether to pay out.

Before everyone turned in, Plakakis joined Vergos and Mockett for dinner. Around the table, the men got to talking about their families, and how they came to be in such a remote part of the Middle East. Both Vergos and Mockett had grown daughters in their home countries, and the surveyor mentioned that he had a crop of grandchildren, whose exploits delighted him when he was in England. That prompted Vergos to turn to Mockett with some unsolicited counsel. "At your age," he said, "it's better to stay with your grandchildren." Why run around a dangerous place like Yemen? Vergos repeated the advice: "You can go back to your country and enjoy your grandchildren."

Toward noon the next day, Mockett descended from the *Brillante* to the floating crane, his survey complete. To Plakakis, it was obvious that he was perplexed by what he'd found—or, perhaps, not found. In earshot of many of the salvors on board, Mockett remarked that he'd seen no evidence of a strike by a rocket-propelled grenade, or of pirates firing their weapons on the tanker—both key elements of what had reportedly occurred. "Everyone could see on his face that he was not happy about what he had seen or what he had been told," Plakakis recalled later. A short time afterward Mockett was gone, steaming back to Aden on the same trawler that had brought him out.

There was little need for Plakakis to stay on the *Brillante*, and he also caught a ride back to the city. More salvors were arriving from Greece, and he helped them get organized, buying provisions and driving to the airport to pick up a team of guards, who would protect what remained of the vessel during its tow to the UAE. He also needed to stop by Nashwan's office to pick up some cash for expenses. When the Yemeni saw Plakakis walk in, he detonated with rage, screaming at his visitor in rapid-fire Arabic. Plakakis could make out only some of what he said, but he did pick out the words "Vassilios"— Vergos's first name—and "*kalabush*," a colloquial term for handcuffs. Only later did he learn why Nashwan was so angry: he apparently hadn't received the $2 million he'd been promised by Vergos, money that Plakakis assumed he needed to pay off others in the Aden hierarchy. (Nashwan denies that he had any role in the *Brillante* hijacking and says he never threatened Vergos. Ba'alawi has also denied wrongdoing. No court has ruled that they were involved in the tanker's destruction.)

Plakakis still had no dry-land place to stay, and he had taken a temporary bed on a Five Oceans tug that was waiting in Aden harbor. He was on a motorboat between that vessel and the port when the driver told him there'd been a bombing in the city center. A Westerner had been killed. Plakakis asked the driver, a young Yemeni, to repeat the name of the victim again and again. He was stunned. Surely, he thought, the man must be referring to someone other than the surveyor Plakakis had met just days earlier. His first instinct was to call Vergos to tell him the sickening news. But when he picked up, the salvor already knew. "I told him to stay with his grandchildren," Vergos said.

Plakakis's story was by far the fullest account of the *Brillante* plot that Veale and Conner had obtained. But they were also certain, even if they could persuade him to aid the insurers, that they didn't want him to testify. In his decades as a cop, Conner had always tried to avoid putting informants on the stand, even—or perhaps especially—when they knew a great deal about an alleged crime. The first and most important reason was simple prudence: appearing in court could expose them to considerable danger. Though provisions exist in English law to protect the identity of witnesses, Conner never wanted them to be the only thing standing in the way of violent reprisal. The second issue was strategic. In the unpredictable environment of a trial, a skilled defense lawyer could push almost anyone into wavering on key details, or undermine their credibility by exposing unrelated misdeeds. After a couple days of cross-examination, even the most robust testimony could start to get wobbly.

Both of those concerns applied to Plakakis. It would be much better, Veale and Conner agreed, to ensure his name got nowhere near the legal proceedings. But if Plakakis was willing to cooperate, they could use him as a secret guide for further investigation. He could direct them to key documents, emails, and financial transactions, which the insurers could demand be disclosed. He knew the names of nearly everyone involved in the *Brillante* operation, people who could be interviewed or called as witnesses. And, not insignificantly, he had extensive knowledge of how Iliopoulos, Vergos, and the other players operated, intelligence that could help Veale and Conner dig into their affairs. He could be an invaluable asset without ever stepping into a courtroom.

They were dismayed to learn that the underwriters' legal team had other ideas. In November 2017, a few months after the detectives appeared at Plakakis's door, Chris Zavos submitted a statement to Nigel Teare, the judge who'd taken over the *Brillante* case, requesting a delay in the proceedings. "I became aware of the existence of a further potential witness in late July this year," Zavos wrote. The insurers needed time to seek a formal statement from him, and, they hoped, to make arrangements for him to "give evidence at the trial," with precautions to protect his identity. That idea was alarming enough for Veale and Conner, but Zavos and the other lawyers soon decided they wanted to go further, by asking the judge to order Plakakis, whose name was still a closely guarded secret, to testify openly. An identified whistleblower, Zavos argued, would add far more weight to their argument than anonymously sourced information. As a lawyer, his first priority had to be securing a favorable result for his client, and that meant using a real name.

Veale and Conner were horrified. Even after years on the case, they felt the insurers and their representatives were treating it like an ordinary commercial dispute. For someone in Plakakis's position, the stakes were much higher than whether a Lloyd's claim paid out. The pair practically begged Zavos and Paul Cunningham to reconsider. "People aren't disposable," Veale nearly shouted during one discussion. But Zavos insisted. In early January 2018, Veale circulated a memo that laid out his views, referring to Plakakis by the code name he and Conner used for him: Zulu 2. "It is the case that one man was murdered," Veale said. "Zulu 2 knows all the main players." If his identity was revealed, his life would be "in immediate danger," along with those of his wife and child. "The only safe option," Veale concluded, "is to corroborate all that he says and leave him and his family in safety."

CHAPTER 25

DON'T LEAVE THE HOUSE

The same day Veale sent his memo warning of the danger to Plakakis, Michael Conner took a train into central London for a dinner at the Little Ship Club, the City's sole yacht club. It was the sort of place where briny older men wearing blazers and striped ties took their wives to enjoy some rip-roaring nautical fun. There was a bar, decorated with oil paintings of wooden ships and long-dead admirals, and a notice board offering classes on rope handling and weather prediction. Members particularly enjoyed the lively sea shanty night, downing pints as they belted out sailors' laments from a time when Britain ruled the waves.

Conner was there as a guest of Roy Facey, David Mockett's old friend who'd been evacuated from Yemen after his murder and had been trying to use his expertise on the country to help the detectives. Facey gave a speech that night about his work for the Aden port authority, in front of a little Yemeni flag on a stand. Conner didn't want to interrupt Facey in full flow, so he reached into his pocket to turn off his phone. Over dinner, the two men shared stories. Facey spoke about his regret at having to leave Yemen, his fond memories of the people and the delicious food. He particularly loved fasoolia, a spicy bean stew served for breakfast, and hadn't had it since. It was funny, he said, the things people missed. Conner brought Facey up to speed on the latest developments in the *Brillante* case. He left the club at about 11:00 p.m. and walked out into the frigid night air.

As he crossed the Thames at Southwark Bridge, Conner was absorbed by the view. On either side of the river, he could see the City's present woven into its past. To his left were the ramparts of Tower Bridge and a decommissioned Second World War battleship, HMS *Belfast*, bristling with guns. Trains clattered past on a railway bridge downstream. Behind him, a cluster of twinkling skyscrapers obscured the insurance district and One Lime Street, the building where Veale and Conner's clients kept the Lloyd's money machine turning.

It was only when he arrived at Waterloo Station that Conner switched on his phone. The screen showed a missed call from Zulu 2. Conner decided it was too late to call Plakakis back and resolved to deal with it the next day. He got home after midnight, and went to sleep giving little thought to what the Greek might have wanted. At about 10:00 a.m. the following morning, his phone rang again: another call from Zulu 2. This time Conner picked up. Plakakis didn't wait for him to say hello. "Michael, Michael, they are outside my house," he stammered. "They are here to kill me."

In an instant, Conner snapped into concentration. He told Plakakis to stay calm and explain exactly what was happening. He would try to help if he could. In his terror, Plakakis was speaking too fast, stumbling over his words, but gradually Conner was able to piece the situation together. It had started late the previous night. Plakakis was visiting his mother in rural Greece, along with his wife and their three-year-old son. Around midnight, the house phone rang. A woman was on the line, announcing that she wanted to speak to Plakakis, who was outside. Call back in ten minutes, his wife said.

When she told him about the call, Plakakis was wary. Hardly anyone knew where he was staying, and he'd made a point of not giving out his mother's number. The phone rang again. This time, Plakakis listened in silently on another handset as his wife answered. "I'm Mr. Iliopoulos's secretary," the woman said. The shipowner wanted to speak to him. Plakakis's wife said he wasn't in, apologized, and hung up.

Now Plakakis was more than suspicious. There was the lateness of the call, and the timing: not long after Zavos had publicly informed a London court about the existence of a new witness in the *Brillante* case. "That's it," Plakakis said to himself. "They know." After he couldn't get through to Conner, he'd lain in bed awake, trying not to imagine the consequences of being exposed as a police informant.

The next morning, Plakakis heard car engines outside. He looked through a window to see a pickup truck and a gray sedan idling a little way up the road. Inside were a group of bulky-looking men. Peering more closely while trying to remain hidden, he was sure he could see the stocky figure of Vassilios Vergos, his former business partner from Yemen. (Vergos denies that he was present.) As Plakakis watched, the house phone rang. Plakakis ignored it, his heart pounding. It rang again, and then again. A horrifying thought occurred to him. The men were listening from the street, trying to work out which address the phone number connected to. They were trying to find him.

Plakakis had called his contact at the City of London Police, but the detective didn't seem in a great hurry to act. After he pleaded for protection, the officer solemnly informed Plakakis that the force was going to hold a "gold command" meeting to decide how best to respond. While this was the top rung of operational procedure, it wasn't much comfort to someone with potential assassins at his door. Also, the gold meeting wouldn't be taking place until after lunch. Plakakis feared that he and his family might be dead by then. "What the fucking hell is wrong with them?" he cried through the phone to Conner. "What does that mean to me?" Conner tried to speak slowly and calmly. "Go to the middle of the house," he instructed Plakakis. "Get plenty of water. Keep the child quiet. And don't flush the toilet. I'm getting help."

Conner called Veale and quickly agreed on a plan. They would use the same armed security team that had protected Gerry Lallis, the Piraeus lawyer, two years earlier. Conner got his man on the phone and issued his orders. "Get there as soon as you can," he said. "When you arrive, use the codeword Zulu to identify yourselves, then wait for further instructions." The Greek outfit were serious operatives. Armed and highly trained, they wore sunglasses and jeans and zoomed around the country in blacked-out cars like a private SWAT team, guarding politicians and businessmen. Conner knew the group leader as "George." They left Athens as quickly as possible, beginning the two-hour drive to Plakakis's mother's village.

Conner called back to tell Plakakis that help was on the way. Since they last spoke, the house phone hadn't stopped ringing. Plakakis's wife would pick up the receiver and slam it down, only for the ringer to go off again. He told Conner that he could see the men outside pointing into houses, including the one he was in. He didn't know if they were armed. "Michael, I have a hunting rifle. I'm going to shoot anyone that comes," Plakakis said. Conner thought back to his time in the police. He'd lost informants before. While he was hunting Turkish drug gangs in North London, they would dispatch anyone suspected of being a snitch with a hail of bullets. He grimaced at the memory. "Make sure it's loaded," he told Plakakis. Jesus, he thought as the words left his mouth. What if he has to use the gun?

While Conner fielded calls in his living room, his wife overheard him and asked what was going on. After he told her about the situation, she reacted with English poise. "Oh dear," she said. "Would you like a cup of tea?" She put the kettle on. It was only lunchtime, but Conner's cell was already almost dead. He plugged it into the wall and sat on the sofa, his landline also within easy reach, figuring he'd need both.

The landline rang—it was a detective from the City of London Police. "My boss told me you've got to stand down what you're doing," the officer insisted. "He needs to talk to your squad directly." The British cops had learned of Conner's plan and seemed very concerned about who'd authorized the Greek bodyguards to carry out an armed operation directed from London. Conner replied that they couldn't speak to his security team, and he wasn't prepared to give them the number. He'd concluded that the police were too bogged down in procedure to be of any help. "Tell your boss this is a fast-flowing situation that I am handling as I have many times before," he said.

As Conner spoke, his cellphone buzzed: it was George, the leader of the Greek team. Conner could hear their sirens howling in the background. "We are going very fast," George said. They had eight men in two vehicles, and another group was on its way to pick up a third: a van large enough to collect Plakakis's whole family. Conner warned him that the men on the scene might have weapons, but George didn't seem concerned. "Yes, yes, yes," he said, and hung up.

Conner played out various scenarios in his head. It was possible the men had been sent to kill Plakakis, as he feared. It was also possible the authors of the *Brillante* attack had a different strategy, and they were there to bring him back into the fold—perhaps by giving him a choice between violent retribution for talking, or money in return for his silence. Or perhaps Iliopoulos simply wanted to have a frank discussion about how foolish it was to help British law enforcement investigate a fellow Greek, and had sent heavies to reinforce the point.

There was another possibility, albeit a bizarre one. Plakakis might have been making the whole thing up in order to secure protection, or inflate his own importance. After all, Conner only had one person's word for what was happening. He called again to check in. "Michael, they are standing outside the house now," Plakakis said. His voice sounded strange, distant and dreamlike. "Why did this happen to me?" he asked. "This shouldn't happen to me." Conner had dealt with terrified people many times before during his career. Plakakis's fear was real, he concluded. Whatever was happening in Greece, it wasn't an invention. Conner made a note in his phone, which he was using as a logbook: "Mental state deteriorating."

Then Conner's home phone rang once more. The City of London officer was on the line again. "I'm really sorry. I cannot take no for an answer. My boss wants the phone number of your team leader. Now."

"You're not having it," Conner snapped back. "We're in the middle of a live operation."

"You can't run a live operation. You're a civilian."

"You're also a civilian in Greece. So's your boss," said Conner, reminding the cop that his jurisdiction didn't even extend outside central London, let alone to the Greek countryside. As a compromise, Conner suggested his team could deliver Plakakis's family safely to a hotel in Athens. "Then you can have them," he said. "Only once they're safe."

Conner spoke to Plakakis again. The men in the cars had driven a short distance away and were waiting atop a hill, he said. Greece was two hours ahead of London; it would be evening soon. Conner didn't like the idea of

Plakakis being left to fend for himself in the darkness. With Plakakis on one line and George checking in on another, he laid out the next steps.

"Is there a church in town?" Conner asked.

"Yes," Plakakis replied; it was located on a busy road, by a row of cafés.

"Ask your mother to drive to the church." Conner figured that no one would bother to follow an elderly woman. George and the security squad would be there. When George identified himself as Zulu, Plakakis's mother should reply that she was Zulu too. Then she would lead them back to the house. "They're ten minutes away," Conner said.

As soon as they'd finalized the plan, Conner received another call from the City of London detective, telling him again to stop whatever he was doing. "We're about to do the handover," Conner barked. "It's right now." He hung up.

Even though he was setting it up on the fly from his living room, Conner was reasonably confident the operation would go smoothly. If the men were still waiting for Plakakis, he figured they would abandon whatever they had been planning to do after seeing two carloads of security operatives pull up. But there was no way to be sure until it was done. The moments seemed to slow down as Conner sat with one phone in hand, the other on the table next to him, sipping his tea and imagining the scene that was unfolding in Greece.

When Plakakis's mother arrived at the church, she found George leaning up against the side of his car. He gave the gray-haired woman a cheerful wave. "I'm Zulu," he said. "I was meant to tell you that!" she replied. The security expert and the grandmother shared an awkward laugh. He got back in his car and the convoy followed her to the house. When they arrived, George's team fanned out with guns drawn. There appeared to be no one around, and they hustled Plakakis and his wife, son, and mother into the back of their van. Moments later, George called Conner. "Zulu 2 and family all safe," he said. "Four, repeat four, safe." They were on the move. Conner thanked George and dialed the police detective to give him the good news. "You are really lucky," the officer said. Yeah, you're welcome, Conner thought.

Once they arrived in Athens, the Plakakis family checked into a hotel, where Veale had reserved them a room. They were booked on a flight to the relative safety of London the next morning. Greek cops, contacted by the City of London Police, arrived to keep an eye on them. Conner had been on the phone almost continuously for more than twelve hours, and he grabbed a brief stretch of sleep at home. He was up again at 3:00 a.m., heading for the airport to take the first flight to Athens.

After he arrived, he took the security team out for drinks. Conner didn't touch the alcohol himself, but he watched in satisfaction as George and his crew shared beers and shots, marking the end of a successful mission.

Plakakis would be forever grateful to Conner for his decisive intervention. But despite knowing that the *Brillante*'s insurers had funded his rescue, he was furious with the Lloyd's syndicate. He believed they had put him and his family in danger by revealing the existence of a "new witness." That statement could only have referred to him, Plakakis felt, and once the word got out, he was a marked man.

Angry as he was, Plakakis needed money. He was now estranged from many of his business contacts in Greece, and for his own safety he would need to remain in the UK, where he had scant connections, indefinitely. About a week after arriving in London, Plakakis asked detectives from the City force to inform the insurers that he might be willing to help them in their lawsuit. During the first few months of 2018, Zavos and Talbot's Paul Cunningham met him several times to discuss the possibility.

Plakakis told the pair that he wanted to enjoy the same standard of living in Britain as he would at home. Although he didn't want to "suggest anything embarrassing," he reminded them that if he provided evidence in their case, he would have to "live with the consequences for years to come," and needed compensation. On the advice of his attorney, whom the insurance syndicate had hired in order to make him feel more secure during the negotiations, Plakakis proposed a figure of 8 million pounds. That was impossible, Zavos and Cunningham responded.

The insurers had to tread a fine line. It was routine to cover the expenses involved in testifying at a trial, and paying witnesses for lost earnings is permitted in English lawsuits. But large sums are frowned upon as an affront to the integrity of the court, and they couldn't allow the promise of financial reward to taint evidence. Piraeus Bank's lawyers would seize any opportunity to portray Plakakis as an opportunist, willing to tell the insurers what they wanted to hear in exchange for cash. They proposed 250,000 pounds as a compromise. Plakakis thought about it and declined. He needed to survive in one of the world's most expensive cities, and his career was in tatters. Boiling at the injustice of what he'd been through, Plakakis proved to be a difficult negotiating partner. When agitated, he was prone to ranting, reminding everyone that he'd tipped his life into chaos by telling the truth. The discussions dragged on for weeks without agreement, before Plakakis's lawyer abruptly announced that his client was no longer willing to cooperate.

But Plakakis's run of bad luck wasn't over. Zavos and his colleagues had more moves to play. First, they persuaded a judge to issue a witness summons requiring Plakakis to appear at the London trial and provide evidence. He was legally obliged to comply. Then the judge announced that he'd made a decision on the insurers' request that Plakakis be identified by his real name, rather than the pseudonym, Theo Blake, that he'd previously used.

Over the opposition of Veale, Conner, the police, and of course Plakakis himself, Zavos and the legal team argued that the rescue operation in Greece showed that anyone who might want to harm Plakakis already knew who he was. As one of the insurers' barristers put it at a court hearing, "The cat is already out of the bag." The judge agreed. "I find it impossible to resist the conclusion that revealing his true identity . . . will not give rise to a risk to Theo Blake over and above that which already exists," he wrote. He then scheduled the trial to take place in early 2019.

Almost eight years after he first set foot on the deck of the *Brillante Virtuoso*, a vessel he never wanted to see in the first place, Plakakis still couldn't escape it.

CHAPTER 26

JUDGMENT

O n an overcast morning in February 2019, Cynthia Mockett walked down a short, dead-end street toward the Rolls Building, off London's Fetter Lane. On the sidewalk outside, knots of young legal clerks carted overstuffed boxes of files on metal trolleys, a task performed before the start of daily business at the capital's courthouses. Cynthia entered through a set of glass doors, passing the spot where, a little less than three years earlier, officers from the City of London Police had arrested Marios Iliopoulos. After making her way upstairs she sat down in the back of a brightly lit hearing room, which had been set up with a series of plasma screens for viewing photos and documents. There was a buzz of anticipation as the two platoons of lawyers, seated at tables piled high with stacks of paper, waited for the proceedings to begin.

At least some of the insurers' attorneys wanted to keep Cynthia away from the Rolls Building, with one telling Conner that her presence wouldn't be "helpful to our case." On that, as with so much else, the detectives and the lawyers disagreed. But the courtroom was public, with anyone free to enter, and she'd decided to attend anyway. Cynthia was determined to hear the whole story of the events she believed had led to her husband's death, not just the small pieces she'd been allowed so far.

Just before 10:30, everyone stood as Justice Nigel Teare, a sixty-seven-year-old with a fuzz of snow-white hair on either side of his bald scalp, emerged from his chambers, taking his seat at the front. A moment later the lead barrister for Piraeus Bank, Peter MacDonald Eggers, opened the proceedings with a polite "Good morning, my Lord," and proceeded to summarize the key questions of *Suez Fortune Investments Ltd & Piraeus Bank AE v. Talbot Underwriting Ltd & Others.* The case, MacDonald Eggers said, concerned a ship that "was commandeered by armed intruders, who later detonated an incendiary explosive device which caused a substantial fire, resulting in the vessel's total loss." Those facts were not in dispute. What the bank and the insurers disagreed on was the motive for the intruders' actions. Like nearly all civil trials in England, this one would be decided by a judge, not a jury, and it would be up to Teare to determine if the men who boarded the *Brillante Virtuoso* were sent by Marios Iliopoulos, or whether the shipowner and his bankers, who'd given him the money to purchase the vessel, were in fact their victims.

With his direct claim against Talbot and the other underwriters thrown out after his menacing testimony in 2016, leaving Piraeus Bank to continue the suit without him, Iliopoulos would have no say in the matter. He wouldn't even be appearing in court. Shortly after the start of the day's session, MacDonald Eggers explained that, although Iliopoulos had not been charged with any offense, he had been advised by his criminal lawyers not to participate in the trial. Since Piraeus had written off Iliopoulos's loan, concluding he was unlikely ever to pay it back, he didn't have a financial incentive to take part, either. Iliopoulos was debt free and had no reason to care who ended up covering the loss of the *Brillante*. And he was safely in Greece, unlikely to come to the UK while prosecution was even a remote possibility. There was apparently nothing anyone could do to force him to give evidence.

Conner was sitting near Cynthia in the area set aside for spectators, surrounded by perhaps a dozen others. Even without Iliopoulos, the trial was still the culmination of more than half a decade of his and Veale's work. If the verdict went against them, their clients would have to hand over as much as $77 million, a very large award even for Lloyd's—and an embarrassing black mark for Veale's business. The implications went beyond the payout, though, and the fact that Iliopoulos would walk away unscathed. With a loss for the insurers, the whole maritime world would see that it paid to continue scuttling ships, risking sailors' lives in the process.

There was also the matter of law enforcement. Despite Iliopoulos's professed justification for not coming to London, the detectives had very little confidence that police were treating the *Brillante* with the seriousness it deserved. They'd received no indication that charges of any kind were imminent, and whatever investigations had been under way seemed to have stalled. But if the judge clearly ruled that the attack on the vessel was faked—a decision backed by the enormous volumes of evidence they'd helped the insurers amass—Veale and Conner believed the cops might be embarrassed into action. After years of fruitless efforts to get the Metropolitan Police more interested in Mockett's assassination, Cynthia was holding out hope that they were right.

The task of convincing Teare that the destruction of the *Brillante* was a fraud would fall to Jonathan Gaisman, the barrister who'd also represented the insurers when Iliopoulos was on the stand in 2016. With his soft features, Gaisman didn't look imposing, but he had a reputation as a fiercely effective courtroom advocate, with a list of past clients that included the BBC, the Royal Bank of Scotland, and even the government of Russia, defending it against investors in an oil company that had been effectively seized by the Kremlin. (Demonstrating the gymnastic flexibility prized in the British legal fraternity, Gaisman had also advised the financier Bill Browder, one of Vladimir Putin's most tenacious critics.)

Gaisman's specialty was in handling cases of extreme complexity, and the *Brillante* dispute certainly qualified. It would take until midsummer to get through all the hearings, during which he and MacDonald Eggers would present evidence from specialists in marine engineering, salvage, piracy, accounting, and shipboard security, as well as a topic the lawyers called "Yemeni criminality." There would be detailed analysis of Iliopoulos's financial circumstances in the months before the *Brillante*'s last voyage, and of the precise chronology of Poseidon Salvage's response to the attack, the speed of which, the insurers suggested, implied foreknowledge. There would be a mind-numbing debate over what was referred to as "the detachment of the drain-cock," an issue that Gaisman viewed as critically important. A spout on an oil tank had broken off at some point after the *Brillante* fire began, but was later reattached—evidence, according to Gaisman, that someone was trying to cover their tracks.

Veale questioned the wisdom of spending so much time on technical evidence, and on the lengthy questioning of expert witnesses about the minutiae of engineering diagrams and close-up photographs. It would be too easy, he feared, for the trial to get bogged down in angels-on-a-pin details, at the expense of what he believed was an indisputable overall picture. Still, the lawyers had insisted they knew better. As Veale sometimes complained to his partner, they seemed to think that "unless something's written down on a bit of paper, it didn't happen."

Instead of the endless back-and-forth between experts, Veale and Conner were focused on the other parts of the proceedings, which they hoped would make the strongest impression on Judge Teare. For the first time since the *Brillante* was attacked, a court was about to hear from people who were actually there.

"Captain Gonzaga, can you see me and hear me?"

"Yes, sir."

"I want to take you back to the beginning of the last voyage of the *Brillante Virtuoso*."

The video link to the Shangri-La Hotel in Manila, eight time zones away, was patchy. Sometimes the image froze for several seconds, and there was a noticeable lag before questions from Gaisman, in the courtroom in London, reached the other end of the line. If it couldn't be fixed, Teare suggested Gonzaga's appearance might need to be abandoned. But the testimony of the *Brillante*'s captain was critically important, and after some modest improvement, Teare gave his permission for it to proceed.

Some of Gaisman's first questions to Gonzaga were so simple that it was hard to discern what he was getting at. Early in his cross-examination, he asked the Filipino to describe some of the equipment on the tanker's bridge.

"What instruments did you have on the bridge to enable you to see in what direction you were sailing?" Gaisman asked. Gonzaga replied that he had used nautical charts, as well as the Automatic Identification System, a platform for tracking the movement of vessels.

"I rather assume," the lawyer said, "you would mention that there was a gyrocompass on the bridge"—a spinning dial that indicates a ship's heading at all times. "Is that right?"

"Yeah, yeah, yeah."

"Was there also a repeater display on the control panel, which showed you what the heading of the vessel was?"

"Yeah, you can see the repeater also."

"If, say, the second officer came on the bridge at the beginning of his watch, it would be very easy for him to see what the heading of the ship was, wouldn't it, straight away?"

The response came back from Manila without hesitation. "Yeah, we can see by looking at the gyro."

"And at the repeater display on the control panel, correct?"

"That's correct, sir."

Gaisman moved on, his questions sharpening. At one point he asked Gonzaga to imagine a "suspect boat drill," a practice run for responding to the approach of an unidentified vessel. Such drills were a standard part of maritime security training, and the *Brillante*'s crew had conducted one just a couple of months before they ran into trouble. Suppose, Gaisman said, speaking slowly to ensure that he was understood, "During this drill a young officer had put his hand up" to ask a question. "Supposing he had said, 'If the people in the boat have rifles and we can see that they have rifles, would that be something which should increase our concern or diminish our concern?'"

"Increase concern," Gonzaga replied.

Gaisman continued. "Supposing they didn't just have rifles but they also were wearing masks, that would increase your concern even more, wouldn't it?"

At the reference to masks, Gonzaga seemed to grasp where Gaisman was trying to take him. According to the captain's own earlier statements, the men who attacked the *Brillante* had carried assault rifles and covered their faces with surgical masks. And yet Gonzaga had allowed them to come on board, claiming afterward that he believed them to be "the authorities." Suddenly, he began to backtrack. "No, sir," Gonzaga said. Masks wouldn't alarm him. They might be worn "because sometimes it's dust," or to protect against disease—an explanation that, well before the emergence of COVID-19, would have struck few in the courtroom as credible.

Gaisman was trying to show that Gonzaga had ignored every conceivable antipiracy procedure on the night in question, defying his documented training as well as common sense. As the lawyer continued to push him to explain his behavior, Gonzaga's answers became even more strained. "So if somebody tells you that there's a small, unlit boat approaching," Gaisman asked, "it doesn't cross your mind that they might be pirates?" Not necessarily, Gonzaga explained. "Because sometimes there's a small boat coming [to] sell fish." Nocturnal fishmongering—in one of the most dangerous waterways in the world, no less—was a new one, and Gaisman seemed genuinely startled by the claim. "Selling fish in the middle of the night?" he asked.

"Yeah, it's in my previous experience, sir."

"It would be a rather high-risk area just to sell a few kingfish or John Dory, wouldn't it?" The notion seemed too ridiculous to spend more time discussing. "Anyway, let's go on."

Gaisman shifted to what happened later, after the attackers had boarded the *Brillante*, when Gonzaga was alone on the bridge with some of the gunmen. Repeating what he'd previously told investigators, Gonzaga testified that the apparent pirates had ordered him to sail to Somalia—although not, curiously, toward any specific point in that country, which has more than three thousand kilometers of coastline.

With that statement on the record, Gaisman sprang his trap. The ship's navigational logs, he reminded the court, showed that Gonzaga had in fact steered it southwest, toward Djibouti—a placid East African state, fortified with US and French military installations, where it would be distinctly unwise to turn up with a hijacked oil tanker. As Gaisman pointed out, real pirates—experienced seamen, with deep knowledge of oceanic navigation—"would be likely to notice if the vessel was being steered in the wrong direction, wouldn't they?" After all, Gonzaga had helpfully confirmed, in his earlier testimony, that there were multiple instruments on the bridge showing the *Brillante's* heading. The only explanation, Gaisman said, was that no one had any intention of taking the *Brillante* to Somalia, and the ship's captain knew it.

Under a battery of questions, Gonzaga insisted that the gunmen watching over him "didn't know when I sailed wrong direction." Gaisman responded curtly: "So you say, master."

Gaisman's questioning lasted for four days, time he used to dismantle even the most anodyne elements of Gonzaga's story. Although Judge Teare, a model of judicial inscrutability, didn't betray his impressions of the testimony, it was clear to Veale and Conner that the cross-examination had scored point after point for the insurers. Still, they were wary of getting too confident. Their reluctant star witness hadn't yet testified, and they couldn't be sure of what he was going to say.

Dimitrios Plakakis was surrounded by cops. Beamed into the Rolls Building by video link from an undisclosed location, he sat at a table flanked by officers from the City of London Police. Their presence was meant as a warning to anyone intending to hurt him, though it had the unintended effect of making Plakakis appear especially vulnerable. Balding and bespectacled, he looked even more slight than usual. A lawyer for the City force was in the courtroom to monitor his testimony, ready to intervene if he said anything that might compromise his security.

Gaisman had almost no questions for Plakakis, apart from asking him to verify that he was "Theo Blake," the anonymous whistleblower who'd given a long statement to police in 2017, describing everything he'd witnessed in Yemen. Plakakis confirmed that he was, and that the statement, which had been entered into evidence for the civil trial, remained accurate. After just a few minutes, Gaisman asked Plakakis his final question: "Are you attending this court voluntarily or because you have been told to do so by a witness summons?" Plakakis replied that he'd been ordered to appear. "It's not voluntarily," he said.

Gaisman took his seat, yielding the floor to MacDonald Eggers to conduct his cross-examination. "The question I have for you," MacDonald Eggers said after some preliminaries, "is why are you giving evidence today only because there's a court order—a witness summons? Why aren't you giving it freely and voluntarily?"

Plakakis spoke English with a heavy Greek accent, and a translator was standing by in case he asked to switch to his native language. But no one had trouble making out his answer, even if his syntax was sometimes unconventional. "I didn't want to expose my name, I didn't wanted to expose my life," he said. "Unfortunately, for reasons that they had nothing to do with me, police said the underwriters, they decided to give my evidence, to expose my identity, and to find myself in the position I'm here." If it had been up to him, Plakakis said, he would never have testified.

Trying to cast doubt on Plakakis's motives, MacDonald Eggers asked him to explain how he first made contact with the police. Had he approached law enforcement, or vice versa? Plakakis said he'd taken the initiative of going to the police; he believed that he'd witnessed something fundamentally wrong and had a responsibility to come forward—an obligation to his "dignity as a human being," as he put it in his statement.

But if Plakakis had intimate knowledge of a criminal fraud, MacDonald Eggers continued, he could have reported it immediately after it occurred in 2011. Why wait years to tell anyone? "You have to understand me," Plakakis replied. "I was living on the floating crane inside the Aden port, in the sea. It wasn't a case like you go next door to the police and you report something." He had waited until "the time was safe for me"—when he was in London, confident he was beyond Iliopoulos's reach.

MacDonald Eggers kept pressing. Plakakis left Aden a month after the *Brillante* attack, he said, and "had every opportunity, without any fear for your security, to bring this to the attention of the authorities or the police at that time." It was a revealing statement. Like the insurance lawyers who'd so frustrated Veale and Conner, MacDonald Eggers seemed almost willfully blind to the realities of places less well ordered than the City of London. "There was no trust to report the case to the Greek authorities," Plakakis said, because Iliopoulos was "a Greek oligarch," with untold influence in Athens.

"I was afraid about my life." Vassilios Theodorou, the Poseidon crewman who later met with Veale and Conner, had tried to tell a lawyer what he'd witnessed, Plakakis continued. As a result, "he found himself hiding from the world in the Greek mountains." But "I didn't have any mountain to go. I was trying to live a life as a normal person."

MacDonald Eggers moved on to the next part of his strategy: to try to show that the conspiracy described by Plakakis wasn't plausible. This was a central plank of Piraeus Bank's argument—that the fraud alleged by the insurers was too complex, and involved too many people, to have really happened. "Just so I understand it," MacDonald Eggers said, "this alleged conspiracy involves Mr. Iliopoulos and his associates; that's correct?"

Plakakis replied that it was. "And Mr. Vergos," he added.

"The master and chief engineer?"

"Yes."

"Members of the Yemeni Coast Guard?"

"Yes."

The list stretched on, taking in the businessman Sharif Ba'alawi, the Yemeni fixer Ahmed Nashwan, and various others in Greece and Yemen. "That's a very large number of people," MacDonald Eggers declared skeptically. But Plakakis was emphatic. "I was there. I know exactly what happened. I witnessed the thing," he said. "Your belief may be different, because you have different interests. What can I do about that? It's 100 percent true, my whole statement, line by line. I lived through that story. I lived through that in my life. I have damaged my life big time because of this. So I have not any reason to lie."

Plakakis answered MacDonald Eggers's questions for the entire day, speaking in long, digressive bursts that prompted Teare to ask him to keep his replies to the point. For a man who'd needed a court order to testify, he had a remarkable amount to say, and a detailed rebuttal to every attempt to cast doubt on his story. The next day, the bank's lawyer continued to needle him, attempting to pick at his credibility. In his police statement, Plakakis had said he'd known the *Brillante* operation would be dangerous: he feared that the oil on board could explode, or cause a spill on the Yemeni coast. If that was true, MacDonald Eggers asked, "Why didn't you warn someone about these dangers before it happened?"

Again, Plakakis asked the lawyer to consider his circumstances. "I have to remind you I was in the middle of the sea. It wasn't in a flat here in Kensington to call by police station."

"But you had all means of communication available. You could have communicated with anyone, including the insurers, or the police."

Plakakis had remained patient through most of the questioning, but now he began to get angry. "Forgive me for being rude," he told MacDonald Eggers. "Mr. David Mockett, he knew how to communicate and he's where he is." He continued: "Don't ask me questions why I didn't do what I didn't do . . . whatever I did was correct because I'm still alive today. That's all I know."

Neither MacDonald Eggers nor Teare said anything in reply. On a flimsy chair at the rear of the courtroom, Cynthia Mockett was sitting quietly.

The hearings continued for fifty-two days, many of them taken up with microscopic cross-examination of technical specialists with no direct knowledge of what occurred on the *Brillante*. As Veale and Conner had feared, the proceedings felt at times like they were completely detached from the actual events—a procession of paid expert witnesses answering questions that focused, for example, on patterns of damage to the tanker's pipework. "Now, bearing in mind," MacDonald Eggers asked during one memorably futile exchange, "that that angle iron supporting both the pipe which leads to the side flange and then it is bolted to that pipe below, which of course, if it is bolted, that may be, as you say, exerting a downward force on the angle iron, that collapse or that sagging could create tensions and forces within the pipework system which leads to the separation of the flange from the valve body?" The witness's reply: "Well, that was the point I was making."

On the final day, Gaisman got into a debate with Teare on whether "knowledge and belief are different things," which culminated with the insurers' lawyer engaging in a bit of amateur theology. "I mean, religious belief," Gaisman declared, "is obviously one example where, except in the cases of people who are very fortunate in their gifts, you believe what you don't know. 'Credo ut intelligam'"—I believe, in order to understand—"as Augustine said." The attorneys on both sides of the courtroom tittered with amusement.

It was tempting for the detectives to feel the decision was sure to go their way. The insurers' key witnesses had held up well, and they believed they had an overwhelming body of evidence on their side, even if some of it had been clouded through overlong dissection. But overconfidence, they told themselves, would be a mistake. The reluctance of the Lloyd's market to accuse its clients of fraud was only part of why underwriters so rarely took scuttling cases to court. They were also exceedingly difficult to win, with insurers required to prove not only that a vessel was intentionally destroyed but that its owner was directly responsible.

For Cynthia, the trial was notable for how much weight was given to her late husband's work. It wasn't just Plakakis's reference to him. Both sides had cited Mockett's survey, and his photographs were entered into evidence, unchallenged. Every time she saw them being used, she felt a little better. During a break in one hearing, Gaisman took the time to approach her. "There is no doubt that your husband knew exactly what he was looking at," he told Cynthia.

In October 2019, the legal teams returned to the Rolls Building, where Judge Teare would hand down his verdict. No one could accuse him of failing to consider the matter thoroughly. His written judgment ran to more than 130 single-spaced pages, beginning with a detailed summary of the known facts of the *Brillante* case and running through his assessment of key witnesses. Veale and Conner scanned it as quickly as they could, looking for hints of Teare's conclusion, which might be buried deep inside the document. They found it, finally, beginning from paragraph 472. "The armed men who boarded *Brillante Virtuoso*," Teare wrote, "had no intention of hijacking the vessel for ransom and only pretended to be pirates." He'd concluded that Captain Gonzaga and Nestor Tabares, the chief engineer, "assisted the armed men in their task," serving as key players in a conspiracy to which "Mr. Vergos of Poseidon was party." The next lines were the ones the detectives found most satisfying to read. "I do not consider that there is a plausible explanation of the events which befell *Brillante Virtuoso* which is consistent with an innocent explanation," Teare said. And he had no doubt about who was responsible: "The orchestrator of these events was the owner of *Brillante Virtuoso*, Mr. Iliopoulos."

For the lawyers and Talbot's Paul Cunningham, the verdict was met with intense relief. They'd all put their reputations on the line by confronting a shipowner so directly. Zavos had even been accused of organizing illegal investigations in Greece, in a criminal complaint that also named Conner. Such an emphatic ruling from Teare was the best possible outcome, a vindication of all the risks they'd taken. Yet the codes of the London insurance world still applied. None of the *Brillante* insurers wanted to put out a press release trumpeting their victory; it was better, they thought, not to draw excessive attention.

Veale and Conner, for their parts, had mixed feelings about the judgment. Veale recognized it as a professional triumph. Yet he was stung by a sense of regret. There were important witnesses and pieces of evidence he hadn't been allowed to pursue. He thought about Sharif Ba'alawi, who was in business with both Vassilios Vergos and Ahmed Nashwan. At one point Ba'alawi had made contact with someone at Lloyd's, suggesting he was willing to talk. But Zavos never granted his permission for Veale and Conner to seek an interview with him.

For Veale, the missing puzzle pieces were a source of insistent bother, compounded by the knowledge that the verdict might have little or no direct impact on Iliopoulos. With his *Brillante* debt to Piraeus Bank written off, the shipowner was free and clear. Veale's side had won, but he wasn't quite sure he could put the case behind him. Conner, meanwhile, responded to the decision with a shrug. "Not a penny lost in Greece," he said, repeating a line that had become something of a catchphrase when he talked about the *Brillante*. It was a curious sort of victory that allowed the losers to walk away with their position improved by tens of millions of dollars.

After he'd read through the judgment, Conner called Cynthia at her home in Devon to break the news. When he told her what Teare had written, she began to cry. Listening to her, Conner realized that, despite his own ambivalence, the verdict was the closest Cynthia had come to a validation of her husband's life and death—maybe the closest she would ever come. It meant something, even if that meaning had to be found amid insurers and financiers squabbling over the cost of a ship. "David was right," she said through her tears. "I knew he was right."

CHAPTER 27

THE CAPTAIN

I n late 2020, about a year after the *Brillante Virtuoso* judgment, Richard
Veale was back working for the Lloyd's market—on a new case, with a different syndicate of insurers, and a different kind of villain on the other side.
The attorneys on his team were gleefully speculating about how damaging it
would be if a judge in London's High Court ruled against their opponent. He
would be dragged through the mud in the shipping press, they predicted, and
there would be a critical report in *Lloyd's List*, the industry journal that has
chronicled the marine world's triumphs and disasters since 1734. (Despite
the name, the publication is independent from Lloyd's.) The lawyers assumed
this would be devastating for the businessman. Veale disagreed. He had two
words for them: "Marios Iliopoulos."

As far as Veale could see, Super Mario was doing just fine, even after the
decision in London. If anything, he was thriving. Just two months after Judge
Teare ruled that Iliopoulos had orchestrated one of history's most audacious
maritime frauds, a Seajets ferry won "Ship of the Year" at the Lloyd's List
Greek Shipping Awards. Iliopoulos accepted the prize with a speech at a glitzy
ceremony in Athens. Some of the most respected names in the industry were
in attendance, alongside a clutch of Greek politicians that included the country's deputy minister for sport and culture. Wearing a black suit and crisp
white shirt, Iliopoulos praised the vessel's record-breaking speed and envi-

ronmentally friendly turbine engines. "At Seajets, our goals are fully aligned with the goals of all Greeks who want to see Greece, this country with its huge history and culture, smile again and fill the hearts of all Greeks with pride and joy," he beamed. "We believe that society cannot exist without respecting, living, breathing together." Iliopoulos had also won plaudits for his response to the wildfires that tore through the Greek mainland in 2018, killing more than a hundred people and displacing thousands. He'd hired cranes to clear the roads, donated food supplies, and organized special events to provide "psychological support to children affected by the tragedy," according to a press release issued on his behalf.

None of the controversies buzzing around the shipowner seemed to matter. Like irritating flies, he managed to brush them away, never letting them interfere with his business. Back in 2014, Veale had identified another oil tanker that belonged to Iliopoulos's fleet: the *Despina Andrianna*. Proving it wasn't easy. The vessel's ownership was convoluted even by the standards of modern shipping, further obscured by a so-called back-to-back transaction, where an asset is bought by one offshore shell, then immediately sold to another. Veale figured it out when he spotted the signature of a Seajets employee—a woman who'd been seen accompanying Iliopoulos to social events in Greece—in the *Despina*'s paperwork. The entity that owned the ship also shared a phone, fax number, and Piraeus address with Worldwide Green Tankers, a known Iliopoulos shell. When Veale saw that the former captain of the *Brillante*, Noe Gonzaga, had posted a picture of the *Despina* on his Facebook page, he had no doubt who the real owner was.

At the time, Veale passed on the details of his discovery to his contacts at Lloyd's, then thought little more about it. But five years later, in 2019, the US Treasury Department announced sanctions against the *Despina Andrianna* and associated companies, alleging that they had been running embargoed Venezuelan oil to Cuba, to the benefit of President Nicolás Maduro's brutal regime. Though Iliopoulos wasn't named in the order, even indirect international sanctions are among the most serious red flags for corporate compliance departments. Ignoring them can lead to billion-dollar penalties and criminal prosecution. The whole point of sanctions, especially when applied with the global reach of the US government, is to freeze their targets out of the machinery of international finance. Yet Iliopoulos's ventures continued to operate, seemingly unconstrained.

When COVID-19 brought global trade and tourism to a halt in 2020, many maritime businesses faced ruin. Iliopoulos, with typical bravado, saw an opportunity. He bought at least six passenger vessels, at fire-sale prices, from desperate cruise operators whose businesses had shut down. Within a few months he'd sold two for scrap, earning three times the $9 million he paid, according to estimates by trade publications. Like the *Brillante* before them, the *Columbus* and the *Magellan* were dismantled by hand and stripped of recyclable material at Indian and Pakistani shipbreaking yards, some of the world's most dangerous and polluted workplaces. Because of the human and environmental cost, it's illegal for European companies to send vessels to either country to be broken down without first removing all potentially hazardous waste, but the rules are easily skirted by transferring ownership offshore. The other four liners that Iliopoulos bought during the pandemic were, at the time of writing, laid up in Greek ports awaiting their fate. Given his talent for turning old ships into money, they should earn him a healthy return.

Most remarkable of all, Super Mario kept doing business at Lloyd's, according to several sources who asked not to be identified because the contracts aren't public. The Seajets fleet and his bargain cruise ships can't sail without protection, and the world's most important insurance market isn't in the habit of turning away customers. Most of Iliopoulos's vessels are registered for third-party liability insurance with something called the American Steamship Owners Mutual Protection and Indemnity Association. In plain English, the American Club, as it's known, is a kind of global shipowners' collective, pooling resources to cover the cost of damage caused by ships involved in accidents. There are limits to how much clubs like it will pay out, though. For anything major, members of the American Club have to claim extra funds from a reinsurance policy bought through Lloyd's. (A spokesman for the group said that its relationship with Seajets is "routine, unremarkable and legitimate.") To some in the Lloyd's orbit, selling insurance, even in this roundabout way, to someone who'd deliberately wrecked at least one tanker, and probably two, was hard to stomach. To others it wasn't so surprising. The same moral flexibility had allowed the market to survive scandals and financial mishaps for more than three hundred years.

The newest threat to the occupants of One Lime Street was the novel coronavirus, which was expected to cost Lloyd's members at least 6 billion pounds as companies claimed on policies covering unexpected business interruption. Globally, the insurance industry responded with increasingly creative ways to avoid having to compensate clients. Early in the pandemic, an American law firm asserted that since the virus was microscopic and could only survive temporarily outside the human body, the damage it caused wasn't physically quantifiable. Insurers seized on the defense enthusiastically. The first of hundreds of lawsuits to decide the issue began in December 2020, when a New Orleans restaurant sued in Louisiana District Court for the money lost when it was forced to close. The defendants were listed as "Certain Underwriters at Lloyd's, London." The industry's pugnacious attitude toward that and similar claims offered a sharp contrast to its historic ambivalence about scuttling. In the UK, Lloyd's members took a test case on COVID-19 payouts all the way to the Supreme Court, and lost.

The pandemic caused one of the worst years in living memory for London's insurers. Lloyd's had to close its historic Underwriting Room twice in 2020, forcing underwriters and brokers who'd spent a lifetime making deals face-to-face into unfamiliar digital interactions. It was awkward but it worked, just well enough. The market kept on going, even as the Lloyd's corporation, which operates it, swung from a 2.5 billion pound pretax profit in 2019 to a 900 million pound loss in 2020.

Still, Lloyd's would endure. It had weathered storms before. "Actually, when we get under the skin of the results, and get out of Covid, we're really encouraged," chief executive John Neal told the *Financial Times*. From the market's point of view, he said, the next few years offered "really solid trading conditions."

On a balmy summer afternoon, Cynthia Mockett and Michael Conner made the short drive to Drake Memorial Park, a hillside cemetery near Cynthia's

Plymouth home. As they arrived, shadows stretched out from scattered pine trees over the rows of simple plaques laid flat in the earth. Cynthia and Conner followed a neat gravel path through a manicured lawn. There, amid patches of wildflowers, was her husband's plot, marked with an embossed metal slab.

DAVID JOHN MOCKETT

27 MARCH 1946–20 JULY 2011

DEVOTED HUSBAND

DAD AND GRANDAD

ALWAYS MISSED

LOVED FOREVER

"Good afternoon, Captain," Conner said after a few moments of silence looking down on the grave. Then he got down on all fours and began carefully trimming the overgrown grass along the edges with a set of small shears.

The *Brillante* had left its mark on Conner. He was charged in the criminal complaint lodged in Greece by one of Iliopoulos's associates, accusing the insurers and various agents of trying to access private information. While the actions in the complaint had nothing to do with him, he had to take it seriously. So did Veale, who wasn't named as a defendant, but was described in the filing as a "critical and important person" to the case. Conner risked detention under a European arrest warrant, and they were forced to hire Greek defense lawyers at considerable cost. The Talbot syndicate, after initially indicating it was willing to cover Veale and Conner's legal bills, suddenly withdrew the offer. Veale's firm happened to have a separate corporate insurance policy against legal action—but the insurers refused to pay out. The pair had to split the cost themselves.

Conner was left fuming, tens of thousands of pounds out of pocket. His friendship with Veale had also been strained. The two men had argued fiercely about the debt, and Conner felt let down. Then, without explanation, the Greek complaint was dropped. Conner returned to working as a consultant for Veale. They slipped quickly back into their old double act—Metal Mickey and the Accountant, the tough guy and the technician—chasing scammers and swindlers around the world for clients in London's financial district. They were often hired by law firms, though after watching Conner interact with Chris Zavos, Veale tried to keep his partner's contact with attorneys to a minimum.

After Conner finished pruning the grass, Cynthia laid down some fresh flowers. "He always told me he would be the first to go," she said. David would joke that he had to die earlier, because he couldn't bring himself to go on without her. Remembering his words, she smiled. Her husband had wanted to be an organ donor, she told Conner, but that wasn't possible because of the damage caused by the bomb. Instead, she'd agreed to allow the pathologist who'd conducted his autopsy to use his remains to train other forensic scientists. It seemed fitting. "Evidence, dear boy" was one of Mockett's favorite phrases. Cynthia often came to the cemetery alone, to talk to him. She liked to tell him what was happening with the *Brillante* case, and to update him on what the police were doing. "We haven't forgotten about you," she would say.

Not that there had been much recent news. In fact, as far as Cynthia knew, there was none. The City of London Police's fraud investigation into the *Brillante*, the one that led to Iliopoulos's arrest outside court, appeared to have sputtered out, with no charges ever brought. As for Mockett's death, the UK Foreign Office had kicked the case over to the Metropolitan Police anti-terror unit. There it had remained ever since, apparently gathering dust.

In 2018, Cynthia wrote to her local Member of Parliament, Sir Gary Streeter, who said he would try to help. His letters to various police leaders, bearing the House of Commons logo, yielded a handful of meetings and replies expressing condolences, but also making clear it was up to the Yemeni authorities to investigate a murder in Yemen. Given the country's descent into civil war, mass starvation, and disease, that was as good as saying it would never happen. In Yemen, Mockett's death was just one tragedy among millions. "I am afraid that it looks as though both the Home Office and the Metropolitan Police have made up their minds," Streeter wrote to Cynthia in 2020.

Soon after they first met, Conner promised he would help Mockett's widow see the matter through to the end. Now it wasn't clear what sort of ending they could hope for. Conner felt the clearest course to justice could be to use the UK's laws on criminal proceeds, which allow the confiscation of money earned from illegal activities, to pursue the architects of the *Brillante* attack. Whether it was securing a simple fraud conviction, charging Iliopoulos with the deliberate destruction of a vessel, or freezing bank accounts and seizing ships, he believed there were things the British police should have done—and still could. In Cynthia's mind, any response would have been better than what she'd witnessed so far. It was bad enough that the people responsible for destroying the *Brillante* had escaped punishment, financial or otherwise. She'd received no apology, no compensation—not even a payout from Mockett's corporate life insurance—and no satisfactory answer to the question of what her husband had died for.

No longer able to afford the upkeep of the Vicarage, Cynthia had moved out of the family home and into a bungalow nearby. The garden was much smaller, but she kept busy maintaining a colorful display of flowers and growing tomatoes in her greenhouse. It was David who'd encouraged her to take a course in botany, years ago, while he was out of the country working. Although she walked with a slight limp, the result of a hip operation that left one leg shorter than the other, Cynthia could get around the garden briskly, accompanied by a tortoiseshell cat who followed her as she tended the plants.

A few weeks after the *Brillante* lawsuit ended, Cynthia wrote to the chief executive of Talbot, the lead member of the Lloyd's syndicate that insured the tanker's hull. "Congratulations on winning the case," she said. "It was my husband, David Mockett, who inspected the vessel after it had been attacked. His evidence was used during the recent trial." Mockett's report had helped the syndicate defeat a fraudulent claim worth $77 million, she went on. "I am told that Talbot spent £28 million on legal fees. It seems only just that my daughters and I receive some compensation for our loss. Of course, no amount of money can replace David, [but] it would greatly assist my family in our difficult circumstances." She never received any reply.

Cynthia and Conner walked among the trees as the sun slowly set on Drake Memorial Park. Without upright tombstones, the cemetery had a bright, open aspect that she had always enjoyed. She normally spent much of her time there in quiet contemplation, but as she talked to Conner in the fading light, insects swirling overhead, she began to grow angry. She'd lived apart from David for most of their marriage, while he was at sea or in the Middle East. "He was an exciting man," she said. "Nothing was ever dull with him.

The stories he could tell . . ." She shook her head, as though she still couldn't quite accept the reality of his absence. Mockett's retirement was supposed to be the start of a new phase in their lives, one they could finally spend together. "I've been robbed and cheated of years with my husband," she said, her eyes blazing. "It's not right." Conner nodded but said nothing. "It's not right," Cynthia repeated softly. The two of them walked slowly up the driveway toward the exit, leaving the cemetery empty as the sun disappeared behind a smoky haze of white cloud, draping the hills in shadow.

AFTERWORD

O ne day in early 2017, the authors of this book walked the short distance
from Bloomberg's London newsroom to the Royal Exchange, in the heart
of the City, to meet two men who, we'd been informed, could tell us all
about the *Brillante Virtuoso*. The source who'd set up the rendezvous was too
nervous to reveal their names or put us in direct contact with them. "This is
a bigger situation than you know," he'd told us a few weeks earlier, glancing
over his shoulder anxiously. So how were we to spot the men we were supposed
to meet? "One of them has an unusually large head," the source said.

The Royal Exchange is one of central London's grandest meeting places.
Entering through a row of stone columns inspired by the Pantheon in Rome,
we crossed into a central atrium, open from gleaming floor to glass roof. In
years past, it would have echoed with the shouts of merchants, futures traders,
and, for part of its history, the Lloyd's of London insurance market. Today
it is little more than a luxury shopping mall, selling jewelry and overpriced
British condiments. We took a seat at one of the café tables in the center of
the room and began joking about the cranial proportions of the people milling around.

"Is that them?"

"No, his head is only slightly bigger than average."

"That one looks large, but is it unusually large?"

By that time, we'd been investigating the *Brillante* for several months, work that would lead to a feature published in *Bloomberg Businessweek* later in 2017. We knew little of Marios Iliopoulos, and nothing of the dramatic events, involving a pair of Greek whistleblowers, that were just then beginning to unfold. We'd both covered fraud and highly sensitive legal cases before, but we could feel that this story was different. Hardly anyone wanted to talk about it, and those who did insisted on remaining anonymous. No one knew whether the police were investigating, or what the insurers planned to do. It all seemed like a shameful secret.

Finally, our guests arrived. Or, at least, a man fitting the right description appeared, and, after we waved awkwardly, joined us with his companion. Over the next hour or so, they described an intervention by American special forces, a brutal beating in Greece, and at least one other, unrelated fraud connected to the *Brillante*. They explained that Mockett wasn't even the only Briton to have died in Yemen. The two men could give us no proof of any of it, but insisted that, with enough investigation, we would find it was all true. We left the meeting not quite sure what to believe.

By the time we began researching for this book, it was remarkable how many of those stories had turned out to be accurate. David Mockett's friend Roy Facey *had* been extracted from Yemen by an armed American team. Gerry Lallis, the Greek insurance lawyer, had indeed been beaten in Piraeus. The *Brillante* was at the center of not one but multiple frauds, including an apparent attempt to rip off Chinese tax authorities by mislabeling the tanker's cargo. (The architects of this entirely separate ruse must have had no idea the oil was never intended to reach its destination.) And another British citizen really did die in Aden not so long after Mockett: the lawyer Roger Stokes, who worked on behalf of at least one client with a financial interest in the ship, and later sustained a fatal head wound at his home, under circumstances that have never been fully understood.

All the while, the insurance industry has maintained a stubborn silence. Every one of the insurance companies mentioned in these pages declined to formally comment about their roles in the *Brillante* affair. (Allianz, which was part of the group covering the tanker's cargo, said in a statement that it has a "zero-tolerance principle for fraud and corruption" and investigates suspicious claims thoroughly, but couldn't discuss the case.) The Lloyd's market itself went one better. When we sent a document outlining the contents of the book to its media relations team, inviting feedback, they confirmed receipt— and then never responded. The actions of criminals, these organizations seemed to have decided, were none of their business; the less said, the better.

This mindset might have been best exemplified by one of the many London lawyers who has worked for Iliopoulos. Toward the end of our project, we called him to ask whether there was anything he could say about the *Brillante*, even considering the restrictions of attorney-client privilege. Commenting wouldn't be proper, he said: "The case has been resolved in a satisfactory fashion by a senior judge of the realm. I have nothing further to say about it." When he was told that Cynthia Mockett didn't think the matter was satisfactorily resolved, the lawyer responded angrily. "I know nothing about that. Nothing at all," he declared.

It's possible to argue that the *Brillante* case struck a blow against fraud. After all, the insurers did decide to reject Iliopoulos's claim. They didn't have to. Another group of Lloyd's underwriters might have elected to negotiate a settlement and avoid the embarrassment of a trial. On the other hand, many of the people involved believe the lack of criminal or financial penalties for the perpetrators exposed a severe weakness in the system that enables global trade. The *Brillante*, they say, is an open invitation to other crooks, just as the *Salem* was forty years ago. The lesson: maritime fraud is profitable, and even if you are unlucky enough to get caught, you're unlikely to be prosecuted.

Some months after our meeting at the Royal Exchange, we made an important reporting breakthrough: interviewing Allan Marquez, the crewman who let the supposed pirates on board in 2011. After we spoke to him, Marquez asked to be put in touch with the *Brillante*'s insurers in London, who he hoped might be able to protect him from Iliopoulos. We agreed to make the connection. Within hours, someone from the insurers' side told the City of London Police that we had reached a potential witness in their investigation of the shipowner. We were promptly asked to a meeting at the agency's headquarters in Guildhall, one of the oldest civic sites in the City.

It was a tense time. We had concerns about Marquez's safety, and—unbeknownst to us—the police and insurers were dealing with the emergence of Dimitrios Plakakis and Vassilios Theodorou, who would later play important roles in unraveling the *Brillante* fraud. In a conference room, we sat down opposite two detectives and a police spokesman, who asked if we were planning to use Marquez's name in our upcoming article. We said we were considering it, and that the sailor had told us he was eager to speak out publicly. That was unacceptable, one of the detectives said. In the view of the City force, there was a clear danger to Marquez, and they needed to carry out a full risk assessment before he could be identified in print. He added that if we refused to comply, the police might seek a court injunction to block our story from being published—a legal tool used periodically in the UK.

We were taken aback by the demand. Marquez's name and role in the events of July 2011 were already in the public domain. Statements he'd given to private-sector investigators were disclosed in US litigation related to the *Brillante*, accessible to any of the millions of people with a login for the federal court records system. Not only had the City of London Police never attempted to contact Marquez, they'd never even read those statements. When we asked what legal precedent the detectives planned to use to block the identification of a witness who'd already been identified, one of them replied, "We'll find one." They had a room full of lawyers downstairs, he said.

After consulting with Bloomberg's legal team and sending a Filipino colleague to meet with Marquez and make sure he was comfortable going on the record, we published his comments in our *Businessweek* story. In the end the police didn't try to stop us; either they changed their minds or they were bluffing. Not long afterward, a City of London detective flew to Manila to finally interview Marquez. But the crewman's account, which shed alarming new light on the case and implicated Iliopoulos in the fabrication of evidence, didn't lead to a breakthrough in their investigation. Instead, the inquiry appears to be dormant at best. One of the lead detectives left to join the compliance team of a British bank; another died of COVID-19. At the time this book was finalized, we knew of no law enforcement agency, anywhere in the world, that was seriously looking into either the *Brillante* fraud or the killing of David

Mockett. The Metropolitan Police, whose counterterrorism unit previously examined the latter, said in a statement that there were very limited circumstances in which British officers could investigate a murder overseas. "The Yemeni authorities have overall responsibility for the homicide investigation," a spokesman said. The force offered its condolences to the Mockett family.

Cynthia Mockett and Michael Conner haven't given up on their campaign for justice. In November 2021, Cynthia's Member of Parliament, Sir Gary Streeter, introduced a brief debate in the House of Commons about her husband's death and the *Brillante Virtuoso* case. It was late afternoon and the historic chamber's benches were nearly deserted after a busy session debating women's rights and a looming energy crisis. Streeter, reading from prepared remarks, described the attack and its aftermath. "It was all a massive fraud that Captain Mockett was in the process of uncovering—for that, he was killed," he said. Streeter called on the Minister for Security to encourage the British police to do what Conner had long urged: to treat the burning of the *Brillante* as an act of piracy, allowing the perpetrators to be prosecuted under UK maritime law. The evidence was there waiting to be used, in London and Athens. "Even now," Streeter said, "it is not too late."

For insurance executives and police officers in London, it may be embarrassing, or difficult, to confront the reality of maritime fraud. But in Yemen, asking questions about the *Brillante Virtuoso* can be considerably more challenging. One after another, Yemeni journalists we tried to hire to assist with research were initially enthusiastic—but then, once they learned more about the nature of the project, said they were too busy, or simply fell out of contact. A writer we approached elsewhere in the region was warned by a Yemeni friend not to take the assignment, because it could put her in danger. "These are bad people," the writer was told.

There are probably only a handful of people alive who know the details of what happened to David Mockett. One of them may be Sharif Ba'alawi, the Yemeni-Somali businessman who acted as a middleman between Aden's

Greek salvors and their local partners. When we reached him by phone in 2017, Ba'alawi responded to almost every question with blank denials, telling us he knew nothing about the attack on the *Brillante* or Mockett's assassination. He was simply a contractor, he said, providing food and diesel for salvage crews. We later learned that he'd been jailed in the United Arab Emirates, apparently accused of trading with Yemen's Houthi movement, which some regional governments consider a proxy for Iran. Despite repeated attempts, we were unable to contact him in prison.

With Ba'alawi out of reach, we focused on finding Ahmed Nashwan, the gun-toting Aden fixer who, according to both Plakakis and Theodorou, was at the center of the *Brillante* plot. He wasn't easy to track down. Some of our Yemeni contacts thought he'd been killed, one of the more than 200,000 dead in the country's ongoing civil war. But just weeks before our book deadline, we reached one of Nashwan's former employers, who unexpectedly set up a meeting in Cairo, where Nashwan now lives along with a significant chunk of the Yemeni diaspora.

Like Ba'alawi, Nashwan denied any wrongdoing, saying that he was "an ordinary citizen," not a "big successful businessman." While he confirmed that he was in business with the Greek salvor Vassilios Vergos, Nashwan insisted that he had no involvement with the hijacking of the *Brillante*, and no idea who killed Mockett. Somewhat improbably, given Mockett's prominence in Aden, Nashwan claimed not to even know who the Briton was. "I do not ask for people's blood," he said. "I swear to God almighty: I did not participate in the extortion of the insurance company."

At one point in our reporting, a legal expert shared an anecdote about a Greek shipowner he'd worked with. There had been an accident involving a tanker, which was spilling oil into the Atlantic. The lawyer asked what went wrong. "Do you want the truth about what happened, or the facts?" the shipowner replied. To him, the two were rarely the same. The facts were what happened; the truth depended on your perspective, and your interests.

We heard many versions of the truth about the *Brillante Virtuoso*: from private investigators, police officers, judges, insurance executives, officials in far-flung ports, Filipino sailors, and Arab businessmen, each with different and sometimes contradictory recollections. Before we could complete this project, we wanted to hear from the men who were said to have devised the plan to destroy the ship, putting in motion everything that followed.

Vergos never agreed to an interview, so in the summer of 2021 we sent him a detailed letter inviting him to comment. His first response, delivered over WhatsApp, was a crying-with-laughter emoji. In a brief phone conversation afterward, he did not deny working with Iliopoulos to torch the *Brillante*; indeed, as Judge Teare pointed out in the 2019 trial, he never denied it at any point during the insurance litigation. He did, however, accuse Plakakis and Theodorou of fabricating allegations against him, describing them as people who "imagine things in order to blackmail." As for David Mockett, he said, "How would I know who killed him?" It was a violent period in Aden; as Vergos correctly pointed out, innocent people were dying regularly on the city's streets. "I'm really sad about the gentleman who lost his life," he said.

Beginning in 2016, we tried repeatedly to open a line of communication with Iliopoulos. One of his lawyers told us he was passing on our requests, but had "no instructions" to help us beyond that. Another claimed he didn't know how to contact his former client. We sent emails and letters to his companies, but Super Mario ignored them all.

Then, just two days before our *Businessweek* feature was due to be published, we received a letter from a London law firm that specializes in "reputation management" and said it was acting for Iliopoulos. We were warned that our article might contain "outrageous allegations" against their client, including the "unfounded" suggestions that he was in any way responsible for the destruction of the *Brillante* or Mockett's death. The lawyers said that Iliopoulos vigorously denied such allegations, and threatened us with legal action if we published an article that contained them. After we ran our story, we never heard from them again.

In 2021 we wrote to the shipowner's employees, a close associate, and a public-relations agency he had worked with recently, including an eight-page memorandum listing eighty-one points on which he was welcome to comment. In reply, we received a brief letter from Carter-Ruck, another firm of libel specialists, which was now representing him. "Our client categorically denies any allegations of wrongdoing and does not propose to respond to baseless allegations," it said.

One of our attempts to reach Iliopoulos, however, did reveal something about how he operates—and how determined the shipping industry can be to obscure the connections between what goes on at sea and the men who profit from it. In addition to emails, we sent printed copies of our memo, in English and Greek, by courier to Seajets's headquarters in Piraeus. There is no doubt that the ferry line is controlled by Iliopoulos: he is routinely described in the Greek media as its owner, and in 2016 he testified in London that it belonged to his family. Company press releases have described him as either its chief executive officer or "head of strategic planning and development."

We were surprised, then, to get a call from a befuddled courier-company manager shortly after sending the documents. Seajets was refusing to take delivery, he said. At their offices, staff had insisted that they knew of no one named Marios Iliopoulos at that address.

ACKNOWLEDGMENTS

This book would not exist without the support and enthusiasm of our editors and managers at Bloomberg, who saw the potential in the story from the start. We owe a lasting debt to Nick Summers, Jim Aley, Megan Murphy, and our indefatigable lawyer, Randy Shapiro, all of whose wisdom and determination made our 2017 *Businessweek* feature possible. More broadly, we have had the good fortune to work for a series of bosses whose commitment to ambitious long-form journalism, and to helping us do whatever it takes to deliver it, has never wavered, including Brian Bremner, John Fraher, Alan Katz, Jacqueline Simmons, Heather Harris, and of course Joel Weber. A special thanks goes also to Jeremy Keehn.

Telling the full story of the *Brillante Virtuoso* was a daunting journalistic undertaking. In the Middle East, Mohamed Ali Zidan, Mohammed Komani, Wafa ST, Vivian Nereim, and Hala Nasreddine provided crucial assistance. Ioannis Papadopoulos in Athens was a relentless and astonishingly resourceful researcher, and this book is far richer for his work. In the Philippines, Yas Coles tracked down sources under extremely trying conditions. Cam Simpson, Abigail Fielding-Smith, and Tom Finn shared wisdom and contacts. Kit's friend Kosta was an invaluable consultant on matters of Greek language and culture. Greg and Lucas Jackson allowed their basement to be transformed into a writer's den. And Kevin Baker brought some Hollywood glamour to the world of narrative nonfiction.

When it came time to write, we were lucky to draw on the wisdom of Liam Vaughan and Tom Wright, who trod the path of executing complex, highly sensitive book projects long before we set off. Joel Lovell was a perceptive and unfailingly thorough first reader; that these pages make sense to anyone who hasn't spent several years learning about shipping, salvage, and the workings of the Lloyd's market is thanks in large part to him.

Though it seems silly in retrospect, we worried at the beginning of this process whether there was enough in the *Brillante* case for a book-length work. Could the events of one night in the Gulf of Aden, we wondered, really serve as the basis for a ninety-thousand-word narrative? Luckily for us, our brilliant agent Ethan Bassoff had no such doubts—and was a tireless advocate for making that story a reality. The team at Portfolio—Adrian Zackheim, Niki Papadopoulos, Kimberly Meilun, and most of all our gifted editor Noah Schwartzberg—were also believers from day one, and their confidence lifted us at our most difficult moments. Noah deserves a special thanks for expertly guiding two first-time authors through the process of turning an intimidating mass of reporting into something people might want to read.

For reasons that will be obvious to anyone who's read this far, many of the sources for that reporting cannot be named. But they chose to speak to us, at considerable personal or professional risk, because they had decided the truth about the *Brillante Virtuoso* shouldn't remain a secret. For that, we will be forever grateful. Our gratitude to Richard Veale and Michael Conner, similarly, will have no expiry date. Understandably skeptical of us at first, they have over the last five years given us an extended peek into a world that's usually hidden from view—and patiently answered thousands of silly or pedantic questions in the process.

The deepest thanks among our sources, however, are reserved for Cynthia Mockett. Opening up to a pair of strangers about the worst trauma in one's life can't be anything but excruciating. But Cynthia did it anyway, and with exceptional grace and good humor. We can only hope that this book captures her husband's remarkable character—and helps, in some small way, to bring the Mockett family the justice for which they are long overdue.

ACKNOWLEDGMENTS

No acknowledgments can adequately express the love and appreciation we feel for our families, and the ways they aided us throughout this long journey. Matt's parents, Barry and Debra Campbell, were early and careful readers, suggesting improvements large and small. With her characteristic mix of affection, emotional intelligence, and no-bullshit reasoning, his wife Lauren Myers-Cavanagh guided him out of countless narrative and reporting dead ends—and kept him laughing all the while. Theo provided a daily dose of the kind of uncomplicated joy that only a toddler can elicit, while releasing the tension in more than a few video calls with a high-speed Zoom bombing.

Kit's two older children, Callum and Isla, helped with cover ideas—including by putting crayon to paper for some excellent concept sketches. Baby Lachlan had the exceptional courtesy to wait until just after the manuscript was submitted to come tumbling into the world. Jim and Bee took grandparenting to heroic levels when schools closed during Kit's book leave. And in addition to her boundless love and support, his wife, Lindsey Macmillan, kept his feet on the ground throughout the process, not least when reminding him there was more to life than "that bloody boring boat."

INSERT PHOTO CREDITS

Page 1 top: courtesy of Gerolf Drebes

Page 1 middle: courtesy of Dimitris Tamvakos

Page 2 bottom: US Navy photo by Chief Petty Officer Raynald Lenieux via DVIDS

Page 3 top: courtesy of Nicholas Sloane

Page 3 bottom: courtesy of Nicholas Sloane

Page 4 top: courtesy of Adam Greaves

Page 4 bottom left: courtesy of Cynthia Mockett

Page 4 bottom right: courtesy of Cynthia Mockett

Page 5 top: courtesy of Roy Facey

Page 5 bottom: AFP via Getty Images

Page 6 top: courtesy of Cynthia Mockett

Page 6 bottom left: photo by Chet Susslin/Bloomberg via Getty Images

Page 6 bottom right: courtesy of echoflorina

Page 7 top: courtesy of Michael Conner

Page 7 bottom: INTIME Photo Agency

Page 8 top: courtesy of Cynthia Mockett

Page 8 bottom: courtesy of Kit Chellel

NOTES

4 **One Turkish official:** Victoria Clark, *Yemen: Dancing on the Heads of Snakes* (New Haven and London: Yale University Press, 2010), loc. 287, Kindle.

4 **A Scottish officer:** Clark, loc. 564.

4 **In the 1960s:** Clark, loc. 1541.

4 **"When are you people":** Clark, loc. 2090.

5 **In Hadhramaut, mud palaces:** Clark, loc. 123.

5 **Those peaks had:** Freya Stark, *The Southern Gates of Arabia: A Journey in the Hadhramaut* (New York: Modern Library, 2001), 4.

8 **By April, Al Qaeda militants:** "Rival Demos Pack Yemen Capital Under Security Net," Agence France-Presse, Apr. 29, 2011.

9 **A July 2011 report:** "Yemen's Turmoil: The Southerners Flex Their Muscles," *The Economist*, Jul. 2, 2011.

10 **After building up some experience:** Gunnar M. Lamvik, "The Filipino Seafarer: A Life Between Sacrifice and Shopping" (Doctoral diss., Norwegian University of Science and Technology, 2002), 161.

11 **Seafarers are responsible:** *Review of Maritime Transport 2020* (New York: United Nations Conference on Trade and Development, 2020), 20.

11 **All told, there were twenty-six:** Lamvik, 92.

11 **The tankers share the ocean:** "Merchant Fleet by Flag of Registration and by Type of Ship, Annual," United Nations Conference on Trade and Development, accessed Jan. 4, 2020, https://unctadstat.unctad.org/wds/ReportFolders/reportFolders.aspx?sCS_Chosen Lang=en.

12 **Along with larger tankers:** "World Seaborne Trade by Types of Cargo and by Group of Economies, Annual," UNCTAD, accessed Jan. 4, 2020, https://unctadstat.unctad.org/wds /TableViewer/tableView.aspx?ReportId=32363.

12 **Tankers began carrying oil:** Daniel Yergin, *The Prize* (New York: Free Press, 2008), 51.

12 **A decade and a half after:** Yergin, 54.

14 **Something happened to sailors:** Rose George, *90 Percent of Everything* (New York: Picador, 2014), 115.

14 **There were more than 170:** "Key Facts and Figures," EU Naval Force—Somalia, accessed Jan. 4, 2020, https://eunavfor.eu/key-facts-and-figures/.

15 **Often occurring hundreds of miles:** Jeffrey Gettleman, "Suddenly, a Rise in Piracy's Price," *The New York Times*, Feb. 26, 2011, https://www.nytimes.com/2011/02/27/weekin review/27pirates.html.

15 **More often the crews:** Kaija Hurlburt et al., *The Human Cost of Somali Piracy* (Broomfield, CO: One Earth Future Foundation, 2011), 15–17.

16 **They had a reputation:** Peter Apps, "Have Hired Guns Finally Scuppered Somali Pirates?" Reuters, Feb. 13, 2013, https://www.reuters.com/article/us-somalia-piracy -idUSBRE91B19Y20130212.

21 **Three of them died:** Nivell Rayda, "Ransom of $1.9m Frees 26 Sailors," *The Australian*, Oct. 25, 2016.

31 **It's standard practice:** Ioannis Theotokas and Gelina Harlaftis, *Leadership in World Shipping: Greek Family Firms in International Business* (London: Palgrave Macmillan UK, 2009), 29.

31 **This lack of transparency:** Guillaume Vuillemey, *Evading Corporate Responsibilities: Evidence from the Shipping Industry* (Paris: HEC Paris, 2020), 4.

32 **As one chronicler put it:** William Langewiesche, "Anarchy at Sea," *The Atlantic*, Sept. 2003, https://www.theatlantic.com/magazine/archive/2003/09/anarchy-at-sea/376873/.

34 **The story was picked up:** Michelle Wiese Bockmann and Alaric Nightingale, "Million-Barrel Tanker on Fire Off Yemen After Grenade Attack," *Bloomberg News*, Jul. 6, 2011.

34 **Reuters and the Associated Press:** U.S. Congress, House, Africa, Global Health, and Human Rights and Terrorism, Nonproliferation, and Trade Subcommittees of the Committee on Foreign Affairs, *Assessing the Consequences of the Failed State of Somalia*, 112th Cong., 1st sess., 2011, https://www.govinfo.gov/content/pkg/CHRG-112hhrg67305/html /CHRG-112hhrg67305.htm.

36 **After 9/11, Lloyd's members:** "Lloyd's of London Raises Loss Estimates from World Trade Center Attacks," Associated Press, Nov. 27, 2001.

37 **Lloyd's is the place:** Godfrey Hodgson, *Lloyd's of London* (New York: Viking, 1984), 9.

37 **Dolly Parton's breasts:** "Going Out on a Limb," Lloyd's of London, accessed Jan. 20, 2021, https://www.lloyds.com/about-lloyds/history/innovation-and-unusual-risks/going -out-on-a-limb.

37 **Lloyd's began life:** Hodgson, 49.

38 **The insurers of the *Tiger*:** Hodgson, 151.

38 **"letters of marte":** Steven Johnson, *Enemy of All Mankind* (New York: Riverhead Books, 2020), 42.

40 **"It's the beginning":** "Lloyd's Workers Set to Jacket In," *The Sunday Telegraph*, Jun. 17, 2007.

40 **It provided "an interesting life":** Hodgson, 31.

40 **Member firms competed to hire:** Gavin Finch, "The Old Daytime-Drinking, Sexual-Harassing Ways Are Thriving at Lloyd's," *Bloomberg Businessweek*, Mar. 21, 2019, https:// www.bloomberg.com/news/features/2019-03-21/the-old-daytime-drinking-sexual -harassing-ways-are-thriving-at-lloyd-s?sref=lmS4F5Vf.

41 **After some discussion:** Elizabeth Luessenhop and Martin Mayer, *Risky Business: An Insider's Account of the Disaster at Lloyd's of London* (New York: Scribner, 1995), 66.

41 **After an earthquake:** Hodgson, 65.

41 **Every year its members:** "Lloyd's Pocket Guide," Lloyd's of London, accessed Jul. 20, 2021, https://assets.lloyds.com/assets/pdf-history-lloydspocketguidev7digital/1/pdf-history -Lloydspocketguidev7digital.pdf.

41 **On average, about 30,000 pounds:** Lloyd's, "Pocket Guide."

42 **During the Vietnam War:** "Ian Posgate: Buccaneering Underwriter Who Made a Fortune as the 'Goldfinger' of the Lloyd's Insurance Market," *The Daily Telegraph*, Jul. 13, 2017.

42 **Shipping disasters, while regrettable:** Hodgson, 41.

49 **Yemen's strongman president:** Ginny Hill, *Yemen Endures: Civil War, Saudi Adventurism and the Future of Arabia* (Oxford: Oxford University Press, 2017), 221.

49 **In 2010 British and Emirati:** Mark Mazzetti and Robert F. Worth, "U.S. Sees Complexity of Bombs as Link to Al Qaeda," *The New York Times*, Oct. 30, 2010, https://www.nytimes.com/2010/10/31/world/31terror.html.

63 **In 2010 the UK ambassador:** Mohammed Sudam, "Suicide Bomber Targets British Ambassador in Yemen," Reuters, Apr. 26, 2010, https://www.reuters.com/article/yemen-explosion/wrapup-2-suicide-bomber-targets-british-ambassador-in-yemen-idUSLDE63P1GO20100426.

65 **Even fingerprinting wasn't:** Lawrence Wright, *The Looming Tower* (New York: Vintage, 2011), 368.

67 **The US had been stepping up:** Mark Mazzetti, "U.S. Is Intensifying a Secret Campaign of Yemen Airstrikes," *The New York Times*, Jun. 8, 2011, https://www.nytimes.com/2011/06/09/world/middleeast/09intel.html.

68 **One group of researchers estimated:** Anna Bowden et al., "The Economic Cost of Maritime Piracy," One Earth Future working paper, Dec. 2010, 10.

69 **Specifically, the money:** *Pirate Trails: Tracking the Illicit Financial Flows from Pirate Activities off the Horn of Africa* (Washington, DC: World Bank, 2013), 61.

72 **Margaret Thatcher, who led Britain:** Robert Chessyre, "Thatcher's 'Boot Boys': When the Unholy Trinity of Police, Press, and Government Took Root," *The Independent*, Sept. 15, 2012, https://www.independent.co.uk/voices/comment/thatcher-s-boot-boys-when-unholy-trinity-police-press-and-government-took-root-8139816.html.

78 **Partly for reasons of self-preservation:** Hill, preface.

78 **"There are many versions":** Hill, preface.

85 **Sometimes they caused the wrecks:** Joseph N. Gores, *Marine Salvage: The Unforgiving Business of No Cure, No Pay* (Garden City, N.Y.: Doubleday, 1971), 16–17.

86 **Under the industry's traditional rules:** Gores, xviiii.

87 **High-profile spills:** Ron Bousso, "BP Deepwater Horizon Costs Balloon to $65 Billion," Reuters, Jan. 16, 2018, https://www.reuters.com/article/uk-bp-deepwaterhorizon/bp-deepwater-horizon-costs-balloon-to-65-billion-idUKKBN1F50O6.

88 **Traditionally, the NCIS focused:** Deedra Allison, "NCIS Brings Law Enforcement Expertise to Counter-Piracy Operations," *NCIS Bulletin*, Summer 2010, https://ncisahistory.org/wp-content/uploads/2020/05/NCIS-Bulletin-Summer-2010.pdf.

90 **They take neither:** *Pakistan Shipbreaking Outlook* (Brussels: Sustainable Development Policy Institute, 2014), 4–30.

90 **Of the materials on board:** Ghulam Dastageer, Subuk Hasnain, and Ayesha binte Rashid, "The Ugly Side of Pakistan's Ship-Breaking Industry at Gadani," *The Wire*, Dec. 28, 2016, https://thewire.in/south-asia/ugly-gadani-ship-breaking.

90 **Despite efforts by activists:** NGO Shipbreaking Platform, "NGOs Denounce Dangerous Working Conditions After Major Explosion at Gadani Shipbreaking Yard in Pakistan Killing at Least 21 Workers," press release, Nov. 2, 2016, https://shipbreakingplatform.org/press-release-ngos-denounce-dangerous-working-conditions-after-major-explosion-at-gadani-shipbreaking-yard-in-pakistan-killing-at-least-21-workers/.

92 **On average, roughly half a million:** *The Inquest Handbook: A Guide for Bereaved Families, Friends and Advisors* (London: Inquest, 2016), 14.

92 **Since the 1980s:** John Woodcock, "I Will Never Bury My Daughter," *The Observer*, Apr. 5, 2009.

93 **Once, in a newspaper interview:** Olivier Vergnault, "On Call 24 Hours a Day in a Job That Dates Back 800 Years to Norman Times," *Herald Express* (Torquay), Feb. 1, 2011.

96 **But his words carried:** Holly Watt, "Briton Killed for Standing Up to Pirate Fraud Gang," *The Telegraph*, Jun. 28, 2012, https://www.telegraph.co.uk/news/uknews/defence/9363580 /Briton-killed-for-standing-up-to-pirate-fraud-gang.html.

98 **Sailors call this pitch-poling:** Sebastian Junger, *The Perfect Storm: A True Story of Men Against the Sea* (London: HarperCollins, 1997), 135.

98 **Then there are fires:** Victoria Gill, "Have Rogue Orcas Really Been Attacking Boats in the Atlantic?," *BBC News*, Nov. 2020, https://www.bbc.co.uk/news/extra/buqvasp1rr/orcas -spain-portugal.

99 **A proud Dutchman:** "Jan van Speijk (1802–1831)," City Archive Amsterdam, accessed Feb. 5, 2021, https://www.iamsterdam.com/en/amsterdam-qr/centrum-oost-de-plantage /jan-van-speijk.

99 **A *New York Times* correspondent:** Jamie L. Jones, "The Navy's Stone Fleet," *The New York Times*, Jan. 26, 2012, https://opinionator.blogs.nytimes.com/2012/01/26/the-navys-stone -fleet/.

99 **In 2009, for example:** Brian Skoloff, "Ship Set to Be Sunk for Reef; 'Vandenberg' to Anchor Wrecks in Keys," *South Florida Sun-Sentinel*, May 26, 2009.

100 **The Romans knew it:** Frederick Martin, *The History of Lloyd's and of Marine Insurance in Great Britain* (London: Macmillan and Co., 1876), loc. 33, Kindle.

100 **It was a tale:** "Crime in Ancient Greece," *The Police Journal*, Jul. 1, 1929.

100 **The moneylenders of antiquity:** "Demosthenes, Against Zenothemis," Perseus Digital Library, accessed Feb. 8, 2021, http://www.perseus.tufts.edu/hopper/text?doc=Perseus %3Atext%3A1999.01.0076%3Aspeech%3D32%3Asection%3D10.

101 **He knew the ship:** Martin, loc. 2960.

101 **"Few industries offer such opportunities":** Hodgson, 172.

102 **In a given year:** "The Sailor's Friend; Maritime History," *The Economist*, Jul. 8, 2006.

102 **The official parliamentary reporter:** "Breach of Order (Mr. Plimsoll)," *Hansard*, HC Deb 22 July 1875 vol 225 cc1822-9, https://api.parliament.uk/historic-hansard/commons/1875 /jul/22/parliament-breach-of-order-mr-plimsoll.

105 **Pierrakos lost a couple more:** Hodgson, 183.

105 **It was "the grimmest period":** Arthur Jay Klinghoffer, *Fraud of the Century* (London: Routledge, 1988), 61.

105 **This chaotic situation:** Hodgson, 175.

105 **The crew of one vessel:** Barbara Conway, *Maritime Fraud* (London: LLP Professional Publishing, 1990), 5.

106 **More than half:** Hodgson, 184.

106 **A port official became suspicious:** Conway, 101–5.

107 **The British rescuers:** Klinghoffer, 3.

107 **As far as anyone could see:** Allister Sparks, "$50 Million Loss in Con Job," *The Washington Post*, Mar. 2, 1983, https://www.washingtonpost.com/archive/politics/1983/03/02/50-million -loss-in-con-job/4a5d727a-b3ea-4c29-97fd-0ff466b72710/.

108 **He then ordered:** Klinghoffer, 52.

108 **In return for slipping:** Klinghoffer, 38.

108 **The sailor's testimony:** Klinghoffer, 75.

108 **US federal prosecutors convicted Soudan:** Greg Nolan, "Architect of Huge Tanker Fraud Caps His Career with a Jailbreak," *The Journal of Commerce*, May 30, 1988, https://www .joc.com/architect-huge-tanker-fraud-caps-his-career-jailbreak_19880530.html.

109 **One investigator claimed:** Hodgson, 192.

109 **The Greek commercial fleet:** Theotokas and Harlaftis, 7.

111 **To raise more funds:** Hodgson, 117.

111 **Instead, the market adopted:** Michael Ford, *Marine Insurance Fraud in International Trade* (London: Witherby, 1993).

111 **Claims departments, responsible for investigating:** Baris Soyer, *Marine Insurance Fraud* (Abingdon, UK: Informa Law, 2014), chapter 1, 1-5.

112 **By some estimates, maritime crime:** Soyer, chapter 1, 1-1.

116 **Zavos's firm, Norton Rose:** Elizabeth Fournier, "Top Law Firm Profits Smash Through £5bn," *CityAM*, Sept. 4, 2012.

119 **Everyone had seen news reports:** See, for example, "Yemen Car Bomb Victim David Mockett 'Killed by Fraudsters,'" *BBC News*, Jun. 28, 2012, https://www.bbc.com/news /uk-england-devon-18632369.

119 **If the destruction:** Hodgson, 191.

122 **He went on to work:** Michael Gillard and Laurie Flynn, *Untouchables* (Edinburgh: Cutting Edge Press, 2004), 533.

123 **By the time he retired:** "Top Officer Lost Job Before Death," *BBC News*, Sept. 29, 2005, http://news.bbc.co.uk/1/hi/uk/4294264.stm.

125 **In October 2012:** Eddie Wren, "Mystery Surrounds Death of British Lawyer in Yemen Who Died 'After Answering His Door Covered in Blood,'" *Daily Mail*, Oct. 12, 2012, https://www.dailymail.co.uk/news/article-2216864/Mystery-surrounds-death-British -lawyer-died-answering-door-covered-blood-Yemen-home.html.

125 **"It was just a silly":** Joanne Butcher, "Mystery over Tyneside Lawyer Found Dead in Yemen," Oct. 12, 2012, *ChronicleLive*, https://www.chroniclelive.co.uk/news/local-news/mystery -over-tyneside-lawyer-found-1372744.

126 **Both, the NCA said:** The request from the NCA was documented in US Naval Criminal Investigative Service records, disclosed in 2019 to the authors under the Freedom of Information Act.

126 **Given the rampant corruption:** Ian Urbina, *The Outlaw Ocean: Crime and Survival in the Last Untamed Frontier* (London: Vintage, 2019), 171.

131 **It appeared to be drawn:** Andrew Erickson and Austin Strange, "China and the International Antipiracy Effort," *The Diplomat*, Nov. 1, 2013, https://thediplomat.com/2013/11/china -and-the-international-antipiracy-effort/.

134 **The litigation would ultimately drag:** *In the Matter of the Alexandros T*, The Supreme Court of the United Kingdom, [2013] UKSC 70, 6.

147 **The marine assets:** "Merchant Fleet by Country of Beneficial Ownership, Annual," UNCTAD, accessed Feb. 5, 2021, https://unctadstat.unctad.org/wds/TableViewer/tableView.aspx.

148 **To this day they are:** "Tsipras Thanks Shipowners over Changes to Voluntary Tax Deal," *Ekatherimini*, Feb. 27, 2019, https://www.ekathimerini.com/238133/article/ekathimerini /news/tsipras-thanks-shipowners-over-changes-to-voluntary-tax-deal.

148 **Some of the longer-lived:** Theotokas and Harlaftis, 31.

148 **The Second World War:** Geoffrey Jones and Paul Gomopoulos, "Aristotle Onassis and the Greek Shipping Industry," *Harvard Business Review* 805(141) (May 2005): 4.

148 **Despite the demands of fighting:** Gelina Harlaftis, "Cornerstone of Greek Shipping: 100 Liberties," *Ekatherimini*, Jul. 19, 2012, https://www.ekathimerini.com/143279/article /ekathimerini/life/cornerstone-of-greek-shipping-100-liberties.

148 **The vessels were awkwardly designed:** Marc Levinson, *The Box* (Princeton, NJ: Princeton University Press, 2016), 25.

149 **Sixty percent of the growth:** Theotokas and Harlaftis, 13.

149 **They vied to dominate:** Arthur H. Richter, "Niarchos to Add 2 'Super' Tankers," *The New York Times*, Aug. 1, 1955, https://timesmachine.nytimes.com/timesmachine/1955/08/01 /84152846.html?pageNumber=37.

149 **The London office was meant:** Elias Kulukundis, *Bold Coasts* (Athens: GC Eleftheroudakis SA, 2018), 122.

150 **The very first vessel:** Laleh Khalili, *Sinews of War and Trade: Shipping and Capitalism in the Arabian Peninsula* (London: Verso Books, 2020), 238.

150 **By 1959, over half:** Jones and Gomopoulos, 20.

150 **Other financial sleights of hand:** Gelina Harlaftis, "The Onassis Global Shipping Business, 1920s–1950s," *The Business History Review* 88, no. 2 (Summer 2014): 260.

151 **As a high school student:** "Marios Iliopoulos: The Take-off of Seajets and Its New Plans for the Aegean," *Deal News Online*, Jul. 7, 2019, http://www.dealnews.gr/roi/item/265435 -ΜΑΡΙΟΣ-ΗΛΙΟΠΟΥΛΟΣ-Η-απογείωση-της-Seajets-και-τα-νέα-σχέδιά-του-για -το-Αιγαίο#.YMF_ii0RoQ9.

161 **In his written judgment:** *Suez Fortune Investments Ltd & Piraeus Bank AE v. Talbot Underwriting Ltd & Others,* [2016] EWHC 1085 (Comm), http://www.bailii.org/ew/cases/EWHC /Comm/2016/1085.html.

162 **As for Iliopoulos's promise:** The relevant passage in Flaux's judgment is as follows: "The strategy emerged even more clearly when Mr. Gaisman QC pressed Mr. Iliopoulos on the fact that it was the owners who had the motive for hacking into the emails. Mr. Iliopoulos clearly lost his temper and effectively threatened the insurers and their legal representatives from the witness box in a disgraceful manner, thereby exposing, as I pointed out to him, what his real motive now is: to build up a case against the insurers and their representatives in Greece. With this intemperate and menacing evidence, Mr. Iliopoulos lost any remaining shred of credibility."

167 **There was lucrative employment:** First Witness Statement of Richard Julian Veale, *Suez Fortune v. Talbot Underwriting*, Sept. 28, 2017.

174 **The only way to get:** Witness Statement of Richard Veale, 14–15.

174 **Theodorou had helped:** In his 2019 judgment, for which detailed citation information is included on page 256, Justice Nigel Teare said the following of Veale's account of his interactions with Theodorou:
"Mr. Veale, an insurance investigator, gave evidence that Mr. Theodorou, one of the local salvors who boarded the casualty, told him (over six meetings between September 2016 and May 2017), that the fire on the vessel had been planned in advance by Mr. Iliopoulos. There is no reason to doubt Mr. Veale's evidence that Mr. Theodorou told him the matters which Mr. Veale said he did. Mr. Veale gave his evidence in a forthright and compelling manner. No particular reason was advanced during his cross-examination which suggested that this evidence should be doubted. However, whether Mr. Theodorou's statements to Mr. Veale were true is another matter. He did not sign a statement, wanted a large sum of money for his evidence, was not available to be cross-examined and there are problems with his evidence (identified by counsel for the Bank as 13 'inaccuracies or inconsistencies'). Although counsel for the Underwriters emphasised that 'the core' of the accounts of both Mr. Theodorou and Mr. Plakakis was strikingly similar and that they told the same 'essential story,' I consider that what Mr. Theodorou said to Mr. Veale can only be accepted as true to the extent that it is supported by other compelling evidence."

179 **He admitted that much:** Witness Statement of Allan Briones Marquez, *Suez Fortune v. Talbot Underwriting*, Aug. 28, 2017.

180 **Tabares would say:** Day 14 transcript, *Suez Fortune v. Talbot Underwriting*, 48–52.

181 **Tabares denies that:** In his judgment, Teare said the following of Marquez, who did not testify in person in the 2019 trial:
"I am unable to place any weight on the evidence of threatening behaviour by Mr. Marquez. It was not tested in cross-examination. It was denied by the chief engineer and Mr. Paikopoulos."

However, I find it impossible to resist the conclusion that those who said that the armed men announced themselves as 'the authorities' did so because they had been requested to do so, and not because it was the truth."

183 **Iliopoulos completed the course:** "Results Ritsona Hillclimb 2017," accessed Jul. 19, 2021, http://www.rallycross-photo.com/heuvelklim2/results-ritsona-hillclimb-2017/.

184 **The backup Audi:** Vassilios Sarimbalidis, "Marios Iliopoulos' Audi R8 Le Mans Caused Panic Among the Spectators," *Zougla*, Apr. 13, 2017.

191 **According to the account:** Witness Statement of Theo Blake, *Suez Fortune v. Talbot Underwriting*, Oct. 25, 2017. "Theo Blake" was the pseudonym used by the City of London Police to protect the identity of Dimitrios Plakakis.

193 **He apparently even had:** Embassy Nairobi, "Somalia—Political Perspectives from Dubai," WikiLeaks Cable: 08NAIROBI2619_a, dated Nov. 20, 2008, https://wikileaks.org/plusd /cables/08NAIROBI2619_a.html.

193 **Rumored to be a veteran:** Lucas Winter, "The Adaptive Transformation of Yemen's Republican Guard," *Small Wars Journal*, Mar. 7, 2017, https://smallwarsjournal.com/jrnl/art /the-adaptive-transformation-of-yemen's-republican-guard.

195 **As he recounted:** Witness Statement of Theo Blake, 9.

199 **Vergos was happy:** Witness Statement of Theo Blake, 16–24.

200 **Eager to build:** U.S. Congress, Senate, Committee on Armed Services, Ongoing Efforts to Combat Piracy on the High Seas: Hearing before the Committee on Armed Services, 111th Cong., 1st sess., 2009, https://www.congress.gov/event/111th-congress/senate-event /LC6133/text?s=1&r=1229.

200 **It received about $30 million:** Jeremy M. Sharp, *Yemen: Background and U.S. Relations*, CRS Report No. RL34170 (Washington, D.C.: Congressional Research Service, 2011), 15.

200 **In the final phase:** Sally Healy and Ginny Hill, *Yemen and Somalia: Terrorism, Shadow Networks, and the Limitations of State-building*, MENAP/AFP BP 2010/01 (London: Chatham House, 2010), 11.

201 **Early in 2011:** Margaret Coker, "U.S. Military Aid Is Available for Hire in Yemen," *The Wall Street Journal*, Jan. 4, 2011, https://www.wsj.com/articles/SB1000142405297020420 4004576049660513491614.

203 **Vergos repeated the advice:** Witness Statement of Theo Blake, 33–34.

208 **This time, Plakakis listened:** Day 19 transcript, *Suez Fortune v. Talbot Underwriting*, 52–55.

213 **On the advice:** Day 19 transcript, 64.

221 **Although Judge Teare:** In his judgment, Teare said the following of Gonzaga:
"A feature of his evidence, however, was a failure to answer difficult questions. For example, he maintained that he believed the intruders to be the 'authorities' because they wore uniform and 'authorities' with arms had boarded his vessel in West Africa and other places. When his evidence as to this belief was probed he tended to repeat his belief and the reasons for it without answering the question put. That suggested that he was unwilling to answer the question perhaps because he had no credible answer to give.

"Another feature of his evidence was a tendency, on occasion, to give answers which were surprising and lacked reality. For example, when asked whether he was concerned at the approach of a small boat he said he was not because it might have been a boat selling fish. He was asked whether the fact that those approaching in the small boat not only carried arms (which he accepted would heighten his concern) but also wore masks was a reason for yet more concern. The master said he did not think so. When asked why, he said that the masks might protect against dust. When it was pointed out that the boat was at sea, he said that the masks might be protection against infection. He later suggested that the men might be wearing masks to avoid a bad smell. These answers suggested that, having appreciated where counsel's questions were going, he was prepared to say whatever was necessary to avoid making admissions which might later prove to be damaging."

222 **"There was no trust"**: Day 17 transcript, *Suez Fortune v. Talbot Underwriting*, 46–47.

225 **His written judgment ran**: *Suez Fortune Investments Ltd & Piraeus Bank AE v. Talbot Underwriting Ltd & Others*, [2019] EWHC 2599 (Comm), http://www.bailii.org/ew/cases/EWHC/Comm/2019/2599.html.

225 **"The armed men"**: The relevant passage in Teare's judgment is as follows:

"Having considered all of the evidence in the case and counsel's detailed submissions on that evidence and having stood back from the detail to view the story as a whole, in the round, I have reached several firm conclusions.

"First, the armed men who boarded BRILLANTE VIRTUOSO with an IEID did so with the intention of starting a fire on board the vessel. They had no intention of hijacking the vessel for ransom and only pretended to be pirates. They activated the IEID for the purpose of starting a fire on board the vessel.

"Second, the master and chief engineer assisted the armed men in their task. The master decided to drift off Aden to make it easier for the small boat carrying the armed men to come alongside the vessel and then permitted the armed men to board the vessel. The chief engineer in all probability provided the accelerant for the IEID and the additional fuel to enable the fire to spread from the purifier room. There is no clear evidence as to what the accelerant and additional fuel consisted of, but it may have been diesel oil as suggested by the fire experts.

"Third, Mr. Vergos of Poseidon was party to the conspiracy to damage the vessel by fire. He was aware that there was to be a 'fake' attack by pirates and once he knew that that had occurred and that the vessel was on fire he proceeded to the casualty. On arrival he failed to take obvious precautions to prevent the spread of the fire. When it appeared that the fire was about to go out he, or one or more of his salvage team, damaged the drain cock to the diesel oil service tank so as to cause the resurgence of the fire.

"Fourth, the orchestrator of these events was the owner of BRILLANTE VIRTUOSO, Mr. Iliopoulos. It is improbable that the armed men, master, chief engineer and Mr. Vergos took part in the conspiracy on their own initiative. By contrast Mr. Iliopoulos had a motive to want the vessel to be damaged by fire, namely, the making of a fraudulent claim for the total loss of the vessel in the sum of some US$77 million which, if successful, would solve the serious financial difficulties in which he and his companies were at the time. Moreover, his involvement is consistent with his early telephone calls to FOS and Poseidon between 0300 and 0400 on 6 July reporting that the vessel was on fire and positively indicated by the striking coincidences that (i), although it is clear from the VDR audio record that the armed men identified themselves as 'security,' almost all of the crew in their early statements said that the armed men identified themselves as 'the authorities' and (ii) that the statements of those few crew members who said that the armed men identified themselves as 'security' were amongst those not disclosed to the Underwriters until, some years later, the Owner's solicitors disclosed them. Only Mr. Iliopoulos had reason for the crew to tell an untrue story. Thus the evidence relating to the loss, the crew's untrue evidence in their early witness statements that the armed men described themselves as the authorities and Mr. Iliopoulos' motive for setting fire to his vessel amount to a cogent and compelling case that the events were orchestrated by him. The case against him is strengthened by what is known of his character from the findings made by Flaux J. and by the inference that the documents he was unwilling to disclose would have supported the case against him. I have therefore concluded that Mr. Iliopoulos was the instigator of the conspiracy."

229 **"We believe that society"**: Seajets, "SEAJETS' WorldChampion JET Wins the 'Ship of the Year 2019' at the Lloyd's List Greek Shipping Awards 2019," press release, Dec. 11, 2019, https://www.prnewswire.co.uk/news-releases/seajets-worldchampion-jet-wins-the-ship-of-the-year-2019-at-the-lloyd-s-list-greek-shipping-awards-2019-866040484.html.

229 **He'd hired cranes**: Seajets, "Greek CEO Wins Award for His Humanitarian Efforts During the Tragic Fires in Greece," press release, Jul. 24, 2019, https://pressreleases.responsesource.com/news/98118/greek-ceo-wins-award-for-his-humanitarian-efforts-during-the/.

229 **But five years later**: U.S. Department of the Treasury, "Treasury Sanctions Companies Operating in the Oil Sector of the Venezuelan Economy and Transporting Oil to Cuba," press release, Apr. 5, 2019, https://home.treasury.gov/news/press-releases/sm643.

230 **He bought at least six**: Jonathan Boonzaier and Harry Papachristou, "Cruiseship Sold by Royal Caribbean Emerges in Fleet of Greece's Marios Iliopoulos," *TradeWinds*, Mar. 23, 2021, https://www.tradewindsnews.com/cruise-and-ferry/cruiseship-sold-by-royal-caribbean-emerges-in-fleet-of-greeces-marios-iliopoulos/2-1-985218.

231 **Early in the pandemic**: David Yaffe-Bellany, "U.S. Businesses Are Fighting Insurers in the Biggest Legal Battle of the Pandemic," *Bloomberg Businessweek*, Nov. 2, 2020, https://www.bloomberg.com/news/features/2020-11-02/should-insurers-have-to-compensate-businesses-for-coronavirus-lockdowns.

231 **In the UK, Lloyd's members**: Lucca de Paoli and Jonathan Browning, "Insurers Face More Covid Payouts as U.K. Court Appeal Fails," *Bloomberg News*, Jan. 15, 2021, https://www.bloomberg.com/news/articles/2021-01-15/insurers-face-covid-payouts-as-appeal-of-u-k-court-ruling-fails.

231 **From the market's point**: Ian Smith, "Lloyd's of London Braced for £6bn Covid Hit," *Financial Times*, Mar. 31, 2021, https://www.ft.com/content/75ce339e-2586-46fd-ae96-1c3e2df24875.

INDEX